British Studies Series

General Editor JEREMY BLACK

Published

Forthcoming

(*List continued overleaf*)

F. J. Levy **Politics and Culture in Tudor England**
G. I. T. Machin **The Rise of British Democracy**
Allan Macinnes **The British Revolution**
Thomas Mayer **Britain, 1450–1603**
Michael Mendle **The English Civil War and Political Thought**
W. Rubinstein **History of Britain in the Twentieth Century**
Howard Temperley **Britain and America**

A History of Britain, 1885–1939

John Davis
Fellow in Modern History and Politics
The Queen's College, Oxford

St. Martin's Press
New York

A HISTORY OF BRITAIN, 1885–1939

Copyright © 1999 by John Davis

St. Martin's Press, Scholarly and Reference Division, 175 Fifth Avenue, New York, N.Y. 10010

First published in the United States of America in 1999

This book is printed on paper suitable for recycling and made from fully managed and sustained forest sources.

Printed in Hong Kong

ISBN 0–312–22033–2 clothbound
ISBN 0–312–22034–0 paperback

Library of Congress Cataloging-in-Publication Data
Davis, John, 1955–
A history of Britain, 1885–1939 / John Davis.
p.   cm. — (British studies series)
Includes bibliographical references and index.
ISBN 0–312–22033–2 (cloth). — ISBN 0–312–22034–0 (pbk.)
1. Great Britain—History—Edward VII, 1901–1910.   2. Great
Britain—History—George V, 1910–1936.   3. Great Britain—History–
–George VI, 1936–1952.   4. Great Britain—History—Victoria,
1837–1901.   I. Title.   II. Series.
DA566.D38   1999
941.08—dc21   98–40372
                                                                        CIP

To Carolyne

Contents

Acknowledgements

A book of this sort is an exercise in multiple plagiarism. I have tried to acknowledge all the secondary works from which I have directly taken material in the bibliography, and I hope that nobody is aggrieved. With no archivists or copyright-holders to thank, I should perhaps begin by expressing my gratitude to my publishers for believing, as few did, my repeated assurances that this book would appear one day. I am also grateful to my 'focus group' of Pallavi Aiyar, Katharina Böhmer and Maya Priestley for product-testing the manuscript, and to Katharina in particular for perceptive scrutiny and properly sceptical criticism when most needed. Frédérique Lachaud most kindly allowed me to flat-sit for her in Paris during the three consecutive summers when most of this book was written. Above all I must thank the dedicatee for putting up with me, as always.

JOHN DAVIS

The Queen's College
Oxford

ix

List of Abbreviations

BBC	British Broadcasting Corporation
BUF	British Union of Fascists
COS	Charity Organization Society
CPGB	Communist Party of Great Britain
ILP	Independent Labour Party
INL	Irish National League
IRA	Irish Republican Army
LCC	London County Council
LRC	Labour Representation Committee
NEC	National Executive Committee (Labour Party)
NLF	National Liberal Federation
NUCA	National Union of Conservative Associations
NUSEC	National Union of Societies for Equal Citizenship
NUWSS	National Union of Women's Suffrage Societies
SDF	Social Democratic Federation
TUC	Trades Union Congress
UAB	Unemployment Assistance Board
UGC	Unemployment Grants Committee
WSPU	Women's Social and Political Union

Introduction: A Liberal State

Addressing an Edinburgh audience in August 1884, the Prime Minister William Gladstone claimed that his Liberal Party embodied the 'solid and permanent opinion' of the British nation, at least since reform of the parliamentary system in 1832. Since then, Gladstone argued, ten out of twelve parliaments had had a liberal majority. The eleventh, that elected in 1841, had begun as a Tory parliament but had evicted a Tory government for a Whig–Liberal one in 1846. Only the 1874 parliament had been irredeemably Tory, and its Tory majority had been caused by Liberal divisions. In the age of reform the Liberals – and their Whig predecessors – had been the natural party of government.[1]

It may be debatable how liberal Britain had been in the 1830s and 1840s, but the Britain of the third quarter of the nineteenth century clearly was a liberal state. The central tenets of British liberalism – the freedom of speech and association, religious freedom and the freedom of the press – were so well established as to be virtually beyond discussion by the 1870s. All educated Victorians understood that these liberties were rooted in the defeat of Stuart absolutism and divine-right monarchy in the constitutional battles of the seventeenth century. The great majority accepted that this achievement had been consolidated in the years 1828–35, when civic equality had been granted to Roman Catholics and Nonconformists, when the parliamentary system had been reformed to reflect the contemporary distribution of wealth and population, and when local government had been placed on a democratic foundation. By this largely peaceful overhaul of her *ancien régime*, Britain was believed to have replaced a system based on patronage and executive manipulation with one founded upon proper representative principles. However starry-eyed this view, it probably is the case that the British state was more transparent and accountable in the second half of the nineteenth century than ever before or since.

What really turned liberalism into a comprehensive philosophy of government, though, was the fusion of this political and constitutional liberalism with economic liberalism in mid-century. Economic liberalism was rooted in the prescriptions of the British economic theorists of the late eighteenth and early nineteenth centuries. In policy terms it implied principally the pursuit of freer trade through the relaxation of tariff duties, and the pursuit of price stability by fixing the value of paper currency to that of a given amount of gold. In the 1820s Tory governments had used these methods as tools of economic management, in the hope that economic success would weaken the critics of the political system and take the steam out of the movement for parliamentary reform. When reform none the less followed in 1832, the division had widened within Tory ranks between those who considered free trade and sound money correct in principle and those who saw them as inimical to the true values of Toryism. The catastrophic split over the Tory Prime Minister Sir Robert Peel's abandonment of the protective duties on corn in 1846, which many of his followers considered fatal to the party's core rural support, reduced the party to an agriculturalist rump and denied it majority office for a generation.

The Corn Law split did not instantly create a free trade *bloc* in parliament – indeed the 1850s were a decade of party instability – but it provided the precondition for such a *bloc,* which was then reinforced by Britain's economic success in the years after Corn Law repeal. Arguably free trade was as much a symptom of that success as its cause – a dominant economic power tends to value free trade in principle as a means of lowering artificial barriers to its dominance – but Corn Law repeal had been a very conspicuous political victory for the forces of free trade, and the fact that it was followed by an unprecedented period of sustained growth led many contemporaries to attribute economic success primarily to free trade policy. After the embittered arguments over trade policy in the 1840s, free trade almost ceased to be a matter for debate: Sir Thomas Farrer, Permanent Secretary at the Board of Trade from 1867 to 1886, who did more than anybody else to mould Britain's trade policy in the second half of the nineteenth century, believed that challenging free trade was like questioning the rules of grammar.[2]

The mid-century discovery that the combination of political and economic liberalism strengthened the state rather than weakening it created the liberal consensus which Gladstone described. The *ancien régime* values of 'old corruption', protectionism and religious discrimination appeared fundamentally wrong, and the Tory Party was discredited by association with them. This was the real effect of the free trade triumph, but it should be acknowledged immediately that free trade itself – the progressive removal of protective duties – was virtually the only area in which clear policy prescriptions flowed directly from the general acceptance of liberal values.

It was not even clear that international free trade implied domestic *laisser faire*. The two were intellectually closely related, of course, with a common ancestry in classical economics, and they tended to share the same advocates, but *laisser faire* – the principle of non-intervention in the economy and society – created the greater problems. Certainly *laisser faire* was the guiding principle of what would now be called macro-economic policy. The British state avoided, in most respects, the vexatious regulation of private industry. At the heart of free trade policy was the principle that British tariffs should not privilege particular British producers at the expense of the community as a whole. Duties on sugar, coffee or tea, grown overseas, were therefore acceptable, but duties on corn were not. Domestic industrial policy was framed with the same aim of even-handedness towards British producers, with government neither interfering with nor discriminating against them unnecessarily. Parliament was ready to regulate monopolistic public services like the railways or the private water and gas companies. It would intervene to effect desirable social objectives even at the expense of constraining industry: child labour had been regulated in the 1840s in the knowledge that this would affect the hours worked by adults, and in the 1870s parliament opted to give trade unions a protected legal status. In general, though, the state left industry alone.

In social policy, though, the economic case for non-intervention was always much weaker. If Britain's economic success had been aided by liberalising trade and industry, industrialisation – and the urbanisation that accompanied it more extensively in Britain than anywhere else – created social problems which the market could not necessarily solve. The state's response, in the decades when Gladstone's liberal consensus was being formed,

showed no overriding commitment to *laisser faire*. In the two most
pressing areas – public health and the relief of poverty – legislation was in fact highly prescriptive, though the appearance of the
minimal state was preserved by the extensive devolution of
executive power to local authorities. On the whole, sanitation
and disease control raised little controversy: despite some exceptions which have been well aired by historians, the objective
of improving the quality of urban life and lowering the community's vulnerability to disease was not one which encountered
much criticism, and in recent years the role of public intervention
in lowering nineteenth-century mortality rates has received fresh
emphasis from medical historians. Poor relief posed more difficult problems, in the absence of any consensus upon the community's obligation to rescue individuals from poverty. The
notorious Poor Law Amendment Act – the 'New Poor Law' – of
1834 had attempted to create a self-regulating system, by which
poor relief would be offered in the workhouse at a level and in
conditions so unappealing as to deter all but those incapable of
work, so that the genuinely destitute would identify themselves
and could be treated separately from the merely workshy. It was a
system really designed for a stable rural economy, subject to
endemic underemployment but not to cyclical collapse. It did
not adapt well to the circumstances of growing industrial towns,
sucking in rural migrants with no guarantee of work, and vulnerable to the volatility of the industrial economy. Workhouse casual
wards became magnets for the vagrant unemployed, whom the
authorities controlled by resort to something close to prison discipline. In practice these disciplinary methods were often
extended to the genuinely destitute – the elderly, the crippled,
the blind, the mentally ill – as well. The central Poor Law Board
felt it necessary to remind local authorities as early as 1839 that
the law had not envisaged a punitive régime: the workhouse
'ought not to be used for punishing the dissolute or rewarding
the well conducted pauper'.[3] By then, though, the workhouse
had already acquired the stigma that would surround it until its
abolition. It consequently became difficult for Poor Law guardians to make 'respectable' victims of industrial slump or similar
accidents of life enter the workhouse as a condition of receiving
relief. The practice of giving out-relief – a dole offered without
the obligation to enter the workhouse – became widespread,

although it greatly weakened the deterrent purpose of the system. As out-relief cost the authorities less than accommodation in the workhouse, as well as being less politically contentious, Poor Law guardians faced a continual temptation to rely upon it, and when urban unemployment mounted in the late 1870s both central government and a growing lobby of Poor Law reformers called for restrictions upon its use. By then a system marked by its initial reputation for meanness and still despised by its clients had become the most extensive and costly public relief system in the world – a far cry from the principles of *laisser faire*.

The point could be reinforced in the field of education, in which the state intervened in 1870 to augment the very limited provision of schools by voluntary agencies (generally the churches) in most industrial towns, and in areas such as food adulteration, the subject of legislation in the 1870s. In general, exceptions to the rule of *laisser faire* counted for more than the rule itself in Victorian social policy. What all of this shows is that while international free trade remained a largely unchallenged good, and non-intervention was the accepted general rule in economic affairs, few were prepared entirely to entrust the shaping of society to the market. John Stuart Mill, the leading mid-century Liberal thinker, argued for regulation of the hours of labour and intervention in education in his generally orthodox *Principles of Political Economy* in 1848, while the final chapter of his *On Liberty*, eleven years later, explored the appropriate extent and limits of the state's interference with the individual. If free trade was a liberal dogma, *laisser faire* was merely a rule of thumb. The bifurcation of the two principles would become clear in the 1900s, when the Liberal Party rallied in defence of orthodox free trade while its most advanced thinkers were exploring the ways in which state intervention could benefit the poor.

Non-economic issues raised still more difficult questions. In religion the legislation of 1828 for Nonconformists, 1829 for Roman Catholics and 1858 for Jews had reduced legal discrimination against groups outside the Church of England while maintaining the state's identification with an established church. The minority episcopalian church in Ireland had been disestablished in 1869, but the established churches – Anglican and Presbyterian respectively – in England and Scotland enjoyed majority support which would work against their complete disestablishment. Yet Nonconformity, strong in many industrial centres, had gained greatly from the process of parliamentary reform, with the greater representation of manufacturing towns in 1832 and the expansion of the urban electorate in 1867, and Nonconformists' enhanced political presence ensured greater criticism of the privileges still enjoyed by the established churches. Once-contentious issues such as the obligation to pay church rates might appear ephemeral today, but the potential for controversy in the most prominent religious question, that of the extent of the established church's control over public elementary education in England and Wales, remains evident, and that issue convulsed the Liberal Party when the first national Education Act was passed in 1870. Liberalism prescribed religious toleration, certainly, but it was unclear how far it prescribed the weakening of the established church.

Similar ambiguities existed in foreign policy. It is true that for one of the architects of the free trade order, Richard Cobden, there existed a direct link between liberalism in economics and liberalism in international relations. Cobden, who had led the campaign against the Corn Laws in the 1840s, believed that protective duties distorted the natural flow of trade, and that an unfettered system would allow countries to specialise in those products which, by virtue of climate, resources or labour skills, they were best equipped to produce. Mercantilist trade wars would therefore become unnecessary, and the whole imperial ethos of conquest and expansion would become outmoded. There was an inherent truth in this, in that the free trade state, by denying itself the revenue from protective duties, limited its capacity to afford expensive standing armies and colonial bureaucracies. The problem was that Victorian Britain had inherited an extensive overseas empire amassed in the heyday of mercantilist conquest in 1780–1820. She showed no sign of giving this empire up and, indeed, steadily increased it throughout the nineteenth century. Whitehall tried to square the circle by various efforts to limit imperial liability – by refusing to assist speculative colonial ventures which overreached themselves or ran into native opposition, for instance, or by devolving the cost of local administration and defence on to the shoulders of the English settlers in the white colonies of Canada, south Africa, Australia and New Zealand. None the less, the inescapable reality of an extended empire ensured that British foreign policy always covered more than the simple defence of British security and home trade. It created strategic imperatives which governed British actions, notably the defence of the route to India, Britain's largest colonial market, and the protection of ragged colonial frontiers against native insurgents and rival powers. However minimalist British government might become at home, a superpower required an assertive foreign policy; once again the first principles of liberalism offered no clear guide to how a liberal superpower should behave.

Thus behind the consensual support for the general principles of liberalism, there was much to debate in prominent areas of policy. The political developments of the 1840s and 1850s ensured that these debates would take place within the Liberal Party. The 1846 split had left the Tory Party diminished and discredited, easily dismissed by John Stuart Mill as 'the stupid party', as it could never have been under Peel. In consequence the Liberal Party which eventually coalesced in 1859 was extremely broad in range. A Liberal might be an aristocrat or a working-class politician, an industrialist or a professional, an Anglican or a Nonconformist, an evangelical or a secularist, an imperialist or a pacifist, a Whig or a Radical, an ex-Tory or an ex-Chartist. Loose talk of the party as a 'coalition' is inappropriate, but its breadth almost guaranteed major differences in the formulation of policy. If the Liberal Party was a natural party of government, it was one which was prone to fracture *in* government: every Whig and Liberal administration between 1830 and 1895 would end in internal division in the House of Commons.[4]

At the risk of being over-schematic, it is possible to identify three main groups in the Liberal Party. The Whigs, the largely aristocratic leaders of the party, still dominated its high command. They cherished a political tradition rooted in the defence of parliamentary government and Protestantism by the opponents of James II in the 1680s. Whiggery might conceivably never have developed beyond a particularistic defence of aristocratic independence, but the Whigs of the early nineteenth century had embraced both religious pluralism and parliamentary reform in order to demolish the Tory one-party state that had developed from the 1780s, and Whiggery had broadened its range. It remained, though, a doctrine of unabashed élitism. The Whig idea of progress entailed enlightened and educative leadership of the people by the Whig élite. Whig social policy retained a paternalistic tinge. In religion, the Whigs valued the principle of church establishment as a buttress of the social order. Whiggery had few articulate advocates in this period, but this weakness was offset by the Whigs' prominence in government and by the tightly knit nature of Whig society. The effective Whig leader from 1870, the Marquess of Hartington (later the eighth Duke of Devonshire), was connected by blood or marriage to much of the remainder of the 'Grand Whiggery', including the Dukes of Sutherland, Westminster and Argyll, the Grey family and the earls of Halifax, Zetland and Northbrook. Many in this group entered politics as a matter of course, and took office for granted when their party was in power. The top-heavy nature of Gladstone's second administration, formed in 1880, with ten out of a Cabinet of thirteen either peers or connected to the aristocracy, prompted much comment; in reality the Whigs depended heavily upon their prominence in the top posts to offset the expansion of the political system beneath them. Though much liberal thought was meritocratic in principle, the political system would remain an élitist one in practice as long as money and social standing conferred political power. When this began to cease to be true in the 1880s, Whig insecurity, and disenchantment with reformist liberalism, became evident.

The second main group is the larger and more diverse category of 'moderate Liberals': the Liberals of the suburbs, particularly around London, of the professions, of the universities and of the City. This group was distinct socially from the Whigs (though many City figures were connected with Whiggery) and distinct denominationally from the predominantly Nonconformist Radicals. In their distrust of demagoguery and of evangelical enthusiasms, though, they were closer to the Whigs than the Radicals. Many were social conservatives, but this largely urban group had been lost to Toryism by Tory support for agricultural protection in the 1840s. The extension of the parliamentary vote to working-class householders in 1867 worried many of them, and there are clear signs of a shift to Conservatism in the City, in outer London and in the universities from the late 1860s, though this would not produce unambiguous effects until the political weight of the suburbs was enhanced by the redistribution of parliamentary seats in 1885.

The third group were the Radicals. Radicalism in the early nineteenth century had been characterised by hostility to the aristocratic order, to its monopoly ownership of land, to the protectionism and mercantilism that nourished it and to the established Anglican Church which supported it. The goals of Radicalism were consequently to diminish the political advantages attached to social status, to free up the land market, to end the perks conferred by law upon the landed interest, from the Corn Laws to the Game Laws, and to erode the privileges enjoyed by the Church. The collapse of the early-nineteenth-century Tory state, bringing parliamentary reform and the repeal of the Corn Laws, reduced the aristocratic character of the British polity, and the emphasis within Radical politics shifted accordingly. The voice of the secular 'philosophic Radicals', eager to produce a rational democracy in Britain, waned in the mid-Victorian period, and with the achievement of household democracy in the boroughs in 1867 some rationalist Radicals worried about the intellectual fitness of the new electorate. The extension of the urban vote in 1867 did, though, galvanise politics in many of the centres of provincial Radicalism, particularly in the industrial north, and the new organisations created to handle the wider electorate became platforms for the provincial civic élite. This translated to the national stage an urban Radicalism concerned less with the iniquities of the landed order and more with the battle between Church and chapel. Provincial Liberal Radicalism in England became almost synonymous with political Nonconformity, and Nonconformists increasingly looked to the Liberal Party to realise their political aspirations. Initially these revolved around ending religious discrimination, in such matters as compulsory Church rates or the denial of the right of burial in Anglican churchyards, but as these grievances were removed, Nonconformity concerned itself more with the direct attack upon the principle of church establishment, and with the attempt to moralise public life. Disestablishment climbed the political agenda in the 1870s, though the weakness of the cause in England limited its progress. Most English Nonconformists were concerned more with raising the moral conduct of the state, which meant promoting an ethical foreign policy and regulating the liquor trade and other agents of vice.

This web of doctrines makes it hard to place the late-Victorian Radical on a modern ideological spectrum ranging from individualism to collectivism and dominated by questions of class, wealth and welfare. There was an implicit egalitarianism in the Radical attack upon privilege, but most Radicals also supported *laisser faire* as a means of attacking the economic privileges of the wealthy. John Bright advocated giving the vote to the urban working man, and promoted the repeal of the Corn Laws to lower the working-class cost of living, but opposed legislation against the adulteration of food as an infraction of *laisser faire*. The Bradford woollen magnate Alfred Illingworth considered the royal family 'only a set of outdoor paupers' and wanted support for disestablishment to be made a test for Liberal Party membership; he supported trade unionism in his workplace but fought to break the major strike in the Yorkshire woollen industry in 1891. Nonconformity made some men sympathetic and others hostile to social reform. In the last quarter of the century Nonconformist ministers like Andrew Mearns and C. Fleming Williams in London argued that improvement of the moral condition of the poor depended upon improvement of their material condition and identified themselves with movements for housing and other social reforms, while other Nonconformists feared that social politics would weaken denominational politics. All could be described as Radicals.

Mid-Victorian liberalism thus covered a wide ideological range, ensuring scope for disagreement in many areas of policy. Not in every area. Whilst the modern reader might look first to economic and social disputes for an explanation of a party's disintegration, these issues were not the most prominent areas of Liberal contention. The two main pillars of Peelite economic liberalism – free trade and sound money – were so widely accepted as to be almost beyond debate in the mid-Victorian years. The question of state intervention in the economy was, as has been argued, less clear cut, and there were essential differences between the residual paternalism of many Whigs, the *laisser faire* leanings of Moderate Liberalism and the moral suspicion of the free market entertained by some Nonconformists. Economic slowdown from the 1870s would accentuate these differences, but they were not the principal causes of Liberal dispute. Significantly, there was little pressure from below to depart from the principles of the minimal state even when economic slowdown became obvious. The lessons of mid-century ran deep for most working-class Radicals: the Tories were the party of protection and the dear loaf, of privilege and profligacy, while the Liberals were 'the party of cheap food and high wages'.[5] Though the New Poor Law might appear to modern observers the Achilles' heel of the Victorian state, Gladstone could unblushingly invoke 'the spirit and courage of the Parliament of 1834' to a workhouse audience in 1879.[6] Without a major controversy to stimulate debate, as the Corn Laws had done in the 1840s, economic policy remained a matter for connoisseurs; neither Whiggery nor Radical Nonconformity was much motivated by economic issues.

Real contention existed elsewhere. It is hard for the student in a secular age to appreciate the pervasiveness of religious controversy in Victorian Britain, particularly as these battles were largely fought within Protestantism. Religious issues separated the parties, but they also divided the Liberal Party. Whigs and Radicals alike objected to the use of the church establishment to force a narrow creed upon the nation, but the differences between them remained divisive. The Whigs, almost exclusively Anglican, believed in church establishment as a badge of national identity and a guarantor of social stability, but they sought an establishment broad enough in doctrine to be as inclusive – and therefore 'national' – as possible. This latitudinarianism appeared spiritually inadequate to the largely evangelical Nonconformist Radicals, most of whom would have preferred a religious pluralism in which no one denomination was favoured with the privileges of establishment. While English disestablishment remained impracticable and Nonconformists continued to gain the removal of specific grievances, disagreement could be contained, but the difference of outlook between latitudinarian Whiggery and sectarian Nonconformity was a profound one, which burst out on occasions such as the debate over religous teaching in schools at the time of the 1870 Education Bill. The divisions over religious issues during Gladstone's first ministry in 1868–74 foreshadowed the later, fatal, division over Irish Home Rule. Gladstone, an Anglican from an evangelical background, shared the Nonconformist belief in the spiritual laziness of most Whigs,

and although he would never accept the case for English disestablishment, his emotional and idealistic approach to politics
resembled that of political Nonconformity, with important consequences.
     Foreign and imperial policy produced similar divisions. The
Whigs loved the empire and many of them did well out of it, as
colonial governors or in other official positions. Empire preserved overseas something of the aristocratic paternalism that
was withering in the face of economic liberalism at home. A
commitment to Britain's extended world role induced in most
Whigs a belief in *raison d'état* as the guiding principle of British
foreign policy. Many Radicals, on the other hand, relieved their
doubts about the morality of empire by convincing themselves
that the white man's burden could be borne responsibly, and
advocated an ethical foreign policy. The tension between these
two approaches was demonstrated in 1876, when Gladstone, by
then out of office and no longer Liberal leader, launched a personal campaign against Turkish massacres of Bulgarian Christians
and against the Disraeli government's pro-Turk foreign policy.
Most Nonconformists rallied to support Christians abroad suffering at infidel hands. Most Whigs, contemptuous of the populist
nature of Gladstone's crusade, were reluctant to subordinate
raison d'état to idealism in foreign affairs. Moderate Liberalism,
less susceptible to the ethical imperatives that moved
Nonconformity, largely sided with the Whigs. Again the divisions
anticipated those over Home Rule.

* * *

The mid-Victorian Liberal Party, then, was a party which agreed
on core political principles but was capable of bitter disagree-
ments on policy – not all of them arguments over details. Recur-
rent internal friction was a fact of Liberal life, and one which the
party contained with reasonable success so long as it remained
confident in its core principles, but the party's internal disputes
reveal some of the fault lines which would widen in the 1880s.
     During the 1870s government became more difficult. The end
of the mid-Victorian boom and the onset of a world-wide industrial slowdown from 1873 raised questions of economic policy
which had been dormant for a generation. They could be con-

sidered, though, at leisure: the slowdown did not create the urgent public order problems typical of the more volatile industrial economy of the 1840s. The depression was apparently monetary in origin, as the decision of various industrial nations to imitate Britain's gold standard sterilised gold in the vaults of central banks and prompted an international price fall. Falling prices made life easier for the majority of the urban working class, and the last quarter of the nineteenth century saw the expansion of leisure industries – football, the music hall, pubs and the popular press – which depended on working-class disposable income. The loudest complaints came from manufacturers hit by falling profits and 'dumped' foreign goods, who called for protection and for the watering down of the gold standard by a parallel silver standard to offset the shortage of gold. The Fair Trade League was formed in 1881 to lobby for industrial protection, but it represented a minority of industrialists – and a negligible proportion of Liberal industrialists – and achieved almost nothing.

The effects of the agricultural depression which gripped most of northern Europe from the late 1870s were much more profound. The agricultural crisis was rooted in transport improvements which allowed the shipping of wool and frozen meat from Australasia and, above all, of bulk grain from the American plains to glut European markets. Apparently unlimited grain imports meant that farmers could no longer rely upon high prices when harvests failed, and a succession of harvest failures in the late 1870s and early 1880s underlined their vulnerability. The lack of any policy response to the *industrial* depression reflected the tangential position of industrialists in the British political order, but the landed classes still dominated British politics and agriculture's plight was harder to ignore. The triumph of economic liberalism had been marked by withdrawal of the privileges previously conferred upon landed society in 1846; the agricultural depression would test the professed neutrality of Britain's liberal state.

The insecurity of the landed élite in the early 1880s was heightened by the decision of Gladstone's second government in 1884, after four barren years in office, to extend household suffrage to agricultural labourers. After a protracted crisis and the threat of obstruction in the House of Lords, the measure was passed along with a comprehensive redistribution of parliamentary seats. In the long run the Conservative gains from the latter measure probably outweighed the radical effects of the former, but it was franchise extension which impressed contemporaries. 'I don't see any hope for the Tories anywhere or anyhow', the Liberal Home Secretary Sir William Harcourt wrote to his wife in 1884.[7] It became a commonplace of political discussion that the extension of the 1867 urban franchise to the counties had made Britain a democracy, although some 40 per cent of adult men and all women still lacked the parliamentary vote. It was against this backdrop of economic depression and democratic change that the events of 1885–6 unfolded.

1 Liberal Disintegration

The party realignment of 1886 was produced by a complex political crisis, in which the issue of Irish Home Rule provoked the defection from Liberalism of a varied group comprising landed Whigs, suburban and professional 'moderate' Liberals and a handful of Radicals. By 1890 it was clear that the split was irreversible, and that British politics had shifted to the right. The Liberal defectors gave the 'Unionist'[1] alliance of Conservatives, Liberal Unionists and Radical Unionists a natural majority in the House of the Commons and an overwhelming majority in the Lords, ensuring a Tory advantage that would last twenty years.

Rural Depression

In Britain as in continental Europe the agricultural depression provided the setting for a rightward political movement, though the British experience differed in many ways from the European. The essence of the problem was the same: the entry in bulk of extra-European grain, meat and wool into European markets. Railways had opened up the American prairies, the Russian plains and the Australian outback; cheap, long-distance steamship transport allowed the invasion of European markets which had previously been protected from such competition by transport costs. With substantial extra-European imports guaranteed, European producers became vulnerable to the vagaries of the weather, as the effects of a poor harvest could no longer be offset by high prices, and the late 1870s brought a sequence of bad harvests. Governments across continental Europe responded by introducing agricultural protection, often harnessed to industrial protection, creating a powerful producers' lobby sheltered by tariffs. In Britain, with its large urban population, the decision had been made in 1846 not to shield agriculture from foreign competition; the delayed effects were felt from the mid-1870s. In two decades from 1875 cereal prices halved,

15

and wool prices suffered a similar decline. Meat, livestock and dairy prices began to fall, though less steeply, from the early 1880s. In the worst-hit areas the fabric of rural life was destroyed: Norfolk villages lost their builders, blacksmiths, tailors and shopkeepers, and 'became almost entirely dependent upon Norwich and other large towns for supplies of common necessities'.[2]

The agricultural depression hit some of the most powerful men in the land: the Tory leader Lord Salisbury saw his farming rents fall by 20 per cent in the years after 1874. He could fall back upon buoyant urban rents, as could the Dukes of Bedford and Northumberland and many other aristocratic victims of rural depression, but he still lamented the decay of the rural order. Those without an urban safety-net worried more, and the talk of landed society in the early 1880s was freighted with foreboding. 'A strange dread of something vague and imminent over society' was noted by the Tory peer Lord Carnarvon in 1881: 'it reminds one of what what one has read of as heralding great revolutions'.[3]

English landed society became in the 1880s more defensive, more sensitive to imagined threats to property and more protective of social status and political authority. The agricultural depression obviously threatened class harmony in the countryside, and hostility to landlords grew in the traditional strongholds of rural radicalism, like Norfolk and Lincolnshire, but in general the custom in the English countryside of annual rent adjustments meant that the shock of the depression was transmitted directly to landlords. There was no 'feudal reaction' in England, no widespread class warfare between landlords and tenant farmers. Agricultural labourers were the more frequent victims of the recession, as the shake-out of labour which had begun after Corn Law repeal was accelerated. Where possible they drifted to the towns, ensuring that the rural depression had urban consequences.

'The great secret of earning a profit nowadays,' one rural observer was told in 1892, 'is to keep down the labour bill.'[4] The exodus of agricultural labour to the towns was not a new phenomenon, but after 1875 it owed more to the shedding of labour in the fields than to the magnetism of industry. In fact the urban economy had always had difficulty coping with rural immigrants in industry's slack years. From the 1870s, though, surplus labour became a regular feature of the urban economy, at the root of many of the most prominent urban problems of the last two decades of the century – overcrowding, unemployment and the crisis in the Poor Law system.

Urban Crisis

The rural influx hit the large cities harder than the factory towns. London suffered in particular. The capital was surrounded by arable counties, which felt the impact of depression more intensely than the grazing areas. Since the 1850s, high rents and wages had driven labour-intensive industry out of London, and much of the central area was devoted to commerce and services. London also became the main British reception centre for the waves of poor Russian and Polish Jews fleeing the pogroms that followed the assassination of Tsar Alexander II in 1881. London was being forced to absorb two separate waves of immigrants at a time when its economy was not attuned to receive them. Most of the crises which so exercised social commentators in the 1880s were centred on London and reflected the difficulties occasioned by the rush of population into its poorer quarters: the panic over slum housing prompted by Andrew Mearns's 1883 pamphlet *The Bitter Cry of Outcast London*, which led to a Royal Commission; the concern over sweated labour which produced a House of Lords Select Committee investigation in 1888; and the campaign against unemployment in the mid-1880s, fuelled by socialist-organised protests in 1886, leading to the clash between protestors and the Metropolitan Police at Trafalgar Square on 'Bloody Sunday' in November 1887.

In the 1880s London became the poverty capital of Britain. Her labour surplus became an object of public concern, and the very word 'unemployment' entered the *Oxford English Dictionary* in 1886. The capital's poor were examined in minute detail in Charles Booth's street-by-street surveys of London life, beginning with the poor of the East End in 1887, studies which made urban poverty a pressing political issue. The settlement movement, which conveyed Oxbridge men into the East End to live among and educate the poor, began with the foundation of Toynbee Hall in Whitechapel in 1883. Successive Lord Mayors of London ran charitable appeals for the relief of distress and the improvement of slum housing.

The danger that poverty could breed unrest was inescapable in a difficult period when assumptions about steadily increasing prosperity were being challenged. In fact the headline-making episodes of anarchy, such as the stoning of the Carlton Club in 1886 or 'Bloody Sunday' the following year, were isolated. The revolutionary Social Democratic Federation, which organised the unemployment protests, was never a mass organisation. London did, though, develop a socially oriented working-class Radicalism, highly critical of the existing order, and espousing doctrines which many equated with socialism. The dominant influence was the American writer Henry George, whose doctrines of land reform proved extraordinarily tenacious. George was an amateur economist who applied traditional rent theory to modern urban conditions in his *Progress and Poverty* of 1880, and in his British lecture tour of the following year. George argued that the mono-poly powers enjoyed by landowners – because land was of finite supply – allowed them to channel the community's wealth into their own pockets. 'The great cause of inequality in the distribu-tion of wealth,' he argued, 'is inequality in the ownership of land.'[5] His work provided an explanation for the urban paradox of poverty amidst plenty: parasitical landlords, creaming off the products of the community's labours, worsened the quality of life for all. To right this wrong George and his followers advocated a punitive tax on rent or even the nationalisation of land.

The idea of the landlord as parasite had a long intellectual history; George's ability lay in popularising the doctrine. This was what many contemporaries found worrying, and the excoria-tion of 'socialism' in the early 1880s – otherwise puzzling in view of the weakness of socialist movements – referred principally to the attack on landed property. George's doctrines alarmed an already nervous landed class. There was a ready audience for attacks on landlordism; with up to 35 per cent of the income of an urban working-class family being absorbed by house rent, land reform appealed to many who would never have negotiated Ricardian theory. The popularity of land reform encouraged Radical Liberals to take up the issue. The Cabinet Radicals Joseph Chamberlain and John Bright lionised George on his visit to Britain in 1882. Chamberlain, a Londoner who had enriched himself as a manufacturer and created a personal political base in Birmingham, noted the popularity of land reform among urban working men. He cultivated a materialistic politics which he considered appropriate to the emerging democracy, stressing the paradox that growing prosperity had not brought proportionate improvements in the conditions of the poor. He identified himself with a 'Socialism' which he defined, unrigorously, as 'every kindly act of legislation by which the community has sought to discharge its ... obligations to the poor'.[6] He developed a provocative rhetoric aimed at the landed classes – enriched, as he claimed, by the labour of others – and attacked the aristocratic leaders of his own party as readily as the landed Tories. Joseph Chamberlain became the first national politician to attempt to build a career upon the grievances of the urban poor.

Wales, Scotland and Ireland

The agricultural downturn hit most severely those regions of Britain with no substantial industry to absorb surplus rural labour. In mid- and north Wales, in the highlands of Scotland and in most of Ireland there was no easy escape from the land. European governments safeguarded rural populations through agricultural protection, but the Celtic fringe belonged to a British state which considered protection heretical, and it was denied any economic panacea. In all three countries the response was a reaction against features of English domination. In Wales, where this reaction was most muted, calls for the disestablishment of the Anglican Church reached a climax in 1883, after which resistance to Church tithes became widespread. In the highlands of Scotland the crofter community, already living in a state of wretchedness, reacted to deeper privation by a comprehensive attack upon its Anglicised landlords and the established Presbyterian Church. Constitutional action, such as the formation of the Highland Land Law Reform Association in 1883 and the election of five crofter candidates to parliament in 1885, was accompanied by unconstitutional action, beginning with rent strikes in 1881 and culminating in extensive agrarian vandalism in 1884. Faith in direct action was strengthened by the apparent success of agrarian protest in Ireland: 'if we had been more of a landlord-shooting and outrageous class in Orkney, we would have had telegraphic communication long before now', a witness told the commission set up to investigate the problems of the highlands in 1883.[7] In 1884 a Liberal government sent a gunboat to police British subjects on the Isle of Skye; in 1885 the Queen's writ was said no longer to run there.

The linkage of constitutional and unconstitutional protest in the Scottish the highlands imitated precedents in Ireland. There the agricultural crisis had devastated a rural economy which had recovered well from the disaster of the 1840s famine. Poor harvests from 1878 to 1881 had ended the post-famine recovery and revived traditional social tensions. Landlords, more Irish than English, responded by a short-termist insistence upon collecting rents from farmers who were often unable to pay. In 1879–81 no farmer felt safe from eviction. The effect was to radicalise the naturally conservative farmers, who already dominated the Irish county electorate, and to encourage the fusion of nationalist politics and agrarian protest which characterised the Irish national movement from 1879. In that year the leader of the newly established Land League, Michael Davitt, agreed a joint programme with the leader of radical nationalism, Charles Stuart Parnell, advocating an Irish parliament, extended peasant proprietorship and the formation of a popularly based Irish party in parliament. This fusion allowed a land movement which was strongest in the west and among tenant farmers in Ulster, to join forces with a political movement strongest in Leinster and Munster. Parnell's own political skill facilitated the creation of a pan-Irish popular movement which transcended the country's substantial social and regional differences. It also straddled the line between legitimate and illegitimate action – Parnell possessed, as his follower William O'Brien recalled, 'the supreme gift, so rarely to be found in Ireland, of knowing when it was wisdom to be moderate and when it was wisdom to be extreme'.[8] Extremism, in the years of the Land War down to 1882, was characterised by the calculated use of crimes against public order. Meanwhile the sixty Home Rulers returned in the 1880 election played the Westminster system, pushing parliamentary procedure to breaking point with filibusters and the exhausting protraction of debates. This tactic proved sterile, and was abandoned at roughly the point that the Land League was proscribed,

giving way to the more conventional Irish National League in
1882. Nationalism entered a moderate phase which lasted until
the worsening of the agrarian economy in 1885, but the Parnel-
lite movement had already placed itself, in the eyes of much
English opinion, beyond the pale of constitutional politics.

The Evolution of Urban Politics

In Britain as in Europe, therefore, agricultural depression had
political repercussions. The political crisis of the mid-1880s
gained its particular piquancy, though, from the conjunction of
these developments with the separate evolution of the political
system prompted by the enfranchisement of much of the urban
working class in 1867. The Second Reform Act, giving the vote to
male householders in borough seats without any minimum property or rateable value qualification, really had been a 'leap in the
dark'. It was rendered more liberal than its creators had
intended in 1869, when the requirement that voters pay local
taxes in person was removed. The urban electorate more than
doubled immediately after the Act, but rose by a further 40 per
cent between 1868 and 1884, as the 1869 voters were included,
and as local organisations became better at identifying eligible
voters. This large group of novice voters provided problems and
opportunities for political managers. In many borough seats, and
particularly in towns where the major employer was the MP, the
new enlarged electorate might behave as deferentially as the old
one: in Hartlepool the local magnate Christopher Furness controlled the town for the Liberals, and challenging him there was
said to be like fighting the Pope in Rome. At the other extreme,
the ten boroughs into which London was divided before 1885
contained so many electors as to be unmanageable, and they
were shunned by those anxious to appeal to the new democracy.
It would be the major provincial centres which provided electorates large enough not to be controlled by a single magnate
or landowner but compact enough to be manageable, and it
would be these cities which produced the men who made careers
out of organising the new electorate: Archibald Salvidge and
A. B. Forwood in Tory Liverpool, Joseph Chamberlain and
Francis Schnadhorst in Liberal Birmingham.

In every borough, though, the enlarged electorate enlarged the role of local activists. The party associations set great store by their ability to unearth new voters and remove their opponents' supporters from the list. At election time in particular the efficient canvassing of voters became critical. As the electorate grew, it became increasingly necessary to enlist volunteer labour for these tasks: the black arts of electoral bribery, which had always carried the risk of legal penalties, now also became impossibly expensive. The 1880 general election produced an orgy of dubious expenditure. It also produced a consensus for reform of the system which allowed the Corrupt Practices Act to pass relatively easily in 1883. The Act imposed spending limits on individual candidates in proportion to the size of their electorate, enhancing the value of the volunteer.

In both parties, therefore, the post-1867 period saw the emergence and growing importance of the local political association. National federations of these local caucuses were formed: the National Union of Conservative Associations (NUCA) in 1867 and the National Liberal Federation (NLF) in 1877. Local and national caucuses became activist platforms. In return for their unpaid labour, party volunteers expected a recognition of their role in the party, and perhaps a greater say in the formation of policy. The caucus was primarily an urban institution, which advertised the difference between urban opinion and the views of the predominantly aristocratic leaderships of both parties. It was a vehicle for aspiring politicians who felt excluded by their parties' leaders, and it was no coincidence that these years saw the emergence of two front-line politicians who sought to use their parties' rank-and-file to attack their leaders: the Radical Liberal Joseph Chamberlain and the Tory Democrat Lord Randolph Churchill. The two men shared a populist style: demotic rhetoric, an eagerness to cultivate the press, a contempt for political etiquette (including, in Chamberlain's case, Cabinet confidentiality) and a vituperative invective aimed at their parties' 'old guards'.

There were also significant differences. Churchill had not previously been associated with the Tory rank-and-file organisations, and his attempts to use NUCA in 1883–4 savour of opportunism. His concern was narrowly organisational, to gain for NUCA a greater role in the party's processes, and he was easily bought off by Salisbury with the offer of an enhanced propaganda role for the National Union. Thereafter, although NUCA was hardly docile, the more inconvenient resolutions at its national conferences in the 1880s and 1890s, in favour of protection, for instance, or women's suffrage, could simply be ignored. Chamberlain, on the other hand, had been intimately involved in the development of the Birmingham Liberal Association in the 1870s and in the creation of the National Liberal Federation in 1877. He believed that his apprenticeship in the caucus gave him an understanding of democratic politics which his party's grandees could not match, and this confidence in his ability to interpret popular politics lay behind his uninhibited attacks upon aristocracy in 1883–4. He had always seen the NLF's role as more than organisational: at the time of its foundation he had expressed the hope that it would be 'detested by all Whigs and Whips'.[9] Even after his entry into the Cabinet in 1880 he had no qualms about using it to intensify the civil war within the Liberal Party.

The inauguration of the National Liberal Federation in 1877 was an ostentatious event, blessed by the presence of Gladstone, who had relinquished the party leadership in 1875. Though benevolent towards the new organisation, he was concerned that it should not seek a policy-making role. Those on the Whig right, less sympathetic to Radicalism, were concerned that local Liberal Associations might seek to dictate to elected MPs and turn them into delegates of the caucus. The threat was exaggerated, but not entirely imaginary. In areas where a substantial distance had emerged between sitting MPs and the rank-and-file, friction did develop. The formation of democratic Liberal Associations in the London boroughs in the early 1880s put pressure on the capital's several carpet-bagger MPs, many of whom were connected with the largely Tory City Corporation. The threat to Liberal unity was intensified by the redistribution of parliamentary seats in 1885, which covered almost the entire country in single-member constituencies. In the first place the end of the two-member borough seats created in 1867 made it impossible for Liberal organisers to share the representation between 'Whig' and Radical, making disputes more likely. Secondly a network of new seats implied a network of new constituency associations adopting new candidates. In much of the country this process amounted to little more than the endorsement of the local

grandee who would, after all, fund his own campaign and subsidise the association, but where no obvious candidate existed, or
where a sitting MP held views unpopular with the party association, caucuses might attempt to put test questions to candidates
on matters of concern to them. In much of Scotland the issue of
Scottish Church disestablishment – very much an activists' issue,
on which the leadership remained ambivalent – became a frequent test question, and one so divisive as to threaten split Liberal
candidatures in 27 Scottish seats. The divisions evident then
would be reproduced a year later over Irish Home Rule. The
new single-member constituencies, originally a Conservative
device insisted upon by Salisbury to shield suburban Tories
from inner-city Radicals, thus became another cause of Whig
discomfort within their own party. In combination with the 1883
limits on electoral expenditure they threatened the kind of
grandee control of the constituencies on which much Whig
power rested: 'small expense and single-member constituencies
will bring forward any idiot who fancies he is a politician', as the
Whiggish Earl of Durham complained in 1885.[10]

What had happened since 1867 was an inescapable progression
from an élite-dominated political system to one which was, if not
yet democratic, at least more participatory. This evolution
entailed not just the extension of the franchise but also the widening of access to the political process represented by such developments as the emergence of the caucus. The contemporary view
that Britain had attained democracy in the mid-1880s was shaped
not just by the franchise extension of 1884, which only significantly affected the counties, but also by the developments in
borough politics which had their origins in the 1867 reform.

Liberal Dissidents

This broadening of the base of British politics was a natural
process which owed nothing to the background circumstances
of the late 1870s and early 1880s. Nevertheless, Whigs saw their
position within the Liberal Party being eroded at the same time as
they saw their rent rolls falling, rural society disintegrating and
public order coming under threat in Scotland and Ireland. This
conditioned their reaction to the change. Their stock response

was to argue that the leadership of enlightened aristocrats such as themselves was a necessary safeguard in the transition to democracy. This argument was pushed to the point of self-parody in the early 1880s: the Marquess of Hartington, heir to the Duke of Devonshire and the Whigs' parliamentary leader, claimed in 1883 that while the Whigs 'are not the leaders in popular movements, [they] have been able, as I think to the great advantage of the country, to direct and guide and moderate those popular movements'; Earl Granville was said to be 'very careless about what is done, so long as they, the great nobles, have the doing of it'.[11]

These were somewhat precious – arguably self-interested – defences of Britain's *ancien régime*, but the Whig critique of 'democracy' was accepted in essence by significant numbers of men calling themselves 'Moderate Liberals', including many opinion-formers in the universities, the press, the City and other Liberal strongholds in the home counties. The concerns of these men were various, but usually derived from a fear that political developments were threatening the rational, informed democracy that had been their aim in supporting reform in 1867. Some noted the Chamberlainite emphasis upon social conditions, and feared that demagogic politicians would abandon economic rectitude for social reform. A significant group of Liberals connected with the City and the banking community, including G. J. Goschen, Sir John Lubbock and Nathan Rothschild, feared that the rules of classical economics would be bent in the chase for votes. Goschen, the most alarmist of them, thought that 'compulsory division of property would be the law' in twenty-five years' time.[12] Some feared the power of the party machine: those who had once believed that a wider franchise would encourage wider civic responsibility resented the attempts of local wire-pullers to manipulate the electorate. Some feared the prominence of evangelical Nonconformity in many urban Liberal associations. Moderate Liberals tended to be latitudinarians or, in the case of some Liberal intellectuals, agnostic rationalists. They were unmoved by Nonconformist attempts to moralise public life and sceptical of the crusading tone of Nonconformist politics. A similar fault line to that which would open up in 1886 was visible in the debates over religious issues in the 1870s, when Liberal moderates sided with the Whigs in their reluctance to appease Nonconformity.

These considerations combined to sow doubts in the minds of those who had supported reformist Liberalism in the 1860s; of the twenty contributors to the 1867 *Essays on Reform* still living in the mid-1880s, only seven would remain loyal to Gladstone. Gladstone's tendency to depict a world polarised into 'classes' and 'masses' ignored this pivotal group, so influential in moulding metropolitan opinion. The press began to move against Liberalism in the 1880s, as did much university opinion. Late Gladstonian Liberalism conspicuously lacked that vanguard of intellectual advocates that the Edwardian party would later enlist.

For all these reasons, both the Whigs proper and the wider group of 'Moderate Liberals' looked to Gladstone, who resumed the leadership of the party in 1879–80, to provide the kind of conservative leadership that he was temperamentally disinclined to offer, asking him in effect to curb the growing Radical influence within the party. There was, indeed, much that was conservative about Gladstone. He had married into a landed Whig family and was no social leveller. He believed that 'the Anglican Church is divine and (except in ecclesiastical machinery) unalterable';[13] he rejected disestablishment in England and was at best equivocal over the issue in Scotland and Wales. In economic policy he was a 'Peel–Cobden man',[14] committed to the liberal economic consensus of mid-century. He believed in economy in public finance, regretted the 'dearth of sound economists' in the Commons and would 'glory in the appellation of skin-flint'.[15] At the same time a sense of the rottenness of the political system made him less apprehensive about its evolution than many of his colleagues. Of evangelical parentage, he retained the evangelical's concern with sin, conscience and atonement, even while craving the spiritual authority of the historic Anglican Church. He sympathised with the ethical ambitions of Nonconformity even if he did not accept Nonconformists' views on church government. He shared their moral contempt for the latitudinarianism of the Whig aristocracy and for their less-than-spiritual behaviour – Hartington's mistress and racehorses, for instance. A Liverpudlian, he was contemptuous of the metropolitan establishment, which he considered intrinsically corrupt, and convinced of the innate virtue of the poor. He saw the Liberal Party as the agent of the incorporation of the working class into the political system: in 1886 he donated £500 to the cause of labour representation. In 1885 he defined 'the principle of Liberalism' as 'trust in the people, qualified by prudence'.[16] Prudently or not, he attended the inaugural meeting of the National Liberal Federation and several other caucus inaugurations, and became the first national politician regularly to address party conferences. He may not have deferred to caucus Radicalism, as the Whigs sometimes claimed, but he certainly listened to it.

Britain's World Role

This had been most evident in 1876–8, when Gladstone had harnessed the emotions of the rank-and-file in campaigning against Ottoman atrocities in Bulgaria. This campaign had drawn Gladstone back into Liberal politics after resigning the leadership in 1875, and it demonstrated the affinity with the rank-and-file which would characterise his later career. Many Whigs were angered by his invasion of the aristocratic preserve of foreign policy. They resented the attempt to elevate emotive ethical considerations above those of Britain's national interest, which required her to remain friendly with the Ottoman régime. The Whigs believed that foreign policy should be sheltered from the ebb and flow of public opinion; Gladstone welcomed popular support on an issue of principle.

In fact British foreign policy bristled with ethical problems, which would become more plentiful and more pressing as the empire expanded. Much of this expansion occurred during the 1870s and 1880s, with the result that debates within the Liberal party over the legitimate use of British power occurred when the party was already becoming disputatious. Liberalism encompassed several approaches to foreign policy. There remained a significant constituency for pure Cobdenism – the view that Britain should not venture beyond the commercial diplomacy necessary to extend free trade. If commerce was allowed to follow its natural course, trade wars would become unnecessary, as would the acquisition of large parts of the globe to create sheltered markets for British traders. By the 1880s, though, Britain already possessed large parts of the globe and was unlikely to part with them; most contemporaries saw pure Cobdenism as an anachronism. Radicals were uncomfortable about its ethical neutrality – though free trade itself remained an unequivocal good – and Gladstone himself dismissed it as a 'noble error'. By the 1880s Radicalism was more likely to acknowledge the fact of British power and seek to make it a force for good. What Radicals objected to was expansionism for its own sake, and in particular the habit of pre-emptive acquisition that developed during the 'Scramble for Africa' in the 1880s and 1890s: 'slaughtering and invading in order to obtain a scientific frontier and feeble neighbours', in the words of the influential Baptist minister C. H. Spurgeon.[17] The Whigs and Moderate Liberals were not necessarily devotees of slaughter and invasion either, and had endorsed the anti-expansionist message of Gladstone's Midlothian Campaign in 1879–80, but their view of empire was different. Much of the Whig aristocracy served as colonial governors, and a far wider section of propertied Liberalism held colonial investments. The rhetorical endorsement of empire voiced by the Oxford Moderate Liberal G. C. Brodrick in 1885 placed him a long way from the views of Spurgeon:

I like to know and to realise that, travel where I may – in Africa, in America or in the isles of the Pacific Ocean – I cannot travel far without seeing the Union Jack floating over some peaceful and prosperous settlement of my countrymen, with English faces, English manners, English ideas, English religion and English laws, talking of England as their home, cherishing equally the English sentiments of loyalty and of liberty, and speaking that familiar but noble language, which is the glorious inheritance of the English race.[18]

It had been clear since the mid-1870s that the abstentionist principles guiding mid-Victorian imperial policy were no longer adequate. The tension between British and Dutch settlers in southern Africa and the collapse of the Egyptian economy, over-burdened with European debt, showed how easily turbulence could develop in areas strategically or economically important to Britain, leaving governments with the choice between extending or relinquishing Britain's imperial stake. The spread of empire increased the numbers with a financial stake in the colonies – Gladstone himself held Egyptian bonds at the time of his government's decision to put down the Egyptian army revolt and occupy the country in 1882 – as well as those involved in missionary and other enterprises. The interest of continental rivals in expansion increased the pressure on Britain to turn informal influence into formal control. But expansion entailed serious commitments. By crushing Egyptian nationalism in 1882 Britain destroyed the only basis for future self-government in Egypt, obliging her to run the country for the indefinite future. She also acquired responsibility for containing the secessionist movement in the Egyptian dependency of the Sudan, which in time would become a greater liability than Egypt itself. The alarmist fear that a foreign power occupying the Upper Nile region could interrupt the river's flow and harm the Egyptian economy made Britain nervous about other European interest in East Africa. By the mid-1890s Britain occupied the entire region. Actions taken to block other European colonial initiatives were self-evidently provocative, and guaranteed that Britain would be dragged into the continental diplomatic maelstrom, from which she had sought to detach herself for most of the century. The implications of that change were enormous.

Imperial policy therefore proved more complicated than Gladstone had envisaged when crusading against colonial belligerence in the Midlothian campaign. In practice Liberal imperial policy would be hammered out by the 1880–5 Cabinet in response to successive colonial crises, and determined by the relative strength of the interventionist and non-interventionist factions on each occasion. Thus the concession of a large measure of self-government for the Transvaal Boers in 1881 was seen as a defeat for the Whigs, while the decision of Chamberlain and his henchman Charles Dilke to side with the Whigs over Egypt in 1882 fractured Cabinet Radicalism and made occupation inevitable. After Egypt the pattern emerged which would prevail until the Second Boer War of 1899–1902, that while each proposed extension of British power provoked hand-wringing and debate, it would eventually take place. The first bite came in 1885, with the declaration of a British protectorate in Bechuanaland (Botswana) to prevent the Germans in south-west Africa from linking with the Boers in the Transvaal.

The enthusiasm aroused by the successful Egyptian campaign in 1882 demonstrated the popularity of imperial triumphs. One

American observer reported that the average Briton 'likes Mr Gladstone better because a war has been fought under his Ministry'.[19] Colonial campaigns were, though, risky undertakings on unfamiliar ground, and the 1882 expedition was unusual in its efficiency. The Gladstone ministry saw more setbacks than triumphs: the defeat by the Boers at Majuba Hill in 1881, the loss of the Sudan in 1883 and, above all, the death of General Charles Gordon at Khartoum early in 1885, heading an expedition to evacuate Egyptian garrisons from the Sudan. Gordon's death shook the establishment and generated a wave of resentment against Gladstone and his ministry. Arguably the goverment's only responsibility lay in the choice of an unhinged would-be martyr to lead the expedition, but the episode strengthened a growing fear that the Liberals could not be trusted with the empire. This suggestion touched raw nerves on the Liberal right, and would condition the response to Gladstone's proposals for devolution in Ireland in 1886. The reaction against Irish Home Rule would be the more potent because it was treated from the start as an imperial issue.

The 1885 Election

By 1885, then, the disenchantment of the Liberal right wing was evident, and Liberal disintegration widely anticipated. The Cabinet Radicals Chamberlain and Dilke resigned from the ministry in May ('very fair Cabinet today – only three resignations', Gladstone recorded[20]), but further erosion was prevented by the resignation of the government itself in July, defeated in the Commons on a local taxation resolution. Lord Salisbury became Prime Minister at the head of a 'Caretaker' administration, awaiting the general election necessitated by the franchise reform. He, like most, still expected a simple Whig secession from the Liberal Party, in tandem perhaps with obvious fellow travellers like Goschen, who had voted to censure the Liberal government for Gordon's death. The eventual outcome was more complex.

This owed much to the ambiguous result of the 1885 general election. The election had been widely expected to produce a Liberal landslide, on the strength of untested assumptions about the new electors. Chamberlain believed that franchise reform would mark 'the true commencement of the Democratic gospel';[21] his assertive behaviour during 1884–5 and his willingness to risk breaking up the second Gladstone ministry both reflect that view. In the event the Liberals gained 334 seats against the Tories' 250, with the 86 Irish Nationalists holding the balance.

In the light of the claims made by Radicalism since the enlargement of the electorate, this outcome represented a setback. The election demonstrated how difficult it really was to discern the wishes even of this partially democratic electorate, fragmented as it was into single-member seats. The Liberals had offered a form of peasant proprietorship to the new county electors ('three acres and a cow'), and had indeed done unprecedentedly well in the counties, but much of their support proved to have come from voters in disenfranchised small boroughs bundled up in county seats, and their appeal to the rural electorate proper depended rather upon such traditional considerations as the extent of Nonconformity. Village shopkeepers and craftsmen might be Liberals, but many of the labourers – political virgins and often politically ignorant – voted with the farmers and landlords. In the larger towns there were signs that Salisbury's strategy of emancipating the suburban Tory by the creation of single-member seats had succeeded. London, most obviously, was transformed into a Tory stronghold, with the Conservatives claiming four-fifths of the sixty new seats. In most towns where redistribution had made a difference, the subdivision of the borough weakened the borough caucus, as Salisbury had intended, often encouraging a sort of micro-politics in which local issues and allegiances cut across the national forces of class and denomination. Towns with industries threatened by foreign imports might respond to a protectionist Tory candidate – the ribbon-makers of Coventry and the steel workers of Sheffield, for instance – but workers were consumers as well as producers, and miners and agricultural labourers feared the protectionist 'dear loaf'. Anglican charities might win working-class votes for the Tories in cathedral cities – the Liberal at Canterbury was told that payment of voters was preferable to payment of MPs. Dilke found his Chelsea electorate responsive to warnings about the 'dear loaf' that Tory protectionism threatened, and to the purely metropolitan question of reform of the

City livery companies, but London voters were unmoved by the Radical promise of free elementary education. The fate of free education is instructive. It was prominent in Chamberlain's freelance manifesto *The Radical Programme*, and Chamberlain thought it a vote-winner, but the first hint that the abolition of fees in public elementary schools might be funded by disendowing the Church of England provoked a storm of opposition which made the issue a liability. A Church Defence Association was formed, embracing Tories and Anglican Whigs. The defenders of denominational education were galvanised, scoring several victories in the 1885 School Board elections, and the normally Liberal Catholic vote moved to the Tories in defence of Catholic schools. The episode demonstrated, as the whole election demonstrated, the difficulty of identifying the causes that would stir the new democracy: an issue which played well in Birmingham might not run in London or in Liverpool, in Bodmin or in Greenock. The simplicities of the class politics advocated by Chamberlain in particular since the early 1880s were shown up by the complexities of a real election. The 1885 results questioned the moral authority of Chamberlainite Radicalism and emboldened the Whig/Liberal right, which had previously accepted that Radicalism spoke for the masses. The Liberal split came a step closer.

Home Rule

The 1885 election also amplified the power of Parnell's Irish Nationalist Party, at a time when the situation in Ireland was deteriorating rapidly. In September 1885 the British authorities in Dublin reported that anti-English and anti-landlord feeling had reached unprecedented levels, as had membership of the Irish National League. Failure to offer Parnell 'Home Rule or a promise of Home Rule' might see him pushed aside or forced to turn himself into a revolutionary leader.[22] The coercive powers granted by parliament in 1882 would expire during 1885, and some form of constitutional sweetener would be necessary to secure their renewal. Negotiating with Parnell during the summer, Joseph Chamberlain had floated the idea of Irish county councils and an elective central board handling such matters as education, land law and local railway schemes. After the change of government in July, the Tory Irish Secretary Carnarvon, architect of the self-governing Canadian federation in 1867, had embarked upon secret negotiations with Parnell, in the hope that a self-governing Ireland might be feasible within an imperial framework.

Gladstone had convinced himself of the moral case for Home Rule by the spring of 1885. The upsurge of agrarian protest during that year indicated that neither the reform of land tenure of 1881 nor the emergency powers adopted under the 1882 Crimes Act had subdued Irish unrest. Instead the unsolved Irish question had produced 'constipation' in British political life.[23] An immersion in Irish history persuaded Gladstone that Ireland's miseries derived from the denial of self-government in 1800, when the Act of Union had suppressed the independent Irish parliament. The Union, he concluded, had been a 'gigantic though excusable mistake'.[24] He believed previous measures of colonial devolution to have shown that real self-government encouraged loyalty, while coercive rule encouraged rebellion. After the election, which made it probable that the Liberals would return to office when parliament met, Gladstone received ever more alarmist reports about public order in Ireland. It was in this period that he began to contemplate a Home Rule measure based on the Canadian devolutionary legislation of 1840 and 1867.

Gladstone hoped that such a measure could pass by cross-party agreement, and promised Salisbury's nephew (and effectively his spokesman in the Commons) Arthur Balfour to support any Tory Home Rule proposal, but the possibility of such a consensual solution was already fading. Salisbury's view of the Irish question differed profoundly from Gladstone's, and, indeed, from the views of those Tories such as Carnarvon and Lord Randolph Churchill who advocated constitutional concessions. He believed that Irish discontent was rooted in the false promise of self-government with the parliament of 1782, and that purposeful rule from London represented the only valid Irish policy. He saw Gladstone's overtures as offensive – 'his hypocrisy makes me sick'[25] – and buried Carnarvon's proposals in Cabinet in December. The prospect of a bipartisan approach to the Irish question had therefore all but vanished by the time that Gladstone's intention to legislate for Home Rule was leaked to the press by his son Herbert in December 1885. By the time that Salisbury's stop-gap government was defeated in the new House of Commons in January 1886, it was clear that Gladstone would introduce a measure of Home Rule for Ireland.

Unwisely perhaps, Gladstone concocted his proposals in pur-dah, away from the rest of the Cabinet. They reflected the Cana-dian precedents, generally accredited by Liberals with preventing Canada from following the USA into separatism. The eventual scheme proposed a bicameral parliament in Dublin, dealing with all business except those matters specifically reserved for West-minster – 'imperial' matters such as foreign policy, tariffs, the coinage, postage, weights and measures. Westminster would retain control of the Dublin police for two years only. The Irish MPs added to Westminster in 1800 to compensate for the sup-pression of the Irish parliament would be removed. Though Parnell had once contemplated proportional representation to protect the Protestant minority concentrated in Ulster, neither this nor any other safeguard for Protestantism was envisaged. Gladstone shared Parnell's view that Ulster opposition was con-fected by unrepresentative militants in the Orange Order – his most significant misconception in the whole exercise. Home Rule would be accompanied by a land purchase Bill, providing gov-ernment credit to buy out Irish landlords who feared that their estates would be confiscated by a Dublin parliament. Gladstone had been told that they would sell on reasonable terms, and believed that a purchase Bill would mollify opposition in the House of Lords.

By this stage, though, most of his colleagues on the Liberal right did not consider the issue primarily economic. They asso-ciated Irish nationalism with civil disorder and even terrorism, and argued for firmness rather than magnanimity. Hartington, whose nephew had been assassinated by Fenian terrorists in Phoenix Park, Dublin, in 1882, believed simply that 'the Irish are our enemies nowadays'.[26] Goschen felt that Home Rule 'would show every subject race that we were no longer able to cope with resistance if resistance were offered'.[27] Many had, in any case, lost whatever enthusiasm they had possessed for colo-nial self-government. The third Earl Grey, who had advocated colonial devolution in principle as Colonial Secretary in the

1840s, now found that the real thing strengthened his distaste for democracy: colonial parliaments, with universal suffrage and no Houses of Lords, became venues for rowdiness and the politics of the pork-barrel.[28] Some Liberal intellectuals considered the Irishman unfit for self-government – 'his political instincts are those of the tribesman, not those of the citizen', Goldwyn Smith maintained[29] – and argued for an autocracy along the lines of British government in India. In the summer of 1885 the Whigs had made loyalty to Gladstone conditional upon there being no offensive innovations in Irish policy, but the election result and the deterioration in Irish civil order during 1885 had instead prompted Home Rule, and the Liberal right distanced themselves from Gladstone. Eighteen of them voted with the Tories on the motion that brought down Salisbury's caretaker ministry, and Hartington refused to join the new Gladstone government.

Much less predictable was the disenchantment of Joseph Chamberlain. He did accept office under Gladstone in 1886, though the appointment to the Local Government Board, the lowest ranking Cabinet office, symbolised his loss of prestige since the election. He became the leading Cabinet critic of Home Rule, attacking the exclusion of Irish MPs from Westminster, perversely, as a threat to imperial unity. Gaining no satisfaction on this point he literally walked out of the Cabinet in March. His reasons for opposing Home Rule were varied – that it was the first step to Irish independence, that it would not pass but would prevent the Irish from being satisfied with any lesser measure, that it would impede future social reforms – and it is hard to disentangle the ideological from the psychological in his attitude. Edward Hamilton, Gladstone's secretary, believed that Chamberlain was frustrated at his own powerlessness. It is none the less unwise to dismiss his professed motivation. He was not a 'little Englander'. He had helped to push Gladstone into Egypt in 1882, and had been prepared to go to war over Bechuanaland in 1885. In dealing with Parnell in that year he had distinguished carefully between a devolution which handed specified powers to Dublin and one which handed everything to Dublin *but* the reserved powers; he had preferred to govern Ireland by force than to concede Home Rule. His concern that Home Rule would lower Britain 'to the rank of a third rate power'[30] was consistently expressed. The fusion of imperialism and social reform which would eventually become his hallmark was developing in reaction to Gladstonianism. It would prove immensely influential.

* * *

In 1880 the historian J.A.Froude had predicted that Gladstone's Irish policy would 'bring on the struggle, so long foretold, between democracy and the rights of property'.[31] It was a prescient comment. In so far as there was a conflict between property and democracy, Ireland was the most obvious arena for it, since property rights – meaning, as usual in this period, the rights accruing to land-ownership – were less widely accepted in Ireland than anywhere else in the United Kingdom. But the conflict of 1886 was more than a battle between property and democracy. The conjunction of two processes – one the widening of access to the British political system through franchise extension and the growth of party democracy, the other the economic repercussions of the agricultural depression – had encouraged 'democracy' at a time when property felt vulnerable. Many representatives of the Liberal élites, seeing their political position threatened while their economic strength diminished, resented Gladstone's responsiveness to Radicalism. A party which already covered a wide ideological range became precariously polarised. By the mid-1880s the Liberal Party would have had trouble remaining united over any issue requiring a substantial policy initiative, and splits were conceivable over issues only loosely related to property rights, such as church government or imperial expansion as well as Ireland. In the event Home Rule was only tangentially a question of property: had it been otherwise, Chamberlain's defection would not have occurred. The defecting Whigs continued to hanker after a Liberal Party which they could lead in the old manner. Hartington, in his dealings with Salisbury before the 1886 general election, refused to promise not to return to Liberalism after the defeat of Home Rule. A 'party of resistance', binding Tories and dissident Liberals in defence of the status quo, was therefore not the inescapable consequence of the Home Rule split, and the Chamberlain complication made it still less likely. In the event the split did mark the end of the Liberal hegemony, but it was not clear at the time what would take its place.

2 Unionist Ascendancy

The Unionist Alliance

In June 1886 the Home Rule Bill was defeated on Second Reading in the Commons by 30 votes, with 93 Liberals voting against their leader. Gladstone resigned immediately as Prime Minister, the short-lived parliament was dissolved and a general election was called for July. Gladstone, though seventy-six, remained Liberal leader, ensuring that the election became a plebiscite on his policy of Home Rule. This obliged the Liberal Unionists – as those Liberals who had voted to preserve the Union with Ireland christened themselves – to fight alongside Salisbury and the Tories. They secured Salisbury's agreement to dissuade Tories from contesting seats held by Liberal Unionists, so that they faced only Gladstonian opposition, if any. Twenty-nine of the seventy-nine Liberal Unionist candidates were not, in fact, opposed, and many of those who did have to fight faced only an emasculated local Liberal Party.

The co-operation of the anti-Gladstonians increased the electoral strength of the right, and the Liberals lost 144 seats from their 1885 total. Now 316 Conservatives faced 190 Liberals and 85 Irish Nationalists; the Tories could govern with the support of the 79 Liberal Unionists. The Liberal Unionists did not, in fact, consider themselves irrevocably bound to the Tories at this point, but although some Chamberlainites would drift back to Gladstone during the parliament, the circumstances of the split and the fact of having campaigned against their former party made return difficult.

The 1886 election was thus the first step in the consolidation of the centre-right alliance produced by Home Rule, but only the first step. Both Hartington and Chamberlain still believed that the Liberal Party could be saved from its Gladstonian aberrations. Hartington refused to construct a formal coalition for that reason, and, indeed, refused to discount a return to the Liberals. Chamberlain found it difficult to believe that the party upheaval so long anticipated as a consequence of 'democracy' could produce a system dominated by such old régime figures as Salisbury and Hartington, and contemplated co-operation with the Tory Democrat Churchill. Gradually, though, two realities became apparent: first that Gladstone's survival and his undiminished commitment to Home Rule made it very difficult for either group of Liberal dissidents to return, and secondly that the position of the Liberal Unionists within a Tory-dominated alliance was very weak.

They owed their political survival to Tory rank-and-file indulgence: although Salisbury had agreed to urge local associations to give a free run to the dissident Liberals in 1886, he could not *insist* upon their doing so. Only one Tory seat was actually surrendered to a Liberal Unionist, and several Liberal Unionists were forced to stand down in favour of Tories. They gained free runs only where the Tories were already weak. The Liberal Unionists still sat on the Liberal side of the House, with an independent parliamentary organisation to counter the impression that they were Tory prisoners, but in reality their freedom was very limited. Talk of a centrist Hartington Ministry, common after the defeat of Home Rule, was soon stilled. The Liberal Unionists depended upon Tory patronage, and many Tories believed that they could have won a Home Rule election outright, without any concessions to Liberal Unionism.

Co-operation with Salisbury was unlikely to be straightforward for either Liberal Unionist wing. Chamberlain obviously had many fences to mend, having attacked Salisbury and his class in the early 1880s, but co-operation involved difficulties even for the Whigs. They depicted themselves as guardians of a tradition of enlightened reform which was alien to Salisbury, whose most recent contribution to political philosophy had been his 1883 jeremiad lamenting the degradation of modern civic life.[1] Salisbury had resigned from Disraeli's Cabinet in 1867 over parliamentary reform and had spent twenty years mired in defeatism. During this period he had redefined Toryism as a drag on the wheel of democracy – an attitude far distant from the benevolent view of measured progress that Hartington and his Whig colleagues still professed.

Where the Whig tradition was one of enlightened executive leadership, Salisbury was sceptical of the ability of governmental agencies to improve the human condition. He was the last Prime Minister for more than a century to be more than a formal

Christian, and his belief in a divine agency beyond human manipulation made him unambitious about the scope of political action. He was immune to the Disraelian myth of Tory philanthropy, preferring to emphasise self-help, 'one of the most certain and remarkable fruits of the Christian religion'.[2] His scepticism, and a gloomy view of mankind, reduced his political practice to a visionless control of the levers of government. He was no utilitarian, but his detached and unsentimental approach to politics bred a materialistic view of political motivation. He understood patronage as well as any modern Prime Minister, and 'played' the honours system with precision, if not always with restraint. He also understood that executive government rested ultimately on force, and did not hesitate to emphasise the fact in his pronouncements on Ireland. His Irish policy underwent complex changes down to 1902, but underpinning everything was the belief, first voiced in May 1886, that Ireland needed twenty years of firm government before reforms could be contemplated. Like an earlier generation of Tories, he was haunted by the image of the French Revolution – on which he amassed a large library – exemplifying the potential for anarchy within any society where authority collapsed.

He was determined not to make the sort of concessions of principle that he believed his party to have committed in 1829 and 1867: bowing to reformist pressure demoralised supporters without converting opponents. He recognised the possibility of a combination between Lord Randolph Churchill (who became Chancellor of the Exchequer in the 1886 Ministry) and Joseph Chamberlain to pull Unionism to the left, a danger which became a reality in August 1886 when the two men agreed on an updated version of Chamberlain's *Radical Programme*, and in October with Churchill's statement of Tory Democracy at Dartford. Salisbury capitalised skilfully on Churchill's impetuosity at the end of the year, accepting his resignation over a cause – the reduction of the War Office estimates – on which he would have little Tory support. Churchill was replaced as Chancellor by G. J. Goschen, the most conservative of the Liberal defectors. His removal underlined Chamberlain's isolation in supporting a government which Salisbury clearly controlled, and led Chamberlain to approach the Liberals in the hope of reunion. The 'Round Table' negotiations that followed early in 1887 only demonstrated the hardening of attitudes that had occurred even since the Home Rule split; their failure left Chamberlain bound to his new partners and forced to seek constructive legislation from a Salisbury Cabinet.

This proved less implausible than he must have feared. It is true that virtually every measure produced by the Salisbury governments of 1886–92 and 1895–1902 could be attributed to a desire to bolster the electoral position of the Tory Party, to keep the Unionist alliance together or to support some ailing Tory interest: Salisbury's eclectic legislative record is only comprehensible in this light. None the less Salisbury proved ready to adopt revolutionary methods to defend the status quo. Convinced that Irish nationalism could be undermined by reducing the impact of landlordism, this social conservative resorted to what can only be described as social engineering, attempting by means of successive land purchase Acts to scatter peasant proprietors across Ireland. Convinced that the middle class could be won for Toryism if the privileges of the aristocracy and the Church were curtailed, he legislated against Church tithes and errant clergy in 1891–2 and contemplated abolishing primogeniture. Convinced that vital local institutions were essential to curb the central state, he destroyed the county magistrates as administrators and transferred their powers to elective county councils in 1888. Convinced that the financially threatened Anglican voluntary schools were vital to the future of Church and society, the man who had habitually warned of the rapacious nature of democracy raided the public purse to bail them out, underwriting the abolition of school fees in 1891 and subsidising voluntary schools directly in 1897. Convinced that rural society was threatened by the burden of local taxation, he provided central government handouts to rural ratepayers in 1888 and 1896. All this was explicable in terms of maintaining the Unionist alliance, protecting the Union itself or rewarding a Tory lobby, but the cumulative effect was jarring, at times alarming Salisbury himself.

Irish policy presented few such dilemmas, because the central objective of avoiding Home Rule defined itself. Salisbury had little respect for Irish nationalism and, unlike Gladstone in 1885–6, considered the threat to civil order the worst reason for constitutional concessions. Tory policy was shaped in detail by Salisbury's nephew Arthur Balfour as Chief Secretary in Ireland between 1887 and 1891. Balfour believed that the Irish 'ought to have been exterminated long ago ... but it is too late now'.[3] Instead he promoted a form of colonial paternalism, combining police action with economic regeneration. Balfour's arrival followed further deterioration in the condition of rural Ireland, with renewed rent strikes, including refusals to pay even the judicial rents assessed by land courts under Gladstone's 1881 Land Act. The Irish National League (INL) launched its Plan of Campaign, by which what were reckoned fair rents were paid into a fund adminstered by the League. Balfour moved rapidly to proscribe the INL and made unremitting use of the police and the military to enforce the evictions of non-payers. He was unmoved by the INL's attempts to turn the evictions into pieces of political theatre and even by Liberal Unionist qualms over coercion, though their support for new coercion legislation had to be bought with another measure lowering the judicial rents. The benevolent side of policy was what would come to be known as 'constructive unionism' – a programme of economic development embracing the building of harbours and light railways, support for traditional industries and an early form of regional aid in what were termed the 'congested districts'. Land purchase legislation in 1888 and 1891 supplemented this. Though the policy predated Home Rule, state support for the purchase of land by tenants emerged as the principal Unionist alternative to Gladstone's constitutional proposals. Salisbury hoped, if not to cover Ireland with peasant proprietors, at least to create enough of them to dilute the hostility towards landlordism which Parnell exploited. Pouring public money into landlords' pockets did not worry him.

Policy in Ireland was shaped by the emergency which Salisbury inherited. It was never as clear what Salisbury actually wished to do with power in mainland Britain. The legislation aimed at purifying and strengthening the Church of England was probably closest to his heart and, indeed, closer to his heart than to the hearts of many in his party. He considered the Established Church the strongest barrier against 'the spirit of rash and theoretical change'.[4] He made four attempts to pass a measure aimed at making the Church tithe less offensive by ending landlords' power to distrain tenants' property in order to pay it, succeeding eventually in 1891. The analogous proposal to provide optional state grants to reduce or eliminate elementary school fees, designed to save Anglican voluntary schools the opprobrium of collecting them, was his brainchild, promoted despite the doubts of much of his Cabinet and becoming law in 1891. Similarly, Salisbury insisted on pressing the Church Discipline Bill, empowering ecclesiastical courts to punish immoral or negligent clergymen, in 1892, using the guillotine procedure to ensure its passage.

Beyond the Church measures, though, it is harder to discern an overall strategy. Much of what was done was evidently tactical. The victory of the Liberal candidate in the Spalding by-election of 1887, promising allotments for agricultural labourers, led to a hurried Allotments Act (allowing local authorities to buy or rent land which could be made available for allotments) on the insistence of rural Tory MPs fearful of the new county electorate. The need to keep Joseph Chamberlain happy as the 1892 election approached prompted a similar Bill to encourage small holdings, a measure for which neither Salisbury nor the bulk of his party had much enthusiasm. Even the free education proposal was hastened by the fear that a future Liberal government would fund a similar measure by Church disendowment, as Chamberlain had threatened in 1885, or would insist on public inspection of Anglican schools.

The greatest achievement of the 1886–92 Ministry, the reform of county government in 1888, demonstrates the complex of influences shaping Salisburian legislation. A substantial measure of local government reform was desirable to keep the Liberal Unionists happy, allowing them to show that Unionism stood for more than reaction at home and coercion in Ireland. The Chamberlainites had always advocated the democratisation of county government, still in the hands of an unelected magistracy. The right-wing Liberals had seen the strengthening of local government as a means of curbing the growth of the central state, and Salisbury agreed. He did not favour popular election of the reformed authorities, but yielded to the greater need to find a central government subsidy to reduce the burden of county rates and appease rural Tory backbenchers. It was considered inappropriate to make over large amounts of public money to unelected authorities, so the county councils were made elective.

Salisbury none the less ensured that they included a proportion nominated by the elected councillors, in the hope that the peers and gentry would re-enter by that means. Perhaps the most important issue of all, the relationship between town and county government, was casually handled in Cabinet. A new county council for London was created to avoid carving up the capital between three counties, but the number of other towns excluded from county jurisdiction was only settled by a dogfight in the Commons. This random combination of pressures shaped the most substantial Act of the 1886–92 Ministry, a measure which would remain in force until 1974.

By 1891, with allotments legislation, democratic county councils and free education all achieved, Joseph Chamberlain could reflect that much of what he had sought in his Radical days had been effected by his former opponents. The 1886 Ministry, which formally adopted the term 'Unionist' in 1890, had not been the negative government of 'resistance' that had once appeared likely, partly because of the need to retain Chamberlain's loyalty, but largely because Salisbury recognised that reactionary Conservatism would lose votes. There was no escaping the fact, though, that virtually all the Ministry's initiatives had been undertaken with an eye to Conservative electoral strength or the refurbishment of conservative groups in society. This imposed real limits on Salisbury's reformism. He would not take up initiatives which threatened to divide the party. This ruled out fresh experiments in social reform, which had little appeal to the suburban, professional and service-sector voters fleeing from Radicalism in the 1880s. It dictated caution in legislation affecting the relations of capital and labour. An attempt to tighten the law on child labour in 1891 met Tory employer resistance, and Salisbury avoided supporting the proposals for fresh employers' liability legislation from the Tory Democrat Sir John Gorst in 1892 for fear of stirring similar opposition. Chamberlain's optimistic attempt in 1892 to win Conservative sponsorship for an updated version of his 1885 social programme, introducing limitation of the working day, workmen's compensation, labour exchanges and contributory old-age pensions, encountered a predictable snub from Salisbury. Most significantly, Salisbury remained cautious towards the economic heresies of protectionism and bimetallism (the proposal to

introduce a parallel silver currency standard to offset the shortage of gold). He sympathised with protectionism, as did at least
six of his Cabinet, sixty backbench Tory MPs and about 60 per
cent of English farmers. Eight NUCA conferences passed protectionist resolutions between 1887 and 1902. None the less, the
cause offended free traders in both the Tory and Liberal Unionist
parties, disturbed the City of London and alarmed many voters.
Sensing that the issue was ripening after the adoption of the
protectionist McKinley Tariff in the USA in 1890, Salisbury risked
a carefully worded warning at Hastings in 1892 that slavish
devotion to free trade was inappropriate in a protectionist
world: 'it may be noble but it is not business'.[5] Though
Salisbury explicitly renounced duties on food and raw materials,
even the hint of protectionism was thought to have harmed
the Unionists in the 1892 election. Thereafter he avoided the
issue. This was understandable, but it left many urban Tories
aggrieved that a régime happy to throw money at rural
interests in England and Ireland was slow to reward its industrial
supporters.

Liberal Failure

By 1892 the creative limits of Salisburian government had virtually been reached, and Salisbury concluded that he could better
defend property in opposition than in office. With his jaundiced
view of democracy, he accepted that a government with a hand-
some majority in one election might easily to be dismissed at the
next, and prepared for defeat in 1892. A succession of Liberal by-
election victories down to 1890 did indeed suggest a substantial
Liberal victory, but these successes disguised the damage done by
the 1886 split.

The structural damage was obvious. The departure of most of
the party's grandees had so damaged Liberal finances that even
the upright Gladstone was forced to offer honours in return for
contributions to party funds in 1890. The Liberal position in the
House of Lords had been virtually destroyed by the loss of so
many Whig peers. Carnarvon described tellingly the plight of the
Gladstonian front bench in the Upper House, surrounded by
Liberal Unionists 'bitterly enraged and ready to tear them to

pieces'.[6] When Home Rule came before the Lords again in 1893, Liberal peers sought to escape the duty of speaking for it.

The damage to Liberal policy was less obvious but probably deeper. For the first time the party faced the consequences of a failed Gladstonian crusade. Home Rule had not won the support of the electorate but it had become the dominant political issue of the day. It virtually defined the Gladstonian party, as Liberal constituency associations outside the Chamberlainite stronghold of Birmingham rallied to Home Rule. This made the policy harder to drop, as did the Liberals' dependence upon the parliamentary support of the Irish Nationalists.

Nevertheless the airing given to Home Rule in 1886 had demonstrated real flaws in the policy which required attention before it could be run again. The compensation terms offered in the Land Bill had not mollified Irish landlords. Should they be dropped, leaving the landlords to the mercy of the Dublin parliament, or retained, to the annoyance of the Radicals, reluctant as they were to subsidise landlords? Was it safe to ignore the views of Ulster Protestants, when the mere threat of Home Rule in 1885–6 had caused a proliferation of loyalist organisations and when Salisbury's support had stiffened their will to resist? The question of the Irish MPs at Westminster was insoluble. Could they possibly be excluded from a parliament which could still tax Ireland or commit her to a foreign war? If included, could they be allowed to vote on the operation in England of powers to be handled in Ireland by the Dublin parliament? In 1887 the Liberal leadership decided to retain Irish MPs at Westminster, perhaps with restricted voting rights, but this served to stimulate demands for devolution elsewhere in the United Kingdom, particularly in Scotland. 'Home Rule all Round' might have been intellectually neater, and might have suggested a solution to the Ulster problem, but it would have reinforced the Unionist claim that Irish Home Rule was a step towards imperial disintegration. There were also dangers in advertising the extent to which the loss of support in the home counties had turned the Liberals into a party of the Celtic fringe. The Welsh Liberals, virtually monopolising the Welsh parliamentary seats and skilled in the procedures of the National Liberal Federation, pressed the leadership for their own programme of disestablishment, disendowment, land reform and secondary education, gaining approval for disestablishment at the 1887 NLF conference despite Gladstone's lack of enthusiasm. The Scottish Liberals were less Radical – few of Scotland's Whigs had defected in 1886 – but for the same reason they were less ready to subordinate Scottish demands to the overriding objective of Irish Home Rule. Even Gladstone's local association in Midlothian had not declared its support for the policy by the end of 1888. Scottish Home Rule was pressed in compensation, and accepted by the English NLF in 1888. The battles over church organisation in 1885 had encouraged the departure of the supporters of the Presbyterian established church, with the result that disestablishment also became Scottish party policy. Gladstone remained reluctant, but voted for Scottish disestablishment in 1890 when warned by Scottish party organisers that a failure to do so would damage the Liberals north of the border. The warning was probably misguided: Gladstone's action was said to have cost him 600 votes in Midlothian in 1892, demonstrating the danger of activist-driven policy.

There were dangers, too, in allowing too great a share of policy-making to pass to the periphery. The Liberal journalist H. J. Massingham claimed in 1887 that the urban working class would remain indifferent to Home Rule until the party could show 'for the East End docker the enthusiasm which they rightly developed for the Connemara cottier'.[7] The small but active group of Liberals who won London seats in the 1886 election urged greater interest in the social problems of the metropolis, which were receiving enormous attention in the late 1880s. The success of London's Radical Liberals in winning control of the new London County Council in 1889 on a social platform strengthened their claim that a social programme would enhance the Liberals' performance in London. Once again leaders became followers, with both Gladstone and his acolyte John Morley endorsing parts of the London Radicals' programme – land, housing and local taxation reform – during the Council campaign.

The difficulties caused by this profusion of policy initiatives from the rank-and-file were becoming clear by the late 1880s. The passing of the Whigs had strengthened the influence of the National Liberal Federation, which became a playground for local sections and for single-issue lobbies like the temperance reformers. Each group could claim that it represented a vital section of public opinion which the party would alienate at its peril. In the absence of any better guide to public opinion than that provided by local activists, it was easiest simply to tack items on to the party programme, but it became increasingly difficult to keep this programme coherent. This process produced the compendious manifesto adopted by the NLF conference at Newcastle in 1891, a *pot pourri* of Radical causes which embraced Welsh Disestablishment, public control of schools receiving state grants the creation of parish councils, further allotments legislation, more powers for the London County Council and an 'Omnibus resolution' covering popular control of the liquor trade, Scottish disestablishment, reform of the land laws, equalisation of the death duties upon real and personal property and the 'ending or mending' of the House of Lords.

Home Rule stood at the head of the Newcastle Programme. It had assumed fresh tactical significance as a common denominator of Liberalism which the entire party could collectively endorse. Electoral liability or not, it spared the leadership the problem of deciding priority for the rival sectional causes. Home Rule had, though, become more burdensome in itself in 1890, when Parnell was cited in a divorce case, exposing a scandal long whispered about in political circles. Gladstone was pressed by Nonconformist leaders to disown the adulterer – 'what is morally wrong can never be politically right', as the Methodist minister Hugh Price Hughes put it.[8] Ostracising Parnell had its attractions, but his refusal to leave the stage led to a divisive battle within the Irish Nationalist Party, culminating in a split between Parnell's supporters, largely urban and working-class, and his mostly rural and clerical opponents. The Parnellites were in a small minority, but they maintained the fight for most of the decade, long after Parnell's own death in 1891. The involvement of the Catholic priesthood in support of Parnell's opponents was noted by Unionists: Home Rule really did appear to mean Rome Rule. 'The rule of Mr Parnell is now the rule of the priest', declared the *Belfast News Letter*; Salisbury tried to imagine the Archbishop of Canterbury intervening to change the leadership of the Conservative Party.[9] Before 1890 the Liberals had, if anything, gained from the reaction to Unionist policy in Ireland; after the Parnell scandal, it became harder to focus public opinion on the iniquities of coercion, while the divisions within both the Nationalist and Liberal parties were corrosive. The Liberals' loss of momentum after 1890 owed much to Parnell.

In the event the 1892 general election did register the public's disenchantment with the Unionist government, but in a muted way. The Liberals failed to reverse their 1886 losses – largely to Liberal Unionists – in Scotland and the West Midlands, and won around forty fewer seats than the Unionists. They could therefore govern only with the support of the 81 Irish Nationalists (nine of them Parnellites). Gladstone now acknowledged that the Liberals' appeal owed little to Home Rule, but the capricious demands of a hung parliament ensured that a measure twice denied electoral endorsement now gained priority. Gladstone wished to give precedence to British measures in the first full session of the new parliament but was prevented not only by the Nationalists' pivotal position in the new House, but also by the fact that the competition between the two Nationalist sections made it more difficult for the larger group, under John Redmond, to yield over Home Rule. Thus the parliamentary farce of the second Home Rule Bill was played out in 1893. The new measure resembled its predecessor in most respects, though now the Irish MPs would remain at Westminster with full voting rights. It was pushed through the Commons, with liberal use of the guillotine, to be massacred in the Lords by a majority of 419 to 41 – still the largest in the history of the Upper House.

For most of the century the Lords' right to reject a substantial government measure had been more apparent than real. Previous conflicts between Lords and Commons had been resolved quickly in the Commons' favour. Salisbury had been unable to damage the 1882 [Irish rent] Arrears Bill, despite widespread antipathy towards it in the Lords. He had hoped to destroy the 1884 franchise reform, but had been forced to compromise by fellow Tory peers. Home Rule had always been less likely to prompt a damaging 'peers versus people' conflict because of its limited appeal in mainland Britain. During the 1892 election campaign Salisbury had hinted that Gladstone's reticence in clarifying the details of Home Rule would justify the Lords' veto;[10] after the ambiguous election result and the evident horse-trading between Liberals and Nationalists, he was able to claim that no mandate existed. The Liberal leaders knew that they could not chastise the Lords until the peers obstructed something unequivocally unpopular, and it was unclear which items, if any, in the Liberals' variegated programme had real popular support. With little chance either to pass Home Rule or to campaign against the peers, Gladstone brought his sixty-year parliamentary career to a close. Characteristically he did so not with retirement but with resignation on a question of principle – opposing the proposals of Earl Spencer at the Admiralty for a substantial increase in naval expenditure. Refusing to indulge 'the weakness of alarmism',[11] Gladstone resigned in March 1894.

His successor was bound to have difficulty guiding a party without a parliamentary majority and now robbed of its defining policy. Lord Rosebery, who did succeed to the leadership and the premiership, was in any case ill-suited to lead the post-Gladstonian party. In spirit he was a Whig, though a Scottish Whig who had served his apprenticeship in a land where the caucus was weak and Toryism ossified. He was less of a social conservative than the English Whigs who had defected in 1886: he had concerned himself with Scottish urban problems in the 1870s and had presided over the first eighteen months of the London County Council in 1889–90, when its innovative social programme was developed. Inheriting his title in his early twenties, he had spent a quarter of a century in the 'gilded dungeon' of the House of Lords, becoming an enthusiast for Lords reform. This enabled him to pass the undemanding Radical test of frightening Queen Victoria (who once described him as a revolutionary); the Scottish Liberal Association welcomed him to the premiership in 1894 as 'a Radical like ourselves'.[12] He was not, though, a Radical like most of the constituency Radicals of England and Wales. He was a peer with a large rentier income and a hedonistic lifestyle, immune to the ethical concerns of evangelical Nonconformity. Virtually all his Cabinet experience had been gained in the Foreign Office, an aristocratic stronghold proudly impervious to party politics. Rosebery's determination as Foreign Secretary in 1892–4 to continue Salisbury's policy of association with the Triple Alliance of Germany, Austria-Hungary and Italy lay behind the naval build-up over which Gladstone had resigned. His Whiggish enthusiasm for empire had led him in 1884 to accept the presidency of the Imperial Federation League, a lobby group in which he consorted with Tories and protectionists. He believed the post-1886 Liberal Party to be dangerously unresponsive to popular imperial sentiment, and had made the point forcibly to the rest of the Cabinet as Foreign Secretary in holding out for the creation of a British Protectorate in Uganda in 1894. Consistent with his imperialism was his growing unhappiness with Home Rule, and his first speeches as Prime Minister were aimed at attracting Liberal Unionist voters back to the Liberals now that Home Rule had slipped down the agenda. These influences lay behind his enthusiasm for the doctrines of 'national efficiency' – the pursuit of modernising administrative, educational and technological policies designed to enable Britain to prosper in a world of competing empires. He saw 'national efficiency' as compatible with the modern social Radicalism of the London County Council (LCC), but not with the ethical Radicalism of the Liberal sections.

It was the sections, though, which required satisfying after the waste of a session on Home Rule, and the Rosebery government embarked upon the largely theoretical attempt to enact the Newcastle Programme without a Commons majority and in the face of the revitalised reactionaries in the Lords. It is no coincidence that the most substantial measure passed by the Rosebery government was a Budget – by convention immune to defeat in the Lords. Harcourt's 1894 Budget was intended to pay for Spencer's battleships. Setting a precedent that would be followed in 1909, Harcourt made naval expansion the opportunity for progressive reform of the tax system. To meet the largest-ever peacetime estimates, he increased the beer and spirit duties, raised the basic rate of income tax and reformed the death duties. The existing discrimination in these duties in favour of real as against personal property was ended, and estates were taxed at a rate graduated according to wealth, up to 8 per cent on estates over £1 million. The income tax increase was also aimed at the wealthy; various abatements relieved the 'higher paid workmen, clerks, struggling professional men, the smaller shopkeepers, manufacturers and agriculturalists',[13] believed to have voted Tory in 1892. The Budget aimed to correct the situation created by Goschen in 1888, by which a national tax system biased in favour of land was used to subsidise the local tax bills of the country gentlemen. The subsidies remained, but the bias was removed: landowners were made to pay a higher proportion of their own subsidies. They duly complained, not least Rosebery himself, whose failure significantly to alter the terms of the Budget in Cabinet stopped him speaking to his Chancellor for six months. The loudest opponent was the Liberal Unionist leader the Duke of Devonshire (as Hartington had been called since inheriting his peerage in 1891) but Salisbury remained passive, conscious of the political danger of using the Lords' majority to oppose a redistributionary Budget, and aware that the Unionists could offer no other means to finance a naval build-up which they supported in principle.

The 1894 Budget was, though, one of the few achievements of an otherwise barren Ministry. In 1894–5 the Rosebery government tried and failed to legislate on the abolition of plural voting (the right of those registered in more than one parliamentary borough to vote more than once), electoral registration reform, reinstatement of evicted tenants in Ireland, limitation of the working day in the mines, licensing reform and Welsh Church disestablishment. In October 1894 Rosebery announced his intention to reform the House of Lords without consulting his Cabinet. Many of his ministers would have preferred abolition, believing that reforming the Lords would only perpetuate their mischief-making, and Rosebery's only major initiative as Prime Minister came to nothing. With by-elections eroding a majority that was anyway dependent upon the Nationalists, a dispirited government welcomed defeat on an minor censure motion in June 1895 and resigned with alacrity.

The gloomy saga of 1892–5 had raised disturbing questions about the Liberals' capacity as a governing party. Their inescapable connection with the Irish Nationalists had limited their electoral success in mainland Britain. This had left their eclectic programme vulnerable not only in the Commons but also in an increasingly self-confident House of Lords. Salisbury now saw the Lords' veto as a permanent safeguard against Radical initiatives. The veto was not absolute, as the passage of the 1894 Budget showed, but it was much more potent than ten years earlier. The Rosebery government had even tacitly encouraged it by releasing, in 1895, a flood of measures designed primarily to satisfy the party's sections, knowing that few could pass the Commons and that the peers would see off those that did. This programme of first nights, as Goschen called it,[14] represented an unedifying triumph of tactics over policy.

The whole experience encouraged Rosebery's alienation from his party; by the time he resigned the party leadership in 1896 (to be replaced by his *bête noire* Sir William Harcourt) his Liberalism was little more than nominal. It also encouraged a group of younger Liberals – H. H. Asquith, R. B. Haldane, Edward Grey, Ronald Munro-Ferguson, Sydney Buxton – sympathetic to Rosebery and his views, to criticise the influence of the NLF and the 'faddist' Radicals. This 'Liberal Imperialist' group, disproportionately drawn from Scottish Liberalism, university-trained and metropolitan in their focus, had little in common with the English provincial Radicals controlling the NLF. They looked to Rosebery as their mentor, echoing his public enthusiasm for the imperial ventures of Salisbury's 1895 government. During the imperial crises in the late 1890s, they delighted in the embarrassment of their party, accentuating the difficulty it faced in dealing with imperial questions. Though few in number, they were amongst the party's natural leaders, as the return of Asquith, Grey, Haldane and Buxton to ministerial office in the 1900s would show. Their detached and critical stance only increased Liberal discomfiture.

Inertia

Returning to office after the collapse of the Rosebery government, Salisbury immediately sought a dissolution and a general election to exploit Liberal demoralisation. The 1895 election was catastrophic for the Liberals, returning 411 Unionists against 177 Liberals and 82 Irish Nationalists. 'I was prepared for the deluge,' Harcourt wrote to Asquith, 'but not for this earthquake.'[15] Salisbury himself, perhaps for the first time, became aware of the intrinsic Conservative strength in the post-1885 system. Democracy was not the 'régime of surprises' that he had once depicted,[16] nor was the swing of the electoral pendulum as enfeebling as he had previously thought. A Liberal swing in 1892 had produced a tame minority government; a swing to the right in 1895 produced a Unionist landslide. Salisbury's confidence was enhanced by the waning of Chamberlainite Radical Unionism. In

1894 Salisbury had blocked another new social programme – old age pensions, workmen's compensation, industrial arbitration, immigration control – which Chamberlain had suggested for introduction in the House of Lords to revive the reformist credentials of Unionism. Increasingly frustrated that the speeches of Salisbury, Balfour and Devonshire did not contain 'a single creative or suggestive idea from beginning to end', Chamberlain was forced to accept that he was the prisoner of conservative Unionism.[17] His decision to accept the backwater position of Colonial Secretary on returning to the Cabinet in 1895 puzzled many, but it did imply that the pressure for unionist social reform would diminish. 'Happily that seems to be at a discount', Salisbury reflected in 1898.[18]

Home Rule was also at a discount, and the contradictions of Unionist Irish policy became clearer as the Home Rule threat receded. Another land purchase Act was passed in 1896, but by now it was becoming clear that the principal effect of that policy was not to assuage nationalism in the south but to undermine the landed interest in Ulster, where gentry Unionism yielded to a populist loyalism less open to manipulation by English Tories. With Ulster Unionism increasingly dominated by tenant farmers and urban professionals, its links with the predominantly landed Unionism in the south became weaker, beginning a process that would culminate in partition. This was doubtless inescapable, but it was hastened by a gratuitous fillip to Nationalism with the introduction of elective county government in 1898. The haphazard origins of the Irish Local Government Act typified Salisburian legislation. The agricultural rate relief given to mainland Britain in 1896 could not be extended to Ireland without accountable authorities to receive the money. Pressed for the subsidy by Ulster's Unionist MPs, the government created county authorities on English lines. From a Westminster perspective, county councils appeared a minor concession to the constitutional demands of the nationalists. Doubtless they were a poor substitute for a Dublin parliament, but they proved an excellent training ground for Nationalist politicians and accentuated the erosion of landed power.

Salisbury's last seven years as Prime Minister, down to 1902, would be rudderless. The less-attractive features of Salisburian rule – the cronyism and the liberal application of public funds to favoured interests – were accentuated. An honours binge in 1895 scattered baubles so widely that 'you cannot throw a stone at a dog these days without hitting a knight in London'.[19] In 1896 the Agricultural Rating Act found more Treasury money to lighten local taxes in the shires, when many urban ratepayers felt similarly burdened. In 1897 the voluntary schools received another handout, after the failure of an attempt to overhaul the education system in 1896. Less in the way of constructive legislation emerged to offset these political vices than in 1886–92. The major domestic measure, the Workmen's Compensation Act of 1897, was a compromise between Chamberlain's wish to compensate adequately the victims of industrial injuries and the anxiety of his colleagues – and many Tory industrialists – to minimise the costs and the compulsion involved. The Act established the worker's right to compensation for accidents which he had not caused, with the employer taking out insurance against the consequent liability, but it kept the scale of compensation payments low, excluded several industries altogether and allowed employers to opt out by providing their own schemes. Despite its spatchcock nature, the Act gained the qualified approval of the trade union movement. It was, though, almost the only constructive achievement of the third Salisbury government.

Local Initiatives

Several factors contributed to the paralysis of parliamentary politics in the 1890s: Salisbury's lack of legislative ambition, the Whigs' lack of ideas, tension within the Unionist alliance, the Liberals' internal disputes, the Lords' blocking power and their readiness to use it. The criticism of parliament as an institution that would become clamorous during the Boer War was rooted in the 1890s, when Westminster seemed unable to address the most urgent problems of the day. In these years responses to the problems caused or intensified by the industrial and agricultural depressions were more likely to be developed away from Westminster: in local government, in industry, in the nascent labour movement.

The 1890s were the golden age of municipal enterprise in Britain. The most visible innovations in local government came

in London, in response to social crisis in the capital. Surrounded
by arable counties, London had absorbed large numbers forced
from the land during the agricultural depression, as well as most
of the Jewish refugees fleeing persecution in the Russian empire
after 1881, all at a time when the capital was naturally shedding
its labour-intensive industries. The creation of the first London-
wide democratic local authority in 1888 coincided with heightened concern about the capital's social problems, and the first
elections to the new authority were dominated by social
questions. They returned a Council with a Liberal-Radical majority, seeking municipal solutions to social questions. The 'Progressive' majority on the London County Council[20] attacked
London's social problems directly, by a slum-clearance and
rehousing drive, by building municipal lodging-houses for
London's homeless, by creating parks in working-class areas.
Attention was paid to the details of the working-class quality of
life and cost of living: fraudulent traders were harried, subordinate local authorites were pressed to tighten their sanitary operations and to prosecute slum landlords. The tramways were
purchased and operated by the Council, which also attempted
to municipalise the private gas and water companies. The LCC
paid trade union wages to its employees, denied Council con-
tracts to employers who sweated their workforce and carried out
as much building work as possible by direct labour. The 'London
Programme' developed in the early 1890s became a manifesto
for social Radicals on urban authorities throughout the country,
and the Progressives' success in retaining control of the Council
for eighteen years appeared to point the way forward for Liberal
'modernisers'.

Other urban local authorities were less preoccupied with social
problems than was the early LCC, but many towns pursued
comparable policies aimed at economic regeneration and at
improving the quality of town life. Provincial councils were
more likely to be business-dominated than the LCC, and to
concern themselves primarily with infrastructure projects. Such
initiatives as the purchase of the Ribble Navigation Company by
Preston Corporation and the construction of the Manchester
Ship Canal, opened in 1894, were intended to stimulate local
trade. The municipalisation of tramways and electricity undertakings was an extension of the 'gas and water socialism'

practised by many British towns in the third quarter of the century. The corporations of Manchester, Birmingham and other towns supported technical colleges. The widespread development of 'higher grade schools' – essentially secondary schools with a commercial bias to their curriculum – by English school boards was also designed to improve the local economy: more than seventy such schools had been opened by 1900.[21] Another response to local economic problems was provided by the provision of relief works for the unemployed by several local authorities, prompted initially by a circular from Joseph Chamberlain as President of the Local Government Board in 1886. Ninety-six authorities undertook such work in 1892–3, though 31 of them had also established more durable labour bureaux (essentially labour exchanges). Finally the period saw in many cities the more energetic exercise of existing sanitary and town improvement powers, to make urban life more bearable. In Glasgow in the 1880s and 1890s the Corporation launched a working-class housing drive, accompanied by the extension and stringent application of building and sanitary regulations in slum areas. The impetus came from the Glasgow Social Union, a ginger group formed in 1889 by local businessmen, religious leaders and academics to 'prevent... catastrophe by anticipating the demands of the age'.[22] They, like similar groups elsewhere, remind us that while some municipal work was demanded by central government, most reflected local initiative.

A similar process of expansion occurred in English Poor Law authorities. Urban boards of guardians could usually avoid the full costs of unemployment during the industrial slowdown from 1873 by refusing to relieve able-bodied males, but they did have to cope with the other victims of urban life. The hard line adopted towards able-bodied men ensured that the aims of 1834 were realised, in that the workshy were denied relief along with the genuinely unemployed, but this only exposed the mass of urban destitution attributable to other causes. Most relief recipients belonged to those difficult categories that the architects of 1834 had not known how to handle: the sick, the aged, widows, orphans, the disabled, the feeble-minded. The deterrent rigours of the 1834 Poor Law were inappropriate to such cases, particularly after 1886, when the Chamberlain circular urged authorities to final jobs for the able-bodied. The gradual move towards specialist provision for the 'difficult' categories reflected a recognition that the principles of 1834 should not apply to them. The Poor Law authorities were, for instance, the obvious agencies to provide medical services to the poor and became in practice public health bodies. Poor Law infirmaries and isolation hospitals became public hospitals, used by many who were not paupers or whose pauperism resulted only from their sickness. Some Poor Law guardian boards pioneered specialist hospitals dealing with tuberculosis and other diseases, which received a state subsidy on condition that they dealt with *all* local cases, blurring further the distinction between paupers and the rest. The legislation of 1885, protecting medical relief recipients from being denied the vote, reflected public acceptance that the sick should not be treated as paupers.

Public concern for the elderly ran still deeper. The discovery in 1890 that 30 per cent of the population over 65 received poor relief encouraged the campaign for state old age pensions, taken up by Joseph Chamberlain, the Independent Labour Party and others until victory was secured in 1908. Once again, individual authorities produced their own initiatives, such as the alms-houses built by the Sheffield Guardians,[23] but in this area central government encouraged guardians to liberalise policy, moved perhaps by the enormous prospective cost of any state pensions scheme. A succession of circulars from the Local Government Board encouraged guardians to provide books, newspapers, tobacco and tea for the elderly. This relaxation of deterrence was supported by most local authorities and by the public: 'philanthropy has become a national pursuit', complained the New Poor Law's first historian in 1899, attacking these departures from the principles of 1834.[24] If so, it was an expensive one: the total cost of poor relief in England and Wales rose by 34 per cent during the 1890s, mainly through the increased provision for the sick and the aged.[25]

Local politicians during the 1890s therefore experimented in those areas of social policy which parliament was slow to tackle. One consequence was increasing involvement of philanthropic women in public life, which in turn rejuvenated the women's suffrage movement. Women could be elected to borough councils from 1869, to school boards from their inception in 1870 and to Poor Law guardian boards apparently from 1834, though none were before the 1870s. Women remained a tiny minority on local bodies, and few held powerful positions on their authorities, but most of them saw municipal work as the public equivalent of the philanthropy undertaken by many middle-class women in this period, and were less concerned with council power-broking. They argued that they were specially suited to the 'caring' services provided by their authorities, looking after pauper lunatics or workhouse children, pressing for cleaner and brighter class-rooms. In any event, as Lydia Becker, of the London School Board, claimed in 1879, 'political freedom begins for women, as it began for men, with freedom in local government'.[26] Several women later prominent in the suffrage movement began as Poor Law guardians, including Selina Cooper, Charlotte Despard and Emmeline Pankhurst.

At this time the suffrage movement was faltering. Only once since the failure to secure a women's suffrage amendment to the 1884 Reform Act had the Commons even voted on the issue. The predominantly Liberal suffrage movement was divided both by Home Rule and by the 1888 split in the National Society for Women's Suffrage over the affiliation of sympathetic political organisations. Gladstone's declaration against women's suffrage in 1892 divided the Women's Liberal Federation between those who put loyalty to the party before loyalty to the suffrage and those who did not. Against this background of organisational fragmentation, women's practical work in local government helped keep the wider aim in view. Work on Poor Law guardian boards in particular, tightly regulated as they were by central government, underlined the case for the parliamentary vote: both Emmeline Pankhurst and Charlotte Despard claimed to have been convinced of the need for suffrage by their work as guardians. At the very least, service on local bodies that often made Westminster appear the height of decorum exploded the argument that women were unfitted for the rough-and-tumble of politics.

Capital and Labour

Changes in urban life and government were mirrored by changes in industry in response to the slowdown of the 1870s. The revival of protectionism was the most visible effect. Protectionist demands had been voiced in the late 1870s by manufacturers vulnerable to cheap imports, notably in the West Midlands and the West Riding; Birmingham and Sheffield would remain the centres of the movement in England. In 1881 the National Fair Trade League was formed, seeking to capitalise upon the crumbling of free trade orthodoxy across continental Europe. Economic nationalism had still to gain a firm foothold, though, in Britain. The defeat of protectionism in the 1840s had been so complete that to most of the political establishment it remained, in the words of the old anti-Corn Law campaigner John Bright, 'a stupid and impossible proposition'.[27] Salisbury's caretaker ministry of 1885 shelved the issue by appointing the Royal Commission on the Depression of Trade and Industry to investigate the kind of subject that a Royal Commission is least competent to examine; leading Liberals boycotted the Commission in the belief that it was a protectionist ramp, but a plethora of conflicting reports from the Commissioners made legislation still less likely.

Protection and other macroeconomic remedies remained impractical politics, and were irrelevant to many employers in the exporting and service industries. Such men were more likely to respond to the price fall by cutting costs, particularly wage costs, or to enhance productivity by tighter labour discipline or greater mechanisation. These changes invited union resistance and received it in industries with established unions. Patrick Joyce has described how changes in the structure of the cotton industry – the move from family firm to limited company – weakened industrial paternalism in Lancashire, and although the Lancashire cotton industry had been unusual in its mid-Victorian harmony, industrial relations clearly did become more confrontational towards the close of the century. The years 1891–3 saw strikes in the woollen and cotton industries and in the mines. The issues varied in each case, but most of the disputes of the 1890s entailed more than a simple struggle over wages and hours. Behind them was a contest for control of work procedures, – with employers attempting to tighten work discipline, impose piece-rate payment and extend mechanisation, and unions resisting changes in established procedures.

Facing this employer challenge, the established union movement also faced an unprecedented challenge from below – from the ranks of unskilled labour. The growth of trade unionism since the 1870s had been concentrated in trades where unionism was feasible, either because craft skills acquired during a lengthy apprenticeship made the workmen irreplaceable or because the union gained, often with employer approval, *de facto* control over entry to the trade. This meant that the unskilled and the casual, who most needed union protection, were denied it. The attempts to organise unskilled labour in the 1880s owed something to the heightened concern over social issues in this period, but they were aided by the economic upturn of the late 1880s which made it feasible to organise even casual labour. The gas stokers, whose attempts at organisation in the 1870s had been easily resisted, were both empowered by changes in their working procedures and goaded by attempts to increase their workload into a succession of strikes in the 1880s. These culminated in the major national strike of 1889, aimed at securing the eight-hour working day. It was the first significant manifestation of what became known as 'New Unionism', targeting the unskilled, and was followed by the attempt to mobilise the casual labour force in the London docks in 1889. After a high-profile dispute the dockers secured a minimum wage of 6d/hour and other gains. New Unionism spread to other ports and amongst seamen, builders' labourers, transport workers, municipal employees and other previously unorganised groups. It enjoyed some success, but rested on weak foundations. It depended upon such non-economic advantages as the political sympathy of local councils, in the case of the municipal and tramway workers, or the kind of wider public enthusiasm that helped the London dockers. Few strikes in history, as Gareth Stedman Jones puts it, 'have been helped by subscriptions from the City [and] cheered on by stock-brokers'.[28] Such advantages were usually evanescent, however, and New Unionism shrank before employer counter-attack even before the economic downturn of 1892. By the end of the 1890s fewer than 10 per cent of trade unionists belonged to New Unions; the long-term influence of New Unionism depended more upon its success in changing the attitudes of the established unions.

The strength of the older unions had always rested upon excluding the weaker members of the labour force from the bargaining process, which reinforced the sectionalism of individual crafts or trades and did nothing for working-class solidarity. In the 1860s and 1870s they had improved their members' lot by incremental improvements secured through non-confrontational bargaining. Such methods induced a faith in the established industrial order, a confidence in the goodwill of management and, in some cases, a pronounced individualism: 'if Trades Unionists ... don't know where Trades Unionism begins and ends, it is about time they studied Adam Smith and John Stuart Mill' declared Ben Pickard, Yorkshire Miners' leader and epitome of old unionism, in 1897.[29] Men like Pickard saw the strike as a weapon of last resort, usually ineffective. Most old unionists were indistinguishable from Radical Liberals in their politics, and some of them did become 'Lib–Lab' MPs – labour representatives taking the Liberal Whip – after 1885.

New Unionists, on the other hand, resented craft exclusivity and preached working-class unity. Representing men whose only asset was their labour, they tended to see the strike as the first resort. Most New Unionist leaders called themselves socialists, believing in state intervention in labour relations, particularly to limit working hours, and in nationalisation of such industries as the railways and the mines. This pointed them towards political involvement, especially after the collapse of New Unionism as an industrial movement in 1891–2, and distanced them from a Liberal Party which they considered employer-dominated and irredeemably individualistic. The movement to democratise trade unionism and the movement for independent labour politics were intertwined from the start. Where unionists confident in their bargaining power might see no need for political involvement beyond their amicable relationship with Liberalism, and might be prepared to subordinate their needs to the pursuit of Home Rule or Welsh disestablishment, those suffering industrial defeat looked to change industrial law – and the parliament that made that law. James Keir Hardie, who would become Britain's first independent labour MP in 1892, first ran for parliament at Mid-Lanark in 1888 after an embittered and unsuccessful strike in the Lanarkshire coalfield. 'How [is] the system to be changed?', he asked in that campaign: 'it [is] by sending working men to parliament, not lawyers or baronets or the nominees of baronets'.[30]

It was no coincidence that the national Independent Labour Party, formed in 1893, was founded in Bradford, where the limits to trade unionism had been shown in 1891 with the defeat of the textile workers' strike at Manningham Mills. There, as in the Lanarkshire dispute, employers who were prominent local Liberals had used all available power, including the military, to crush the union. Anxious to maximise its support, the Independent Labour Party (ILP) trod carefully in defining its objectives in 1893. The title of 'Independent' rather than 'Socialist' Labour Party was adopted to avoid alienating non-socialist working men, but the party approved a socialist programme – including the eight-hour day and state provision for the aged, the sick and the unemployed – rather than confining itself to the representation of labour. In the 1895 general election the ILP ran its 28 candidates on this programme.

It distanced them from the majority of old union leaders, who saw independent labourism as a dangerous gimmick, but circumstances in the second half of the decade brought the two groups closer. After 1895 the ILP moved to the right. The influence of the New Unionist socialists – Ben Tillett, Tom Mann, Pete Curran – waned, and the party's executive came to be controlled by the four men who would dominate Edwardian labour politics: James Ramsay MacDonald, Philip Snowden, James Bruce Glasier and Keir Hardie. They steered the ILP away from association with the Marxist Social Democratic Federation, which many of the rank-and-file favoured, and towards the trade unions and the sympathetic elements in Radical Liberalism. At the same time old unionism reconsidered its sceptical attitude towards independent labour politics, as employer successes questioned the effectiveness of traditional unionism. In some industries, notably engineering, the spread of mechanisation simply debased the bargaining power of skilled labour; the Amalgamated Society of Engineers was forced to broaden its base by recruiting the semi-skilled men operating the new machines. The entire union movement was threatened by an unexpected development of the 1890s, the resort by employers to the Common Law to exploit loopholes in the definition of trade union rights under the legislation of the 1870s. The Common Law derived from a pre-industrial period and had obviously not been shaped by industrial relations cases, but its interpretation fell to a judiciary unsympathetic to trade unions, and a succession of judgements in the 1890s threatened the unions' legal position. The readiness of old unionists to trust in the benign neutrality of the state, and their consequent indifference to political action, had owed much to the favourable legal framework within which they worked. As this collapsed, they began to interest themselves in labour politics. Above all, trade unionism as a whole was stunned by the successful assault of the Federation of Engineering Associations, the engineering employers' lobby, upon the engineering union in 1897–8. A six-month lockout costing seven million working days ended in almost complete victory for the employers over Britain's most powerful craft union.

These changes persuaded a majority at the Trades Union Congress in 1899 to support the formation of a Labour Representation Committee (LRC), aiming to elect working men to parliament independently of the Liberal and Conservative Parties. The victory was a narrow one, with the giant coal and cotton unions in the minority. Similarly, the decision by the ILP's executive to affiliate to the LRC represented a choice for pragmatic co-operation with trade unionism rather than the impossibilist option of 'socialist unity' and closer association with the Marxist Social Democratic Federation (SDF). Significant minorities opposed both decisions, and the LRC, on its formation in February 1900, remained quite weak, with only 41 unions affiliated. In the longer term, though, it would be the most important of the organisations produced by the grass-roots politics of the 1890s.

* * *

The last fifteen years of the century had seen a profusion of local political initiatives in response to the problems of urban growth and industrial recession. Westminster had been largely by-passed; the laundry worker who told a *Daily Chronicle* reporter in 1895 that 'Parliament is for making war and voting pensions to royalties' was not far from the mark.[31] Much of this local activity was encouraged by the permissive nature of the Victorian liberal state – a state which had devolved executive power to local authorities, which had legalised trade union activity and which had not, unlike Bismarck's Germany, proscribed socialist parties. Yet ultimate power still lay in parliament, and the controversies generated by this micropolitical activity would soon land at parliament's door. Local authority action was straining the inefficient local taxation system, and new forms of local taxation would need new legislation. All local operations required statutory sanction, and where the law was unclear Westminster might have to clarify it. This would prove to be the case with the school boards' experiments in secondary education, and a judgement given against the London School Board in 1901 would eventually force central government to reconstruct the education system. The Poor Law system was clearly under enormous strain, and its accelerating cost was prompting calls from left and right for parliament to reconsider the fundamental purpose of poor relief. The involvement of women in local government made more anomalous their exclusion from parliament and the parliamentary electorate, which only parliament could rectify. Industrial relations law had become ragged, as inappropriate common-law precepts were used to clarify statutes. It would take the shock of the Taff Vale judgement in 1901 to drive the point home, but already it was clear that reform could only be effected by parliament. Finally, the kind of revolutionary change in commercial policy sought by industrial protectionists clearly raised major questions of national economic policy. To list the issues thrown up by the grass-roots politics of the 1890s is to anticipate the national political agenda of the 1900s: protectionism, educational reform, Poor Law reform, women's suffrage, industrial relations legislation, local taxation reform. These issues would be thrust upon Edwardian statesmen in rapid succession, changing the content of national politics.

3 Tariff Reform

National Inefficiency

Like many long-lived régimes, the Unionists were sapped by internal dispute before falling to electoral defeat. The damaging division was less between Tories and Liberal Unionists than between landed and urban Tories. Tory successes in the towns had done much to produce the Unionist ascendancy since the mid-1880s, but Salisbury's cabinets barely reflected the fact in their composition – nobody first elected after 1885 sat in a Unionist cabinet before 1903 – or in their policies. Many urban Conservatives resented the handouts for the landed interest in 1896 and for the predominantly rural voluntary schools in 1897 – 'doles for squire and parson', in Avner Offer's phrase.[1] Having warned for years that democratic governments would raid the public purse, Salisbury appeared set upon proving his point – for the benefit of rural society. Some unimaginative Cabinet promotions, including several of Salisbury's relatives, suggested that the government was becoming a clique. Tory backbench criticism of the government was growing even before it was amplified by the maladroit conduct of the second Boer War.

In October 1899 Britain went to war with the Boer republics of Transvaal and Orange Free State. The ostensible war aim was to secure voting rights for British miners lured to the Transvaal by the gold of the Rand; the concrete object was to roll back the near autonomy won by the Transvaal in the 1880s and to bring it and its mineral riches back into the orbit of Britain's Cape Colony. It would take nearly three years to realise this aim.

The danger that imperial ventures would lead Britain into an unsought war had long concerned foreign policy-makers. During the 1880s and 1890s conflict had threatened with France in north Africa and Siam, with Germany in southern Africa, with Russia on the north-western edge of the Indian empire and with assorted powers in the Far East, as Britain consolidated her imperial position. During the reconquest of the Sudan in 1898 a stand-off at Fashoda on the Upper Nile between Kitchener's army and a small French force threatened war with France. The dispute with the Transvaal, though, involved no other European power, and the Foreign Office's experience of damage limitation was not invoked; instead the High Commissioner at the Cape, Alfred Milner, negotiated personally with the Transvaaler President Kruger, answering to an under-powered Colonial Office.

In fact Milner answered to nobody during the negotiations: he exploited the autonomy traditionally granted to colonial governors to promote very modern views of imperialism and race supremacy. Believing that the British and Boer communities represented 'two wholly antagonistic systems – a medieval race oligarchy and a modern industrial state',[2] he made no real attempt to seek compromise. The Bismarckian Milner and the former Radical Joseph Chamberlain, as Colonial Secretary, both believed that the public could be educated to support an imperial war. During the final sensitive negotiations they projected their case to the British public in a manner scarcely consistent with diplomatic protocol. Milner intended to produce a justification for war rather than a settlement. Anticipating the inevitable, the Boer Republics launched in October 1899 the pre-emptive attack on British Natal which precipitated the war. The cautious Salisbury contemplated gloomily 'a considerable military effort – and all for people whom we despise, and for territory which will bring no profit and no power to England'.[3]

The Boer War has been described as Britain's Vietnam. In both cases military embarrassments followed from a reluctance to accept that a superpower could be troubled by peasant armies. In both cases the peasant army enjoyed the ability to melt into the local community, provoking the superpower into reprisals against civilians which undermined domestic support for the war. Britain was unready for this sort of conflict in 1899, and Milner's diplomacy had outpaced military preparations. A succession of reverses early in the war underlined the point. The Boer defeat was delayed rather than prevented by these early disasters, and British success in pitched battles during 1900 encouraged Salisbury to call a snap election in October of that year. Thereafter, though, the Boers conducted a guerilla campaign which the British found hard to counter. Britain's resort to scorched earth tactics, designed to smoke Boer fighters out of their sheltering communities, was slow to take effect, contributing to impatience at home during 1901. The associated policy of incarcerating whole communities – making the concentration camp a British invention – produced images of inhumanity which outraged domestic and international opinion. Without effective press censorship, the British government was as vulnerable to such exposés as Lyndon Johnson's administration would be to telejournalism in Vietnam. Sir Henry Campbell-Bannerman, the Scottish Radical who had succeeded Harcourt as Liberal leader in 1898, made the most of the disclosures, and his denunciation of these 'methods of barbarism' reached many who had previously thought little about the ethics of colonial warfare.

Initially, though, the Liberals gained little from the government's embarrassment. Nothing was more likely to reopen the divisions which had plagued the party throughout the 1890s than a morally dubious imperial war. On the outbreak of war the Liberal Imperialist group took pleasure in the discomfiture of the left. A sizeable Radical group opposed the war outright, incurring much public hostility. Campbell-Bannerman, though sympathetic to the Radicals, spoke for 'common-sense imperialism'[4] and steered his party away from an outright 'Pro-Boer' position. He could not, though, conjure unity out of discord in the 1900 election. The election was fought at the fleeting moment of euphoria when the formal campaign appeared successful and the guerilla war had yet to begin. It was a disaster for the Liberals, comparable to that of 1895. Although the Unionist share of votes cast was only just over 50 per cent, with 163 Unionist candidates unopposed their real level of support was closer to 60 per cent. Only 184 Liberals were returned to face over 400 Unionists in the new House.

By these means a tired government gained a new mandate. Salisbury, impervious to party criticism, aggravated Unionist disunity by appointing an aged, aristocratic Cabinet, including five of his relatives. Dwindling morale left the régime vulnerable to criticism of its failure to win the war in 1900. In 1915 and 1940 public disquiet at the conduct of war would be contained by the formation of coalition governments, but with no cross-party consensus on war aims in 1901 this option was unavailable. Instead the situation produced the strange anti-political hybrid known as the National Efficiency movement.

Like the two World Wars, the Boer War catalysed public doubts
about Britain's social and political institutions, but where the
coalition governments in the World Wars could channel such
criticism into the drive for a better post-war Britain, public discontent in 1901 remained overtly oppositional. The *ancien régime*
had survived to mismanage the war and few of its critics trusted it
to promote 'national efficiency'. The term became modish in the
light of evident inefficiency in South Africa. There were many
easy points to be scored from Britain's military unreadiness in
1899, but contempt for military ineptitude shaded into general
anxiety about the condition of the people. The link was the poor
health of army volunteers and the high proportion rejected. With
nearly full employment in 1899–1900, recruiting sergeants were
forced to enlist the unfit and the unemployable; the rush to the
colours was not comparable to that of 1914. None the less, the
number of rejections was alarming, and triggered concern about
national physical decline. In the 1900s Britain contemplated
questions of public health, diet, infant mortality, eugenics and
the future of the race rather as she had contemplated questions
of housing, sweated labour and unemployment in the 1880s. She
rejected *laisser faire* and the other Victorian values blamed for
Britain's failings.

What national efficiency actually required was less clear. Education was a universal good. Expertise was preferable to amateurism
in administration. The debilitating conditions of urban life should
be ameliorated: there was no glory, as Winston Churchill put it, in
an empire which could rule the waves but not clean its sewers.[5]
Such mild Prussianisation of Britain was largely uncontroversial,
though easier to invoke than to attain. Beyond that point the goals
of national efficiency became more contentious – compulsory
military service, incarceration of the mentally ill and other aspects
of social Darwinism, which remained minority causes.

The party system and even liberal democracy came under fire
in these years. Given the sterility of the 1890s this is unsurprising.
In that decade Parliament had considered education reform,
pensions, Poor Law reform, regulation of the liquor trade,
Welsh disestablishment and, of course, Irish Home Rule without
making progress in any of these areas. It had devoted inordinate
time to church legislation to little apparent effect (only 33 of 217
Bills on religious subjects introduced between 1880 and 1913

became law).[6] Impatience with what Milner called 'that rotten assembly at Westminster' was evident on the radical Right, though most critics of the system blamed the political parties rather than democracy itself. They called for a centre-right 'ministry of the talents' under a figure standing above the triviality of party conflict. Rosebery, now virtually separated from the Liberals, was most frequently cast in this role, in tandem with various Liberal Unionists – Devonshire, Milner or even Chamberlain. National efficiency was a preoccupation of political salons and the metropolitan Unionist press. Its cross-party pretensions rested more on its hostility to the traditional parties than on real consensual support: most Liberals suspected its authoritarian overtones and opposed such concrete proposals as military conscription. In fact few mainstream Conservatives involved themselves in the movement, its principal adherents being right-wing journalists, military men and the younger generation of social imperialists around Alfred Milner. Such figures were better critics than policy-makers, and despite its hold on public opinion in 1901–2, national efficiency produced very little legislation. The 1902 Education Act may have owed something to the movement, though education was ripe for reform, and the 1913 Mental Deficiency Act – a nasty exercise in eugenics, providing for the compulsory detention of the mentally inadequate – certainly did, but the list ends there. The real influence of 'national efficiency' lay in persuading a generation of articulate right-wing politicians to reject *laisser faire* and to see government intervention in the military, educational and welfare fields as essential for Britain's survival as a global power. They would offer only muted opposition to the Liberals' welfare measures after 1905, ensuring that battle was waged instead over the question of how the reforms were to be paid for, which would prove weaker ground for the Unionists.

Education Reform

Two months after the Boer surrender in May 1902 Salisbury retired, to be succeeded by his nephew Arthur Balfour. The new Prime Minister faced an immediate problem, raised by the decision in the Cockerton case of 1901 declaring that School

Boards had no power to fund secondary education. Although the situation could have been remedied simply by fresh legislation making legal what had been illegal, the case for a simultaneous overhaul of the elementary (primary) school system was pressing. The 1870 Education Act had established a two-track elementary school system in which local School Boards were created in areas where voluntary provision was inadequate. Voluntary schooling was provided almost exclusively by the churches; the Act had been necessary because the Church of England, which provided the bulk of it, was weakest where population grew most rapidly – the industrial towns and cities. Only the Catholics provided adequate denominational education in those towns, like Preston or Stockport, where they were concentrated. School Boards with local taxation powers were created to fill this gap, teaching an undenominational Christianity; empowered to call upon ratepayers' money, they proved better able than the voluntary sector to meet the ever-rising cost of education. Unionist governments were urged by their own supporters to protect Anglican voluntarism, but even without this pressure it was clear that a sector educating 51 per cent of the nation's children[7] could not be allowed to die of neglect. By 1902, 77 per cent of the cost of voluntary schools was being carried by the state,[8] but sixty voluntary schools a year were nonetheless going bankrupt in the early 1900s. Salisbury's usual response of throwing taxpayers' money at the problem – adopted in 1891 to underwrite the remission of school fees for poor parents and again in the handout for voluntary schools in 1897 – was discounted in 1902, with the budget strained by the war. The Chancellor, Hicks Beach, had already raised the income tax and the duties on tea, tobacco and spirits in 1900. In 1901 he had taken a difficult step towards taxing food by reimposing the small registration duty on corn which had lapsed in the 1890s. The Treasury was in no mood for new doles.

The government fell back upon the option that it had rejected as politically dangerous in 1896, that of supporting the voluntary schools from local taxation. This was provocative because local taxes were already strained by the growth in municipal activity since the 1880s, because more people paid rates than paid income tax and because many ratepayers were Liberal Nonconformists who resented subsidising Anglican schools. Local funding implied local authority management of the voluntary schools, and the Bill proposed entrusting both Board and voluntary schools to the county and county borough authorities, creating a uniform network of education authorities in England and Wales for the first time. This meant the abolition of the School Boards, which few Tories regretted, but also raised the danger that Nonconformist-dominated education authorities would simply end Anglican instruction in the former Anglican schools. To prevent this, the Bill denied the new education authorities power to tamper with religious instruction or with the appointment of teachers in those schools; in compensation a clause in the original Bill allowed local authorities to opt out of funding the denominational schools that they administered. This threatened the Bill's original purpose of making the Anglican system solvent, and during its passage through the Commons the clause was altered to *oblige* local authorities to provide rate aid for denominational schools. Nonconformist ratepayers would therefore be taxed to propagate a creed to which they were hostile. In Catholic areas they faced 'Rome on the rates'. When the Act became law, Nonconformists responded with an impressive campaign of non-payment of the education rate. By the time of the Balfour government's fall in 1905 there had been 65,000 prosecutions for non-payment, resulting in 3,000 property auctions to pay the rate and a hundred imprisonments – including an eighty-year-old woman locked up for seven days at Hendon.

The campaign did not kill the Act, but it is generally seen as the first step in the Liberal recovery from the 1900 disaster. The Liberals certainly benefited from the revived enthusiasm of their core supporters, but the reawakening of the denominational obsessives who had given the party its earlier faddist image was a mixed blessing. After the Liberals' return to office in 1905, attempts to revise the 1902 Act would clutter up three consecutive sessions to little effect. More significant was the Act's effect in deepening Unionist discontent. A sizeable minority of Unionists were Nonconformists – mostly Wesleyan Methodists – while shire Tories in former voluntary strongholds found themselves paying an education rate for the first time. Those town Tories who had sought urban rate relief since the farmers' windfall of 1896 faced instead a new local burden – and one which, unlike gasworks and tramways, made no profits. Most backbench Tories had little time for the 'Church Party' of

Anglican zealots which had lobbied Balfour during 1901. Faced with a choice between backing Balfour and backing the Nonconformist revolt they remained in line, but their frustration helps to explain rank-and-file support for Joseph Chamberlain's challenge to the leadership in the spring of 1903.

Tariff Reform

On 15th May 1903, in Birmingham, Joseph Chamberlain called for Britain to renounce free trade, the keystone of Victorian economic policy. He advocated a system of preferential tariffs, by which duties would be imposed upon goods produced outside the British empire, while those produced within the empire would be admitted free. The object of this 'tariff reform' was to encourage the economic integration of the empire, and he accepted that to be meaningful the proposals would have to apply principally to the food and raw materials that were the colonies' main exports. He therefore challenged the principle held to have brought political stability and social peace since the 1840s – that basic food should not be taxed. He did so not as a revenue-raising expedient but in order to safeguard the future of the British empire. This was an ambitious initiative, questioning the foundations of economic policy. Edward Hamilton, the Gladstonian Financial Secretary to the Treasury and no admirer of Chamberlain or protection, recognised immediately that the speech was 'probably the most important political pronouncement made since the Home Rule pronouncement, big with the fate of parties and perhaps of the Empire'.[9]

Chamberlain knew the empire better than most British politicians. He had visited Canada and South Africa and owned an unsuccessful sisal plantation in the Bahamas. Even in his Radical days he had avoided 'Little England' insularity, supporting the occupation of Egypt in 1882. He had opposed Home Rule as a threat to the integrity of the empire. When finally admitted to a Unionist Cabinet in 1895 he had chosen the Colonial Office ahead of more prestigious posts. There he had formulated an adventurous policy of colonial development in West Africa and the West Indies and improved the mechanism of colonial borrowing. He shared the Colonial Office's concern at the colonies' growing tendency to trade outside the empire, having noted Canada's drift into the USA's trade orbit on his visit to the two countries in 1888. Then he had countered a narrow commercial argument with a broad visionary one, appealing to 'the greatness and importance of the the distinction reserved for the Anglo-Saxon race'.[10] By 1902, after the traumas of the Boer War, his language conveyed the same vision with greater urgency: 'I feel sure that the time for small kingdoms has passed away. The future is with the great Empires and it rests with us to say whether our own shall be counted for many years to come as one of the greatest or whether we shall split up into minor, comparatively unimportant, nationalities.'[11]

Chamberlain had toyed with ideas of imperial federation for as long as he had been a Unionist. He had proposed an imperial council, empowered to tax the colonies for imperial purposes, to colonial prime ministers gathered in London for the jubilee celebrations of 1897. Imperial political union was rejected then, and at the next conference in 1902, because the colonies would not yield powers to a British-dominated imperial council. What Britain could offer them was a sheltered market for their agricultural surpluses. Having allowed its own agricultural sector to shrink, Britain had become a complementary rather than a competitor market for agricultural producers, and a very wealthy one. The Canadians had introduced tariff preference for British goods in 1898 and maintained it in the face of German hostility. By 1902 they were threatening to remove it unless they received something in return. Chamberlain hoped that the emergency corn duty introduced to pay for the war could, instead of being removed altogether, be retained as a preferential duty benefiting colonial grain.

He secured the Cabinet's agreement to this in principle before embarking on a tour of South Africa after the Boer peace. On returning in April 1903 he found the new Chancellor C. T. Ritchie threatening resignation if the agreement was not reversed. Having failed to convert Ritchie and a handful of other ministers, Chamberlain urged repeal of the duty rather than its continuation without imperial preference. He saw this episode as the latest in a series of snubs with which his Tory colleagues had rewarded his loyalty. He had seen his social reform proposals in 1892 and 1894 blocked, his Workmen's

Compensation Bill of 1897 mutilated by Salisbury and his schemes for the regeneration of the West Indian economy squashed by Hicks-Beach and the Treasury. Beach had also blocked the Chaplin Committee's proposals for old age pensions, another of Chamberlain's preoccupations, in 1899. Worst of all, he had been largely ignored as spokesman for Nonconformist Unionists (Chamberlain was a Unitarian) during the construction of the 1902 Education Bill. These accumulated slights do not explain his decision to propose tariff reform, but they do explain why he chose to launch the proposals publicly before they could be dismembered by Cabinet. Within weeks the formation of two propaganda organisations – the Tariff Reform League, promoting Chamberlain's proposals, and the Unionist Free Food League opposing them – ensured that the Unionists' internal debate would be conducted in public.

Balfour's position was exquisitely difficult. Early indications of public opinion, including a poll of 2,000 voters conducted by the *Daily Mail* in August, demonstrated substantial hostility to food duties. Chamberlain implicitly acknowledged as much in changes to his scheme after its first airing. He sought to make the proposals more palatable to the working class, first by suggesting that tariff revenues could fund old age pensions and then by proposing simultaneous reductions in the existing tea and sugar duties to offset the new duties on other foods. These modifications sat awkwardly together – if there was to be no net increase in the consumer's burden, neither pensions nor any other fresh expenditure could be funded by tariffs – but Chamberlain was no economist and his vision was not primarily an economic one. Balfour's problem was that many Unionists shared Chamberlain's imperial vision passionately, while many more considered free trade an anachronistic liberal fetish, of dwindling relevance in the modern world. Balfour himself, though never an imperial visionary, inclined towards protection as a tool of economic nationalism. He sought to shift the protectionist emphasis away from Chamberlain's imperial concern, which necessarily implied food duties, and towards industrial protection. Britain could reclaim the right to retaliate against unfair competition – 'dumping' or the employment of sweated labour, for example. This was the gist of his rather cerebral pamphlet *Economic Notes on Insular Free Trade*, published in September. Its publication made it clear that Balfour would not go to the stake for free trade. As he explained to Devonshire, who was a free trader, to do so would 'not merely break up the Unionist party: it will shatter each separate wing of the Unionist party, dividing Tory from Tory and Liberal from Liberal'.[12] At the same time Balfour's position fell short of the Chamberlainite ideal. Chamberlain aimed to use imperial preference to strengthen the empire; a retaliatory tariff of the sort proposed by Balfour need have no imperial bias and could conceivably be used against imperial producers. Balfour was concerned with Britain's immediate trading interests, Chamberlain with the long-term future of the empire. The practical difference was slight – Chamberlain himself stressed the dangers of 'dumping' to promote his cause – but it was significant. Though Balfour's proposals were supported by around half the parliamentary party, they were unacceptable both to the free traders and to Chamberlain. The impossibility of maintaining a united Cabinet was acknowledged in September when Chamberlain and three free-trader ministers, including the Chancellor, Ritchie, resigned. In October Devonshire followed them, deciding after characteristic vacillation to end his long ministerial career as a militant free trader.

These resignations diminished the Balfour government, though it limped on for more than two years, passing some substantial measures. Irish Secretary George Wyndham's 1903 Land Act completed the sequence of Unionist land purchase measures by providing new state loans for tenant purchase. The terms were so generous – repayment at 3.25 per cent over 68 years – that the nationalist leader John Dillon feared that Home Rule really would be killed by kindness. The Act rubbed salt into Chamberlain's many wounds: money unavailable for the aged or the colonies could still be found to buy out Irish landlords. In 1905 the Unemployed Workmen's Act was passed in response to alarming levels of unemployment in the previous winter. It was a patchwork proposal to co-ordinate the job-creation efforts of local authorities and charities and define the terms on which the unemployed could be registered for relief work, transferred to labour colonies or even helped to emigrate. It annoyed the charity lobby by providing no guarantee that claimants would be adequately scrutinised. It annoyed students of social conditions like William Beveridge, who thought that it treated symptoms rather than the disease and made no attempt to understand the working of the labour market. Above all, it failed to satisfy the protectionists, who argued that only tariffs could bring jobs. Tariff reform dominated political debate down to the 1906 general election. By then it was clear that the Unionist party had jettisoned free trade. There were fewer than thirty free traders in the parliamentary party, and many of them faced intense criticism from their constituency associations: Ritchie was 'deselected' at Croydon in 1904. Some crossed the floor – most conspicuously Winston Churchill, son of Lord Randolph, in 1904 – but most Unionist free traders were too conservative to enlist for Campbell-Bannerman and Radicalism. Some contemplated union with the Liberal Imperialists, most of whom were free traders, but it became clear that, apart from Rosebery, that group considered Liberal unity the best weapon against protection, and they began their return to the body of the party in 1903. Asquith, always the least disloyal of them, became Chamberlain's most effective critic.

It was virtually impossible to find a protectionist Liberal. Free trade was associated with the party's golden years and still appeared unchallengeable. Even those 'new Liberal' theorists prepared to question economic orthodoxy as it applied to social policy accepted that market forces should regulate international trade. Moreover, working-class anxiety about the cost of living proved that the case for free trade was not merely theoretical. A party which faced many difficulties in its relationship with the politicised working class found this reassuring.

Lib–Lab Relations

The prominence of the tariff battle smoothed the Liberals' dealings with the young Labour Representation Committee. Such dealings had become necessary after the growth in trade union support for the Labour Representation Committee (LRC) during 1902, caused by a single judicial coup: the House of Lords' decision in July 1901 to award the Taff Vale Railway Company damages against the Amalgamated Society of Railway Servants following the railwaymen's strike of the previous year. This was the latest and most damaging episode in the redrawing of labour law by the courts since the early 1890s. The issue of liability for the effects of strike action had been a grey area since the legislation of the 1870s. An 1893 decision implied that individual union officials were indeed liable for damages, but employers had little incentive to sue individuals. The unions themselves, not being corporate bodies at law, had been considered invulnerable to claims against their funds. The Taff Vale decision destroyed this assumption, arguing that parliament could not have intended to leave unions so unaccountable. The case cost the union £42,000, or around two-thirds of its annual income. The decision appeared to make the strike weapon unusable and to empower employers to punish unions with bankruptcy. Those conservative trade unionists who had thought separate labour politics a waste of union funds now acknowledged that a political voice was essential to safeguard the principle of collective bargaining. This helped overcome what were often profound objections to the LRC: the number of affiliated unions rose from 41 in 1901 to 165 in 1904. Of the major unions only the miners remained outside.

It was also clear that labour representation, on the scale that the LRC could realistically expect, would not in itself change the law. This could only be achieved by operating on the major parties. To begin with, the Committee had seen itself as a pressure group, lobbying Liberals and Tories alike in pursuit of labour interests. This stance had been necessary to remove the impression that the LRC was a nest of ideologues and to gain the support of Tory working men, but 'equidistance' was impossible unless the two parties were equally malleable. It ignored the increasingly evident Tory hostility to the unions – 'those cruel associations' as Salisbury had called them[13] – during the 1890s. The enthusiastic Tory response to Taff Vale demonstrated that no reform of labour law could be expected from the Unionists. What might be expected from a Liberal government remained unclear – Liberal lawyers were unenthusiastic about the Trade Union Congress's demand for immunity from damages claims – but removing the Unionists clearly required co-operation with the Liberals.

Local Lib–Lab pacts, with one party standing down in favour of the other to avoid splitting the left-of-centre vote, were already occurring sporadically. At the Clitheroe by-election of 1902 the

LRC adopted the non-Socialist trade unionist David Shackleton ahead of the Independent Labour Party's Philip Snowden in the hope of persuading the Liberals not to run a candidate. The Liberal leadership pressed the local association to support Shackleton, who was consequently returned. The logic of this co-operation was applied nationally in 1903, when Herbert Gladstone, Liberal chief whip and son of the former prime minister, negotiated with James Ramsay MacDonald, secretary of the LRC, an electoral agreement designed to limit the damage that each side could do to the other. The Liberals invited Macdonald to identify the seats which the LRC proposed to fight and undertook to discourage Liberal candidatures in those seats. In return Macdonald agreed to discourage 'wild-cat candidatures' from the LRC.[14] The agreement was secret and its details remain hazy, but it is clear that neither side had the power to enforce it against determined local opposition. It is likely that the seats earmarked for the LRC were those in which the Liberals were so weak that only a labour man could defeat the Unionists – only six of the 45 seats eventually fought by LRC candidates in 1906 had been Liberal in 1900 – and that the seats identified by MacDonald were the only ones in which the LRC had any real strength. The pact would surely have failed, and could hardly have remained secret, had coercion of the localities been necessary on either side. It worked – in that it helped 26 of the 30 LRC MPs elected in 1906 and spared the Liberals more than a handful of LRC challenges – because it entailed little sacrifice for either side. The Liberals, indeed, calculated a saving of £15,000 if the LRC were given 35 straight fights and a gain of ten seats from the Unionists if the LRC stood down elsewhere. The long-term risks of giving the LRC a foothold in parliament were incalculable.

There was much common ground between the two parties. Because most of industrial Britain was Liberal most trade union leaders had been schooled in Liberal politics. They might hate Liberal employers and reject *laisser faire*, but still be moved by the Liberal values of free trade and internationalism, by the rights of small nations, by the canons of Nonconformity or by Gladstone's idealism and ethical drive. 'Gladstone's work has made Socialism possible', wrote Keir Hardie on the great man's death in 1898.[15] The last Gladstone government had introduced the eight-hour day in War Office and Admiralty establishments and in the Post Office, and had introduced an Employers' Liability Bill based on the TUC's blueprint. In some areas Liberal weakness was such that they had little to lose by supporting LRC men. A working-class candidate might appeal to Tory trade unionists who would never vote Liberal – the label of 'independent labour' was a solution to the problem of a politically divided working class.[16] This was most likely in Tory Lancashire, but not only there – half the boot and shoe workers in Leeds were said to be Tories. In some areas – in Manchester, for example, or in the West Midlands – the labour vote was strongest in areas of Tory strength and weakest in Liberal strongholds; such complementarity encouraged Lib–Lab co-operation.[17]

There were also, though, areas where Lib–Lab relations were hostile. Where Liberalism was both strong and employer-dominated, in the West Riding of Yorkshire and the North-East, the pact was resisted by the constituency associations. Samuel Storey, Chairman of the Northern Liberal Federation, warned that the Liberal leaders were rearing 'a serpent which will sting their party to death'.[18] In Scotland, where the Liberal leadership remained landed, Whiggish and hostile to labour, no pact was possible.[19] Associations dominated by Nonconformists, as in Bristol, Leicester and Norwich, feared that the overtures to labour would distract attention from their own agenda. Even where the activists were sympathetic to labour, they knew that contesting elections was the *raison d'être* of a local party; in practice local Liberal organisation withered in areas assigned to the LRC, making the pact effectively irreversible in those seats.

Had political discussion in the years after 1903 been dominated by, for example, the question of trade unions' legal immunities, this friction might have been exacerbated, threatening the emerging 'Progressive Alliance' of labour and the Liberals. Instead the salience of tariff reform helped conceal Lib–Lab differences. Chamberlain's campaign failed almost entirely to rouse organised labour. Most union leaders saw protection as a bosses' creed, looking to the USA, where it was associated with aggressive management. The surprisingly extensive publicity given to Alfred Milner's recruitment of cheap Chinese labour to work the South African mines after the Boer peace helped damage the tariff cause: Milner was close to Chamberlain and it was easy to infer that 'Chinese slavery' embodied the tariff reformers' labour policy. The support of many protectionists for the Taff Vale judgement strengthened the impression of 'plutocratic conspiracy'.[20] Chamberlain's Tariff Commission, established to conduct an ostensibly scientific inquiry into the state of trade, failed to recruit a plausible representative of organised labour to its ranks. His attempt to create a tame labour organisation, the Trade Union Tariff Reform Association, merely advertised his failure to convert the TUC. One LRC candidate in 1906 claimed that Chamberlain believed in trade unions 'as the fox believes in rabbits'.[21] In many industrial areas capital and labour co-operated in defence of free trade. Preston witnessed in the 1906 election 'the unwonted spectacle of the leading capitalists of the town speaking for the Labour candidate, contributing to his election funds and lending him their motor cars'.[22]

On this issue the trade union movement spoke for most of the working class. Chamberlain's suggestion that tariffs might fund pensions or combat unemployment proved less impactive than free traders' images of the 'hungry forties' before the Corn Laws had been repealed. Food duties remained the protectionists' weak spot. The price level had risen gently but steadily since the mid-1890s, threatening to reverse the late-Victorian improvement in working-class living standards. There were industrial communities drawn to protectionism by the foreign threat to their trades – the steel workers of Sheffield or the lacemakers of Nottingham, for instance[23] – but there were simply not enough of them. Most of the enfranchised working class voted as consumers rather than producers, and were alienated by a gratuitous proposal to increase the cost of living. Had tariffs been floated twenty years earlier, at a time of falling prices, rising real wages and industrial slowdown, they might have fared better. Then they lacked a heavyweight political promoter and suffered the hostility of most of the political and economic establishment. By the 1900s they had their heavyweight promoter, and industrial support was substantial, but banking and commerce were scarcely more enthusiastic than before and an enlarged working-class electorate was markedly more hostile. This pointed to the Unionists' defeat in 1906.

The 1906 Election

In December 1905 the Balfour government resigned. Campbell-Bannerman formed a government and called a general election for January 1906. The campaign was dominated by tariff reform. The Liberals' poll of 45.9 per cent was less than 2 per cent higher than the Unionists', but when the 9.4 per cent of the vote cast for LRC candidates – all free traders and most unopposed by Liberals – is added, the scale of the free-trade victory becomes clear. The margin was large enough to produce massive electoral distortion. The Liberals won 401 seats and the LRC another 30, the Unionists only 156. The Liberals had secured a majority which would have appeared implausible only five years earlier. They were not dependent on the 83 Irish Nationalists or the LRC men. The latter none the less attracted much comment. Representing now a party rather than a committee, they adopted the title Labour Party in parliament, their claim to it being strengthened by the fact that they outnumbered the 24 Lib–Labs – trade unionists still taking the Liberal whip. This significant advantage was due almost entirely to the 1903 pact.

Chamberlain had anticipated electoral setbacks, but the scale of the defeat shocked him. The unpopularity of food duties was no surprise, of course, but it had long been an article of protectionist faith that they could be made palatable by association with the cause of empire. Chamberlain and the other imperial visionaries in the Unionist Party placed great faith in a latent enthusiasm for empire in the British working class, at odds with the little-Englandism or internationalism evident on the Radical left. They believed that this sentiment had embarrassed the Liberals frequently since 1886, and that only Salisbury's caution had prevented the Unionists from becoming a genuinely popular national party. The crusade for imperial integration through tariff reform had progressed rapidly in the parliamentary Unionist party, in the constituency associations and amongst Tory supporters in the country. For many of them it had become something of a religion, but it had not converted enough of the electorate. The 1906 result demonstrated how difficult it would be to 'sell' tariff reform on the basis of a greater imperial future. To Chamberlain tariff reform was an imperial project or it was nothing. For all his efforts to sugar the pill with talk of pensions or jobs, Chamberlain was essentially asking the British people to accept a higher cost of living as the price of imperial security.

Their refusal to do so might appear strange, as the late-Victorian and Edwardian period was conventionally the high point of popular imperial fervour. Much historiographical labour has been devoted to examining how the working class was gulled into loving the Empire by pervasive propaganda in everything from music hall songs to biscuit tins. This is valid, but it misses the point. In Britain, as on the Continent, politics had shifted to the right in the 1880s as industrial slowdown and agrarian depression called into question the certainties of mid-century liberalism. Usually this strengthened conservative élites with patriotic leanings, but in continental Europe the political position of those élites had been bolstered by the appeal of agricultural protection to largely rural electorates. In Britain urbanisation was so far advanced by the onset of the agrarian crisis that any attempt to protect rural communities would have been politically risky even had it not been considered intellectually disreputable. The agricultural crisis had therefore accentuated the flight to the towns instead, weakening the rural voice further. The Unionist governments of the 1890s had consequently steered clear of protection despite much sympathy for the cause. Jingoism was perhaps a substitute for protectionism, but without the material advantages that protection promised it proved a largely superficial one. Chamberlain was justified in pointing out that the world's leading superpower not only failed to organise her empire economically but dogmatically refused to so, but the political dangers of protectionism remained inescapable. Balfour was convinced in 1903 that imperial preference, though desirable, had 'not yet come within the realm of practical politics'.[24] It would not become practical politics for a quarter of a century.

4 Liberalism and Welfare

New Liberalism

The 1906 result ensured that the departure from Victorian values which had been beckoning since the Boer War came not in the form of Chamberlain's protectionist economic nationalism but in the shape of Liberal welfare reform. The tariff debate had emphasised that while international free trade was an indispensable Liberal value, domestic *laisser faire* was not. Chamberlain's pensions proposals, however nebulous, underlined the need for a Liberal social programme: younger Liberals, Campbell-Bannerman was told in 1903, were 'not content to be passive Free Traders'.[1] Two-thirds of Liberal candidates made social reform pledges in their election addresses.

Social reform involved no great upheaval in Liberal principles. Liberal thinkers since John Stuart Mill had adhered to what Mill called 'individuality', which stressed the individual's right to realise his or her social potential, rather than the narrower defence of property rights implied in 'individualism'. Minimal government was advocated by mid-century Radicals because they did not trust the aristocratic state, but where interventionist legislation was necessary for the greater social good – education, for example, or curbs on child labour in mines and factories – it was supported. The economic success of the minimal state in the 1850s and 1860s encouraged the belief that the market was the best wealth creator in normal circumstances, but this was an empirical observation more than a cardinal principle. The last chapter of Mill's *On Liberty* (1859), his strongest defence of the principle of individuality, assessed the circumstances in which society might infringe an individual's freedom, and many subsequent Liberal thinkers showed more interest in analysing these exceptions to the non-interventionist rule than in restating the rule itself. The exceptions became more numerous with the emergence of the social question in the 1880s. The greater prominence of social issues coincided with and encouraged the refurbishment of lib-

83

eral thought in the last two decades of the century. This was characterised by a greater emphasis upon the community's interest in the well-being of its weakest members. Those liberal thinkers influenced by Hegelian Idealism, most conspicuously T. H. Green, Professor of Moral Philosophy at Oxford, stressed the interdependence of the separate members of society. D. G. Ritchie, assessing *The Principles of State Interference* in 1891, emphasised 'the moral function of the state'.[2] Others, less affected by Germanic thought, stressed society's material interest in combating social problems and its consequent right to call upon private wealth to do so. J. A. Hobson argued in *Problems of Poverty* (1891) that individual wealth depended upon collectively conferred benefits – public order, education, sanitation, etc. – and that the community was entitled to a share of the wealth it had helped to create.

The difference between the moral emphasis of the Idealists and the material emphasis of Hobson or L. T. Hobhouse had policy implications. The Idealists sought to use state power primarily to elevate the individual, and in the debates over Poor Law reform in the 1900s Idealists made enemies by their apparent determination to moralise the poor before relieving them. Hobson and Hobhouse had fewer qualms about state charity and became the principal intellectual advocates of the Liberal welfare reforms. In the 1890s, though, both groups combined to create a new faith in the benevolent capacity of the state. 'New Liberal' thinkers remained individualists, but their principal concern was with the ways in which the state could correct those effects of individual competition which threatened to damage society. The municipal enterprise of the late-Victorian period showed how public authorities could improve the conditions of the poorest by building working-class housing or forcing contractors to pay fair wages, and raise the quality of life of the community as a whole by municipalising monopoly public services such as gas, water and transport. The equivalents of these policies at the national level were not always obvious, though, and there were some respects – most obviously the central question of how welfare reform was to be funded – in which municipal practice offered little guidance. 'New Liberal' thinkers tended to be better at justifying the principle of state intervention than at prescribing its practice in detail.

Social Politics

The relationship between political theory and political practice is generally an elusive one. In this case it appears that theories which were not abstruse or inaccessible were received by ministers through the political periodicals, through the heavyweight Liberal press – the *Daily Chronicle* or the *Manchester Guardian* – or through contact with those thinkers, like Hobson and Hobhouse, who moved in political circles. The pervasiveness of arguments for state intervention must have encouraged ministers to proceed with social reform projects, but offered little guidance on precise mechanisms. Thus although no government in modern times has entered office with a stronger intellectual foundation for its policies, the Liberal welfare reforms of 1905–14 still emerged in a somewhat *ad hoc* way.

The frequent suggestion that social reform played no part in the 1906 election therefore needs to be qualified. Free trade was dominant, but free trade was discussed as a social issue, and no politician campaigning in an industrial area could have been unaware of the appeal of welfare questions. It is true, though, that the salience of the tariff question had inhibited any formulation of a welfare programme by the Liberals. In the two years before his death in 1908 Campbell-Bannerman made policy by the traditional means of appeasing the various Liberal lobbies. Labour, or rather the trade union movement, was treated as a Liberal lobby for this purpose, alongside the more familiar Nonconformist groups. These sought above all the amendment of the 1902 Education Act to end the semi-independence of the voluntary schools. This object was simple enough in theory, but in practice it proved impossible to find a settlement acceptable both to Nonconformist supporters of undenominational education and the defenders – both within the Liberals' swollen ranks and amongst the Irish Nationalists – of the Catholic voluntary schools. A Bill was introduced in 1906, endeavouring to increase popular control over voluntary schools and to end religious tests for teachers whilst at the same time, in an attempt to please the Liberals' Catholic vote, allowing denominational teaching in schools where 80 per cent of parents requested it. This uncomfortable hybrid encountered much opposition in the Commons and in the country at large, giving the Lords confidence to emasculate it beyond recognition. It was consequently dropped. Two more Bills in 1907 and 1908, attempting to deal with the Nonconformist grievance that denominational teaching was paid for out of local taxation, were dropped even before they could reach the Lords. Satisfying Labour proved easier. The 1906 Trades Disputes Act reversed Taff Vale, giving unions complete immunity from damages actions despite the misgivings of Asquith, Haldane and other Liberal lawyers, while the 1906 Workmen's Compensation Act satisfied another TUC demand by preventing employers from contracting out of general legislation by offering their own schemes. These two measures became law, as did a further labour measure in 1908, granting the miners the statutory eight-hour limit on the working day for which they had campaigned for twenty years.

There was, though, more to social politics than the satisfaction of trade union demands, and during 1906–7 both Labour and Radical Liberal backbenchers called for a welfare programme. The first two pieces of social legislation – an Act allowing local authorities to provide free school meals for needy children in 1906 and one providing for compulsory medical inspection in schools in 1907 – were introduced by a Labour and a Liberal backbencher respectively. More ambitious schemes required government sponsorship. The absence of any promise of pensions legislation in the 1907 King's Speech drew a concerted protest from the Labour Party, and Asquith, now Chancellor of the Exchequer, promised to legislate. Britain's first state old age pensions scheme was duly enacted in 1908, having been drawn up by Asquith at the Exchequer and guided through the Commons by him shortly after he succeeded Campbell-Bannerman as Prime Minister in April.

Pensions and Dreadnoughts

The case for some state assistance to the elderly had been canvassed since the 1890s. The elderly had been the first to benefit from the humanisation of the Poor Law in the 1890s, and in 1896 and 1900 the Local Government Board had – for the first time under the 1834 system – actually urged guardians to provide outdoor relief (i.e. relief without the obligation to enter the workhouse) to the aged. In 1893 Chamberlain had advocated a state pension to be paid after the age of 65 to those who had made insurance contributions for forty years. Although Asquith exaggerated the drawbacks of contributory pensions in 1908, contributory schemes could not easily cover women or men in irregular employment, and Chamberlain himself disavowed them in 1899. But any proposal to pay pensions from general taxation would raise its own problems: 'the cost will be ruinous', as Edward Hamilton, Assistant Financial Secretary to the Treasury, put it in response to the Chaplin Committee's proposals of 1899.[3] That Select Committee had recommended a 5s weekly pension to those over 65 with an income below 10s a week. Asquith adopted the 5s pension and the 10s cut-off level but raised the age of entitlement to seventy. Though criminals and those receiving poor relief were excluded from the scheme, Asquith aimed at near-universal coverage above the entitlement age and below the income limit. Noting that the German contributory system reached only 126,000 people, Asquith envisaged 572,000 beneficiaries of his proposals.

His calculations made political sense. At first sight they were open to the charge that wide coverage meant a small pension paid at an advanced age. So it did, and although the pension removed 122,000 from the Poor Law, another 300,000 of pensionable age remained on it. Nevertheless, a higher pension more selectively applied would have been divisive, and even 5s was welcomed by those facing the workhouse. All the evidence suggests that pensions were immediately popular on their introduction in 1909. The problem with the scheme arose from its overall cost. Asquith had estimated the annual cost at below £6 million; in the event it totalled £8.5 million in the first full year of operation and over £12 million by 1913, partly because the number of eligible claimants had been underestimated in the first place and partly because of the dropping of the unworkable exclusion of paupers in 1910.

The result was to bring an end to a four-year sequence of budget surpluses. The deficit of £700,000 for 1908–9 was tiny in comparison with those of the Boer War years, but so limited was the scope of peacetime public expenditure in this period that economies were hard to find. The obvious target was defence spending, which accounted for nearly 40 per cent of the national budget. David Lloyd George, the Welsh radical who had replaced

Asquith as Chancellor in 1908 and who faced the funding problems that Asquith had created, hoped to squeeze the armed forces to pay for pensions: 'less money for the production of suffering, more money for the reduction of suffering'.[4] The navy's demand for new Dreadnought battleships to answer the German naval construction plans of 1907 was the most conspicuous capital project in the defence estimates, and Lloyd George attempted to limit the Admiralty to the four new ships acknowledged to be the minimum response. With the Cabinet split over the issue, the debate spilled into the press, which gave the naval case a lurid gloss. 'Is Britain going to surrender her maritime supremacy to provide old age pensions?', asked the *Daily Mail*.[5] In this climate Sir John Fisher, the First Sea Lord, panicked Reginald McKenna at the Admiralty into requesting eight new ships, though Fisher privately acknowledged six to be sufficient, and a strident campaign for the eight was conducted in the right-wing press. The eventual compromise, in March 1909, accepted four ships at once and four more if circumstances required. Circumstances did not require, as reports of German construction had been greatly exaggerated, but the additional Dreadnoughts were none the less approved in July 1909. Annual naval expenditure increased by around 25 per cent over the next two years.

The naval scare had been orchestrated by a hyperactive service chief, Fisher, and by right-wing journalists eager to embarrass the Liberal government; more significant was the eagerness of the Unionist opposition to advertise the government's budgetary difficulties. The background to this was the healing of Unionist wounds after the 1906 election, as Balfour made peace with the tariff reformers. In July 1906 Joseph Chamberlain had suffered a stroke which removed him from politics for the remaining eight years of his life. His successors as tariff reform spokesmen, Alfred Milner and Joseph's son Austen Chamberlain, lacked Joe's standing and originality, and Balfour was able during 1907 to remould the protectionist case to emphasise the tariff as revenue-raiser. What the revenue would be raised for remained at issue. Milner and Austen Chamberlain both called for social programmes more extensive, if anything, than Joseph Chamberlain had envisaged – contributory pensions (before the Liberal proposals appeared), land purchase, housing reform – but W. A. S. Hewins, Joseph Chamberlain's academic adviser, who had Balfour's ear, moved away from this social imperialism. His move reflected party senti-ment. Most grass-roots Tories wanted tariff revenues to pay for existing spending commitments rather than new ones and feared the expansion of the state. They worried that the Liberal govern-ment would be tempted to look for new wealth taxes to balance the budget. Already Asquith had, in his 1907 Budget, taxed unearned income at a higher rate than earned income. He had also aired two options considered by the Select Committee on Income Tax in 1906: the graduation of the income tax, so that the rich paid a higher proportion of their income in tax, and a 'supertax' on incomes over £5,000 a year. The pensions and the battleships approved in 1908–9 were commitments not easily abandoned; the argument that they could only be funded by tariffs gained ground on the Right.

The field was finally cleared for the full-blooded party battle that had threatened since the Liberals took office. It had not erupted over the principle of social reform because so many Unionists had absorbed collectivist views, considering *laisser faire* a relic of the Victorian attitudes which had enfeebled Britain during the Boer War. Surviving individualists – the Unionist Free Traders, the splenetic Rosebery or the independently-minded Liberal MP for Preston, Harold Cox – were politically marginal. But not even the most collectivist Unionist social reformers wished to fund their Bismarckian projects by wealth taxes. Lloyd George's redistribu-tionary 'People's Budget' of 1909 united Chamberlainites, Bal-fourites and Unionist Free Traders in hostility.

The People's Budget

Lloyd George faced a deficit of £15 million in 1909–10. Proposals for a national network of labour exchanges and a system of state-supported unemployment insurance were already under consid-eration in the Board of Trade. The Chancellor had warned the Commons in 1908 that 'I have got to rob somebody's hen roost next year';[6] he understood that change in the tax system would need to be profound if attempted at all, enabling him not merely to clear the deficit but to raise funds for future social measures. In October 1908 he had described the Old Age Pensions Act as 'just the beginning of things', anticipating 'the more gigantic task of dealing with the rest – the sick, the infirm, the unemployed, the widows and the orphans'.[7] Lloyd George envisaged a 'War Budget', designed to wage 'implacable warfare against poverty and squalidness'.[8] The autumn of 1908 brought the rare sight of a Chancellor encouraging spending ministers to spend, in order to strengthen the case for a radical Budget.

The Budget unveiled in April 1909 targeted the rich. It featured an increase in the existing death duties, an increase in the tax rate on earned income above £2,000 a year, an increase in the rate on unearned income at any level, a supertax on incomes above £5,000 p.a. (payable on the amount above £3,000), an overhaul of the duties for liquor licences, and four new land taxes, the most inventive of which was a 20 per cent tax on any increase in value of land, payable when a site changed hands through sale or death. Higher duties on spirits and tobacco were the only items to fall directly on the working class; they were substantial, but did little more than offset the remission of sugar duty in 1908. 'I made up my mind, in framing the Budget,' Lloyd George explained in July, 'that at any rate no cupboard should be barer, no lot should be harder.'[9] The middle class – salary-earners up to £2,000 p.a. – were protected, with no increase in taxes on earned income below that level. As the greatest obstacles to increases in the income tax, they were treated as a politically crucial group.

The 'People's Budget' aimed, therefore, to soak the rich while continuing to soak the poor and treading relatively lightly on those in-between. The wealth taxes were the real innovations, and their impact was enhanced by some demagogic rhetoric from Lloyd George, notably at Limehouse in East London in July. This speech, which highlighted the evils of landlordism, was made with an eye on the House of Lords, 80 per cent of whose members owned more than 2,000 acres of land. All sorts of property-owners might denounce the Budget, but only the Lords could block it.

Dilapidated Dukes

The Cabinet had always understood that the peers might reject the Budget: they had, after all, rejected or mutilated seven major measures since the 1906 election. Though it is often said that they resisted faddist Liberal measures rather than those with popular appeal, this probably exaggerates their tactical sense. The Unionist majority in the Lords had allowed the 1906 trade union and workmen's compensation legislation through because they feared that their party's response to Taff Vale might have cost votes, but they were bold enough to tinker with pensions, while the defeat of Scottish land legislation in 1906 was as unpopular north of the border as the rejection of the Budget. Though by convention the peers could not block a finance measure, their loathing of the Budget weakened that taboo. The experience of commanding the Upper House yet still being in opposition was an unsettling one for the Unionist peers, and the sense of powerlessness that it produced was intensified by Lloyd George's demagoguery. 'The dismal dirge of the dilapidated duke', as Churchill called it, rose above the other noises provoked by the Budget; Lloyd George was execrated in every country house in the land.[10] Constitutional conflict became unavoidable. The government could not allow the Lords a permanent right of veto over Liberal policies. They were being 'Thwarted. Checkmated. Beginning to look silly', Lloyd George had noted, summarising the peers' crimes for the Cabinet in March 1909.[11] At the same time the peers felt that to duck this challenge after defeating less provocative ones would admit impotence and invite more punitive taxation in future. By the autumn it was clear that the Unionist leaders could not restrain the peers; they calmed themselves by counting the possible advantages of rejection. In November the Lords threw out the People's Budget.

The 1906 parliament, with its massive Liberal majority, was therefore dissolved and an election called for January 1910. The constitutional battle between Lords and Commons and the fiscal battle between the Budget and the tariff became intertwined – 'tariff reform means happier dukes', as a Liberal poster put it. The Unionists led with tariff reform, partly to divert attention from the unloveable dukes and partly because they became less inhibited in promoting the policy as it became an alternative to 'confiscation'. This pulled some natural Conservatives back into the Unionist fold. The agricultural community, in England at least, took fright at the land taxes and voted overwhelmingly Unionist. Tory cotton manufacturers in Lancashire, who had voted Liberal in 1906 because they were free traders, swallowed tariffs in the more partisan climate of 1910.[12] Tariffs still told against the Unionists, though, amongst the working-class voters of Lancashire and London, and their failure to recapture these former strongholds prevented them from restoring their pre-1906 ascendancy.

The results have a modern look: a north–south split, with the Liberals strongest in the industrial north and Scotland, the Unionists in the south; and a marked urban–rural division, at least in England. Class voting was clearer than in Victorian elections: 'the workman is beginning to stick by his class in politics, as for years he has stuck by it in industrial disputes', the Conservative *Blackwood's Magazine* concluded.[13] The major parties stood at virtual parity – 275 Liberals against 273 Unionists. In theory, therefore, the forty Labour MPs (their number increased by the affiliation of the miners to the LRC in 1909) and the 82 Irish Nationalists held the balance of power. In reality, though either party might use its leverage to gain particular concessions from the Liberals, neither was likely to put a Unionist government into office. The Liberals remained in power and the election result was taken as an endorsement of the Budget, which passed in April.

The question of the Lords could not be settled so quickly. The pivotal position of the Irish Nationalists allowed them to demand curtailment of the Lords' veto, to remove the obstacle which had encouraged the Liberals to shelve Home Rule since 1906. The Unionist leadership appreciated that substantial reform of the Upper House would be essential if it were to retain its powers, and Rosebery, who had cultivated Lords reform as a pet subject during forty years' observation of the peers' deficiencies, introduced proposals in March to limit the right of hereditary peers to sit in the Lords. The Cabinet itself toyed with reform until it became aware of backbench hostility to any half measures in chastising the peers. The only option short of abolition was a restriction of the veto, which the Lords would not pass without the threat of being swamped by a mass creation of Liberal peers if they refused. Only the King could make peers, and he refused to do so without an unequivocal mandate in a second election. The death of Edward VII in May changed matters to the extent that the parties hesitated to pitch his son, George V, into this maelstrom. In June the government accepted a suggestion emanating from the imperialist Unionist Right – Lord Curzon, J. L. Garvin, F. S. Oliver – for a conference between representatives of each party to settle the constitutional crisis. For five months this 'all-England eleven', as Curzon put it,[14] wrestled with the problem. Their deliberations were interesting for their consideration of Oliver's proposals for regular conferences of party leaders and Lloyd George's suggestion of a government of national unity to deal with the crisis. Both showed how pervasive the 'national efficiency' distaste for party politics still was, but with the Liberals unready to drop Irish Home Rule and the Unionists unready to accept it, no agreement was possible on wider issues. When the conference broke up in November, the Liberals decided to exploit the King's inexperience after all. Asquith and Crewe, Liberal leader in the Lords, secured from him a secret pledge to create new peers if the Liberals won another election. A second election was called for December.

The principal change from January was Balfour's pledge to subject food duties to a national referendum. The referendum appealed in principle to many Unionists as a safeguard against the danger that minority parties or lobbies might bully the Liberals into promoting unpopular measures. A tariff referendum in particular appealed to Balfour as a means of dropping food duties unless they were genuinely popular: a Unionist victory in December would have allowed him to crush the Chamberlainites. In the event the result – 274 Unionists, 270 Liberals, 84 Irish Nationalists and 42 Labour – was virtually the same as in January, and the Chamberlainites turned on Balfour instead.

The December 1910 election cleared the way for limitation of the Lords' veto. The Parliament Bill of 1911 allowed the peers to reject a measure only twice. If passed unamended by the Commons in a third consecutive session the measure would become law regardless of the Lords' opposition. In compensation the maximum period between elections was reduced from seven to five years. With the King pledged to create peers if needed, the Unionist leaders decided not to spin out resistance in the Lords. As a result they brought the hatred of their Diehard right wing upon themselves before the Upper House approved its own emasculation on a hot and tense night in August 1911. Chamberlainites were conspicuous in this opposition, uniting with the backwoods peers and the right-wing press in defence of the Lords and in hostility to Balfour. They failed to defend the Lords, but they claimed Balfour's scalp, forcing his resignation as leader in November 1911.

Satisfying Labour and Ireland

The Liberals none the less paid for their victory in the constitutional battle by acknowledging the peers' powers of obstruction. Although the parliament elected in December 1910 would pass the most important of the Liberal welfare measures, the composite Bill for health and unemployment insurance, in 1911, three sessions would be devoted to passing Home Rule and Welsh disestablishment, as the Lords exploited their delaying powers. These measures were redolent of the aimless eclecticism of the 1892–5 ministries, and it was with undisguised *ennui* that Asquith's government returned to such old issues.

Labour's demands were met with less discomfort. The principal ones emanated from another judicial reverse in the Osborne judgement of December 1909, when the Law Lords had declared illegal the use of trade union funds for political purposes. As the parliamentary Labour Party depended upon union funds to fight elections and to support its MPs once elected, the decision posed a real threat to the party's future. The major parties formulated their responses in public during the two 1910 election campaigns. The easiest answer – the introduction of a state salary for MPs – was acceptable to the majority in both parties, either because they sympathised with Labour MPs facing poverty or because they wished to limit the political activity of the trade unions. It was for this reason that the unions themselves called in addition for statutory reversal of the judgement, which was more contentious. The case had been brought not by an employer but by a Liberal trade unionist; the judgement had been designed to aid similar Lib–Lab and indeed Tory trade unionists. Unsurprisingly the Unionists had decided not to meddle with a decision with which they fundamentally agreed, but many Liberals were also uncomfortable about reversal. With the second 1910 election approaching, however, Asquith had promised Labour both payment of MPs and a Bill to legalise unions' political funds, provided that their memberships approved the funds by ballot and that dissentients could contract out. This fell short of complete reversal, but Ramsay MacDonald, chairman of the parliamentary Labour Party, settled for it. By these means Asquith helped the euthanasia of Liberal trade unionism, though in many unions substantial minorities still opposed the political levy. These measures at least met little resistance in the Lords. The same was never likely to be true of the third Home Rule Bill, introduced in 1912. The Liberals faced a two-year haul to pass a measure for which few of them had much enthusiasm. The party still believed in the principle of self-determination, as the large measure of self-government granted to the newly consolidated Union of South Africa in 1910 showed. Campbell-Bannerman's government had floated a half-way house between devolution and Home Rule in 1907 – a Council four-fifths directly elected to handle Irish affairs subject to the Lord Lieutenant's veto – until the Nationalists vetoed the scheme. But in the context of the battles over welfare, wealth and privilege in 1909–11, Home Rule no longer exerted the emotional pull that it had in Gladstone's day. One sign of the development of Liberal thought was the greater concern with the nature of a Home Rule régime: the former Irish Chief Secretary Birrell anticipated 'a miserable one-horsed poverty-stricken, priest-ridden, corrupt oligarchy' in Dublin.[15] Significantly, where the Gladstonian Bills had kept control of tariffs from the Dublin parliament, that of 1912 reserved old age pensions, national insurance and land-purchase.

The Unionist perception of the issue had changed as well. The various land-purchase measures since 1885, and in particular Wyndham's 1903 Act, had eroded the landed Unionism of the south, leaving the kernel of resistance in the north-east. If anything this intensified Ulster's siege mentality, and Unionism became 'Ulsterised'. This development was encouraged by Balfour's successor as Unionist leader, Andrew Bonar Law. Of Scottish Presbyterian descent, Law understood Ulster Presbyterianism better than Salisbury or Balfour had done. He found it easier than his predecessors to accept that the price of saving Ulster would be the abandonment of the southern Irish Unionists. Where the patrician Wyndham had compared the Ulster Unionists to a contagious disease,[16] Law identified willingly with Ulster resistance, growing rapidly after the reappearance of Home Rule. At Blenheim Palace in July 1912 he argued that the Nationalists' hold over the Liberals made Home Rule 'a corrupt parliamentary bargain', which should be resisted by any means, 'including force'.[17] Two months later half a million Protestants signed the Ulster Covenant, the declaration of resistance drawn up by the Belfast QC Sir Edward Carson. Some signed in blood.

Ironically, the two-year delay built into the legislative process by the Parliament Act gave the Ulster Unionists time to mobilise before Home Rule passed. By 1913 the paramilitary Ulster Volunteers numbered 100,000.[18] The expedient case for a separate treatment of Ulster to ensure Home Rule for the remainder of Ireland was becoming stronger. Early in 1914 Asquith persuaded the Nationalist leader John Redmond to accept the six-year exclusion of any Ulster county opting out in a plebiscite, though Carson rejected this 'sentence of death with a stay of execution for six years'.[19] As the government contemplated coercing Ulster to force the Bill through, 58 officers of the 3rd Cavalry Regiment stationed at the Curragh indicated that they would resign their commissions rather than implement coercion. In the spring and summer of 1914 the Ulster Volunteers and their nationalist counterparts the Irish Volunteers imported large caches of weapons by sea. With Ireland's tribes marching towards civil war, Asquith wished that 'we could submerge the whole lot of them, and their island . . . under the waves of the Atlantic'.[20] Instead the Irish question would be submerged, unresolved, by the First World War.

Poverty, Unemployment and Sickness

The more sectarian the Irish problem became, the more English Liberals sought to erase it from their minds, as Asquith's comment suggests. For most of the Cabinet Ireland was a wearisome if tragic distraction. In 1912 the only way in which the Liberals stood to benefit from taking the issue up again was by clearing it from the agenda for good; by 1914 no solution was visible and the danger of complete breakdown was real. Ministers inched their way down the road that would lead to partition not because they believed in what they were doing but because the consequences of neglect might be horrific. Their views were coloured by impatience towards and some contempt for the Irish. Few now cared about the Irish question; their real interest lay in those social questions left open by the ambiguous election results of 1910.

The 1910 results raised awkward questions about future Liberal policy. In 1908–10 they had taken up a policy with wide appeal – old age pensions – funded it entirely from the Exchequer, invented bold new wealth taxes to pay for it while sheltering the middle class, mounted a powerful demagogic campaign and successfully identified their opponents with the paper tigers in the House of Lords. For all that, the 1910 elections had strengthened the Unionists, who had been denied a majority, probably, only by popular aversion to tariff reform. The intensity of partisanship in 1909–10 had encouraged voters to return to their natural political homes. Those Unionist Free Traders who had not changed party before 1906 appear to have decided that their hatred of Lloyd George's 'Socialism' outweighed their hatred of tariffs in 1910; Lancashire cotton masters and City bankers who made the same calculation[21] epitomised the return of Villa Toryism to the fold. It had been foreshadowed in the ratepayers' massacre of 'extravagant' Liberal borough councils in the municipal elections of November 1906, and in the Tory victory in the London County Council elections in March 1907, which ended the eighteen-year Progressive experiment in municipal social reform.

Liberal policy-makers appear to have calculated after 1910 that no initiative could win over these natural Conservatives, and that future electoral gains would be made amongst the working class, by extending the welfare programme. Asquith had depicted pensions as part of a general assault upon poverty; in 1911 Lloyd George envisaged comprehensive social security, hoping that 'at no distant date [the] State will acknowledge a full responsibility in the matter of making provision for sickness, breakdown and unemployment'.[22] The next steps in welfare were, however, likely to be contentious. Pensions had been easy to justify – society regarded the aged as 'deserving poor' – but a small improvement in the lot of the elderly had triggered a fiscal revolution, two elections and a constitutional crisis. Future welfare initiatives would again raise the question of expense – made more pressing by the money spent on pensions – and might raise trickier questions of principle.

This was already clear from the four-year deliberations of the Royal Commission on the Poor Laws, which had presented a divided report in 1909. The appointment of the Commission in 1905 was an acknowledgement that the 1834 system was breaking down. The Poor Law had always depended upon the stigma attached to it to contain costs; the humanising of relief policy from the 1890s lessened the stigma and eroded its deterrent effect. The cost of poor relief in England and Wales rose by 21 per cent between 1901 and 1906, when other local costs, particularly education, were also rising rapidly. The question of whether to seek new forms of deterrence or to jettison deterrence altogether became urgent. It lay beneath the battle on the Commission between two women with strong views on social policy – Helen Bosanquet and Beatrice Webb – supported by their equally strong-willed husbands. Bosanquet and her philosopher husband Bernard were products of the Idealist strain of Liberal thought which had developed from the 1880s under the influence of T. H. Green, rejecting atomistic individualism and emphasising the interdependence of the individual and the community. They were not the mean-spirited individualists that Beatrice and Sidney Webb caricatured, but taken in isolation their views on poverty conveyed that impression. They emphasised the duty of the individual to contribute to society and the duty of the state to improve the individual rather than demoralise him. Put in concrete terms this could appear ungenerous. The Bosanquets opposed pensions and the watering down of the Poor Law for undermining the individual and corroding character. By the 1900s the Charity Organisation Society (COS), of which the Bosanquets were national figureheads, concerned itself less with its original purpose of curbing indiscriminate charity and more with curbing the *largesse* of guardian boards. Whilst accepting the obvious failings of the 1834 system they believed that able-bodied pauperism was a real evil, reflecting moral weakness in the pauper. Only a clear-sighted destitution authority, advised by experts such as themselves and immune to political pressures and public sentiment, could deal with the problem.

The Webbs objected to the 'deep-rooted censoriousness' of the COS, and its eagerness to control the lives of the poor.[23] Fabian

Socialists with an interest in administrative structures, they analysed the breakdown of the 1834 system. They concluded that the Poor Law system had been founded on *laisser faire* principles, under which the community was responsible for no more than keeping the destitute alive, but that it had subsequently become distorted by assorted welfare functions which it performed badly, because guardians still saw their task as the correction of destitution. Although they accepted the existence of an unemployable class of moral inadequates, they did not consider moral failings the principal cause of unemployment. Beatrice Webb wished to 'Break Up once and for all that Nasty Old Poor Law'.[24] Her Minority Report proposed the removal of all the specialist services – for the sick, the aged, children, the mentally ill, etc. – from the guardians' control and their transfer to the relevant committees of county and county borough councils. To deal with the able-bodied unemployed, the Minority Report recommended, adventurously, that central and local government promote labour-intensive public projects in slack years in the trade cycle. They proposed not relief works, but the rescheduling of work that needed to be done: when the unemployment rate rose above 4 per cent the Admiralty would order a battleship, the War Office commission new barracks, the Office of Works build new post offices to provide jobs. Those who remained idle despite these enticing opportunities would be sent to 'Detention Colonies, of a reformatory type', with a punitive régime that the most illiberal COS guardian would have struggled to match.[25]

Lord George Hamilton, the Commission's chairman, doubted that any government would accept the Webbs' proposals. He and the majority of the Commissioners believed a separate Poor Law authority to be indispensable, placing them closer to the Bosanquets' views than to the Webbs'. The Majority Report was, in fact, largely Helen's work. It recommended that the 1834 Poor Law unions be abolished and that a Public Assistance Authority be established as a committee of each county and county borough. Over a hundred bodies would therefore replace six hundred and fifty, and the new authorities would be large enough to provide specialist treatment for the separate categories of pauper. The able-bodied should be given temporary work, training or 'detention and discipline', as they deserved. Out relief was not to be abolished, but to be given sparingly, subject to prior investigation and subsequent supervision, 'moral and sanitary', of the recipient's home.[26] The Webbs interpreted this as a return to the principles of 1834, which they had always suspected to be the Commission's purpose. They launched the most extensive propaganda campaign ever prompted by a Royal Commission, in favour of their own proposals and against the Majority Report.

The Reports were little help to ministers. The Majority Report proposed a plausible but daunting administrative reform, which would have won few votes even had it not been suffused by the uncharitable attitudes of the Charity Organisation Society. The Minority Report depended upon a contra-cyclical employment policy that was untried and implausible. The odd sight of Socialists calling for battleships and barracks is explained by the limited scope of the public sector at this time: few job-creation schemes could feasibly be implemented on a national scale, and most of those that could were military. They were not uncontentious, though: after the Dreadnoughts row it was hardly practical politics to suggest that the Admiralty could simply whistle up a warship to lower the unemployment total.

It was clear from Asquith's speech presenting the Pensions Bill – before, that is, the Commission reported – that the Liberals would avoid comprehensive Poor Law reform and concentrate upon attacking the causes of poverty. Pensions attacked the poverty of the elderly. In 1909 Churchill's Trade Boards Act attacked low pay, establishing boards of employers, workers and ministerial nominees to set minimum wages in sweated trades, including tailoring, lace-making and box-making. In the same year Churchill also began the attack upon unemployment by creating a national network of labour exchanges, designed to advertise vacancies and spare job-seekers the demoralisation of hawking their services to uninterested employers. The exchanges were also a prerequisite for a more ambitious scheme for compulsory insurance against unemployment, sketched out in principle by Churchill before the constitutional crisis but introduced by Lloyd George in 1911, along with a still wider scheme for sickness insurance.

What became Part II of the 1911 National Insurance Act listed a number of occupations – principally ship-building, engineering and the building trades – covering around a third of the industrial workforce, in which workers would be obliged to pay into an insurance fund which would also receive contributions from their employers and from the state. The system would be administered by the labour exchanges, which would be able to notify claimants of vacancies in their trades. Those not finding work would be paid a small benefit for a period which varied according to their previous contributions to the scheme. The trades covered were chosen because their employment fluctuations were predictable, and because they habitually responded to bad times by laying workers off rather than putting them on short time. Thus occupations with nearly continuous employment, such as the railways, those in which short-time working prevailed and, of course, those with a shifting casual workforce were omitted from what was a carefully calibrated scheme. Compulsion, the most substantial innovation, was essential to meet the obvious risk in a voluntary system: that the least employable workers would join for the benefits while those least vulnerable to unemployment would stay out to avoid the contributions.

The health insurance scheme (Part I of the 1911 Act) was more complex. Seven million people already insured themselves against sickness through friendly societies or trade unions, but benefits were variable and contributions were expensive: a man might pay for years into an insurance scheme only to lose his cover when unemployment – which might induce illness – cut short his payments. Thirty per cent of pauperism, Lloyd George claimed, was due to sickness. He aimed to bring health insurance within the reach of virtually the entire workforce by means of state and employer subsidies. He proposed a similar mechanism to that for unemployment – contributions from worker, employer and the state in the ratio of 4:3:2 – but the coverage would be much wider, embracing types of labour not included in the unemployment scheme: dock and warehouse casuals, cab-drivers, domestic servants and even golf caddies. Employers would deduct their employees' contributions from wages and add their own, conveying the total to the government by purchasing stamps from the post office to be fixed to each contributor's card. The government would remit this money, augmented by the state contribution, to the various 'approved societies' charged with operating the Act. These were principally agencies already involved in working-class insurance: friendly societies, co-operatives, trade unions and commercial insurance companies like the Prudential, which already ran a lucrative business in working-class life assurance. The commercial companies had been able to modify the scheme to protect their own interests, so it did not offer life assurance or widows' pensions. What it did offer was medical care, provided by doctors engaged by the approved societies and paid by them out of contributions, a benefit of 10s per week (7s 6d for women) payable during sickness for up to 26 weeks, a 5s disablement benefit for those still unable to work, sanatorial treatment for tuberculosis, which killed one in three men dying between the ages of fourteen and forty-five, and a maternity benefit of 30s per week for contributors' wives.

Where the pensions scheme had funded benefits out of tax revenues, the 1911 Act obliged those covered by its two sections to contribute to their own protection. It amounted to state-subsidised compulsory self-help. A substantial change of principle was involved: a scheme largely funded by beneficiaries' contributions entailed a far smaller degree of redistribution than one wholly funded by general taxation. For many social reformers, including William Beveridge and Ramsay MacDonald, insurance helped maintain the contributor's self-respect. This was not, though, the principal reason for the triumph of the insurance principle: contributory insurance was adopted simply because the cost of pensions precluded further wholly tax-funded experiments. 'Insurance a necessary temporary expedient', Lloyd George noted optimistically in 1911.[27] National Insurance contributions represented a regressive tax which, like Chamberlain's proposals for tariff-funded pensions, made workers pay for their own benefits.

The drawbacks became clear during 1912–13 as the two parts of the Act were implemented. For those covered, unemployment insurance represented a compulsory wage cut to guard against a danger which, with trade booming, appeared only notional. Sickness insurance was still more unpopular, because it affected more people and more of the low paid. Before the Bill passed, the *Daily Mail* had organised a rally of ladies and their maids at the Albert Hall to protest at the strenuous duty of stamp-licking. Farmers, like duchesses, were unaffected by unemployment insurance but hit by health insurance. They also protested, most colourfully, at Turiff, in the north of Scotland, where one farmer offered a cow in lieu of employer's contribution; the 'Turra Coo' gained immortality on postcards and commemorative crockery.[28]

These were employers' protests which employees were induced to join, but it does appear that the 1911 Act encountered genuine opposition from those it was designed to help. The man who told the South Shields magistrates that his wages were 'twenty-five shillings less Lloyd George' made the point,[29] as did three by-election defeats for the Liberals in six weeks late in 1911. The Conservative Walter Long, touring marginal constituencies in 1913, reported that 'the Socialistic legislation of the Government' was the Unionists' main asset. The Unionists had been wary of opposing the Bill on its way through the Commons, but by 1913 Law felt confident enough to promise its repeal.

Working-class discontent with National Insurance should be seen in context. The evidence is taken from the months soon after implementation of the Act, when many had contributed but few had benefited from the measure. None the less it does appear that the concept of social security – of compulsory protection against the hazards of life – did not have the appeal before 1914 that it would have thirty years later to a generation which had experienced the 1930s slump. Asquith had been right to conclude, as the measure passed through the Lords, that 'the insurance Bill is (to say the least) not an electioneering asset'.[30]

The Land Campaign

The government accordingly turned to projects promising more direct material benefits than National Insurance. In May 1912 a Radical group, including the social observer B. S. Rowntree, the journalist H. W. Massingham and the New Liberal writers J. A. Hobson and L. T. Hobhouse, produced a pamphlet *Labour Unrest and Liberal Social Policy*, advocating a living wage for every worker, wages boards in agriculture and other low-wage trades not covered by Churchill's 1909 Act, railway nationalisation, a housing programme, agricultural development and the reform of land ownership and local taxation. Lloyd George called the authors to breakfast and extracted his own pet projects from their programme. These became the basis for his rural and urban land campaigns, by which he hoped that 'Home Rule and all else will be swept aside'.[31] The rural campaign, launched at Bedford in October 1913, proposed rent controls, a minimum agricultural wage and a rural housing programme funded by the reserves in the National Insurance fund. It was well directed. The English farming constituencies had been amongst the most conspicuous areas of Liberal weakness in 1910, but few were unwinnable: four-fifths of English county seats had been held by the Liberals at some point since 1885. Though pressed by the Unionist Social Reform Committee, a backbench pressure group established in 1911 to press for a positive Tory social programme, Law hesitated to commit the Unionists to substantial rural reforms for fear of alienating landowners and farmers. At the same time he dared not oppose Lloyd George's proposals on account of their evident popularity in the shires.

The urban campaign fared less well. Again Lloyd George proposed a housing drive, but it was to be administered by the urban municipalities who were already in a state of near revolt over the paralysis of the local taxation system. In 1912 and 1913 the Unionists had disingenuously promoted Bills to provide for a £1 million Exchequer grant towards local authority housing, but the government was reluctant to take this road, both because of the expense and because many Liberal land reformers saw state grants to buy up slums as a public subsidy to landlords. Instead Lloyd George entered the minefield of local taxation reform, proposing to allow local authorities to tax property sites separately from the buildings upon them – taxing landlords as well as occupiers, in other words. This could not be done until the site valuation necessitated by the 1909 land taxes was complete, which was not expected before 1916. Lloyd George proposed a temporary Exchequer grant to local authorities and legislation for site value rating, but it was not feasible to enact all this during 1914. If the grants were passed alone, the Lords might use their delaying powers to hold up the site value rating Bill for two years. During this time an election might bring the Unionists back to power, with the opportunity to make the grants permanent and drop the rating reform, thus lining landlords' pockets after all. Stranded in a procedural maze, the government abandoned the whole scheme under pressure from some of its own backbenchers in 1914, along with whatever political benefits the urban land campaign might have brought. Thus died the last of the Liberals' welfare projects.

Labour Unrest

There was little popular reaction to the abandonment of the Liberals' urban programme. Avner Offer suggests that the urban land campaign failed to ignite the towns as the rural campaign had ignited the countryside because it contained no minimum wage proposal.[32] The lesson of events since 1911 was that welfare measures offered an uncertain way of gaining working-class support. This lesson was emphasised by developing labour unrest after 1910, and the growing Liberal interest in wage politics should be seen in this context.

Industrial problems had mounted from the mid-1900s, with a major railway strike averted by government intervention in 1907, with a lock-out of cotton spinners in 1908 and with renewed conflict in the engineering industry, but the recession of 1908–9 took the steam out of this militancy. After 1910, however, years of continuous full employment, rising prices and growing union membership produced a strike wave interrupted only by the outbreak of war. The strikes were concentrated – in the South Welsh coalfields in 1910–11, amongst seamen and waterside labourers in London, Hull and Liverpool in 1911 and 1912, on the railways in 1911, in the mines again in 1912 – but in the immediate pre-war years they caused the loss of ten million working days a year. The pathology of this movement was complex. Though it could not have been sustained without the favourable conditions of rising prices and full employment, these were not sufficient explanations. The pre-war strike wave was coloured particularly by the upheaval within many unions as the growth in membership increased rank-and-file pressure on the leadership, urging them to renounce not only particular agreements but often the whole mechanism of collective negotiation. This period, along with the years immediately after the First World War, saw the flowering of syndicalism – the belief in the use of industrial militancy for political ends. Though not as concerned with revolution or the overthrow of capitalism as syndicalists in continental Europe or the United States, Britain's rank-and-file movement made uninhibited use of mass direct action – sabotage of machinery, attacks on managers and their homes and violence against blacklegs and the police. Above all it sought to alter the hierarchical structure of unions themselves. The influential *The Miners' Next Step*, written by a group of syndicalists in the South Wales coalfield in 1911, criticised the conciliatory habits of union leaders, calling for union power to be decentralised and applied through strike action rather than negotiation.

The Board of Trade's Chief Industrial Commissioner G. R. Askwith accepted as early as July 1911 that Britain had entered 'one of those periodic upheavals in the labour world'.[33] With industrial action affecting a number of vital services, the government also accepted that it could not ignore the disputes. Yet appropriate action was not obvious. 'New Liberalism' was not attuned to class warfare, and Liberal thought had little to say about industrial relations. Industrial policy was made on the hoof. The government inclined towards settling disputes through mediation, and Lloyd George met employers and unions during the coal and rail disputes of 1911–12.[34] A permanent Cabinet committee on industrial unrest was established in 1912, though with no great success. At the same time the government showed itself ready to mobilise police against strikers and to send in troops to the Welsh coalfield in 1910–11 and the ports in 1911. This did little for its relations with the labour movement – the death of a striking miner in a clash with police at Tonypandy in 1910 became a *cause célèbre* – but mediation could also make enemies if it appeared to have the effect of limiting union gains.

More serious still for the Liberals was the effect of rank-and-file militancy on the Labour Party and the consequent threat to the 'Progressive Alliance' of Liberals and Labour. In the 1910 elections the Liberals had confined Labour to the seats assigned under the 1903 pact along with those gained by the miners' subsequent affiliation. After the January election MacDonald had used his party's leverage to secure reversal of the Osborne judgement, and in 1911 similar bargaining produced detailed improvements to the health insurance scheme. MacDonald considered such horse-trading the best use of his party's limited power, but some in his party wished to go further. Many objected to the contributory basis of National Insurance altogether. George Lansbury, pioneer of humane poor relief in Poplar and a signatory of the Minority Report, criticised Labour's support for the Bill in the party's own newspaper, the *Daily Herald*.[35] However sensible the parliamentary party's support for the government, it did create an impression of subservience at a time when trade union leaders were coming under rank-and-file criticism for their moderation. During 1911 forty Independent Labour Party branches were said to have defected to the Marxist British Socialist Party. In these circumstances MacDonald could only resist proposals for a Lib–Lab coalition made by Lloyd George in 1911 and 1912, backed as they were by the threat of more Lib–Lab contests if he declined. In fact a dispute over which party was entitled to fight a by-election at Hanley in 1912 triggered a succession of three-cornered by-elections which lasted until 1914. In five out of twelve contests Labour intervention probably handed the Unionists the seat.

The 1903 pact was breaking down. It would be wrong, though, to see these contests as evidence of the irrevocable rejection of the Progressive Alliance by a Labour Party ready to claim the leadership of the left. The Labour leadership was admittedly no more willing than its activists to see the size of the parliamentary party limited for ever by the 1903 arrangements, and this electoral brinkmanship offered the only means of gaining concessions from the Liberals, but the leadership also knew that Labour could only lose from direct conflict. The party finished bottom of the poll in all the 1912–14 by-elections, just as it had lost all its three-cornered fights in the two 1910 elections. Labour did not yet have the electoral strength beyond its trade union strongholds, and, as Michael Savage suggests in his study of Preston, even where its union base was strong, the failure to go beyond it, to mobilise at community level, limited its power.[36] Duncan Tanner is surely right to conclude that the threat to run 150 candidates at the next election was bluff: Liberal retaliation would threaten some of the party's big guns, and would bring an expensive waste of campaign funds. This did not escape the party's paymasters in the unions: 'the solid phalanx of miners and textiles don't want the Labour members to cast loose from the Liberal party, and MacDonald knows it', Beatrice Webb noted in 1914.[37] As the 1912–14 by-elections showed, large-scale Labour intervention would probably bring a Unionist government, with all sorts of attendant horrors: protection, perhaps with food duties, reinstatement of the Osborne judgement, even a return to Taff Vale. The future Lib–Lab relationship, had war not intervened, would probably have been similar to the actual Lib–Lab relationship in the 1920s, when Labour was the larger party: one of institutionalised tension mitigated by the knowledge that co-operation was essential to keep the Tories out. The rivalry was, though, as inescapable as the need to co-operate; the Progressive Alliance was unlikely to be as stable in the future as it had been between 1903 and 1911.

Votes for Women

However difficult the Liberals found it to 'contain' Labour, they found the accommodation of the political women's movement harder still. The re-emergence of the suffrage movement from the late 1890s reflected women's involvement in social work and local government in those years. The argument, dear to female anti-suffragists like Mary Ward and Violet Markham, that local work was peculiarly feminine – bringing out women's family skills – and distinct from the men's world of parliament, was undermined by Westminster's ultimate control over local matters. The removal of women from London local authorities when the Metropolitan Boroughs were created in 1899 and from education authorities when the School Boards were abolished in 1902 underlined the fact that local authorities derived their powers and their constitutions from parliament. Those women, like the suffrage leader Emmeline Pankhurst, who gained their initial experience of public life as Poor Law guardians, witnessed the minute regulation of Poor Law work by the central government. The experience of Mary Gawthorpe, drawn into suffrage campaigning when her efforts to provide free school meals in Leeds in 1904 were thwarted for want of legal powers, was typical. The elevation of social questions to the national stage during the 1900s, which converted Beatrice Webb to the suffrage cause in 1906, underlined the point.

Two pressure groups had emerged at around the turn of the century to press the case for female suffrage. In 1897 the National Union of Women's Suffrage Societies (NUWSS) reunited the older suffrage movement that had split in 1888. It failed, though, to recruit the members of several smaller women's organisations interested in the economic condition of women as well as the vote, and many members of these groups were drawn into the Women's Social and Political Union (WSPU), founded by Emmeline Pankhurst and her daughters Christabel and Sylvia in 1903. Initially the NUWSS resembled the sort of single-issue pressure group common in late-Victorian Liberal politics, and its membership consisted largely of mainstream Liberals, though like most such groups it disclaimed any party allegiance. The WSPU had a more varied pedigree: the Pankhursts themselves had an ILP background and many who joined it from the older Women's Franchise League were Radical Liberals, but the superior tone of the leaders – said to have held their meetings in evening dress – and their tactical readiness to deal with the Unionists to gain a limited female franchise led the Union's enemies to charge it with Toryism. Initially it had had a significant working-class membership, but as the campaign developed, the Pankhursts' insistence upon the primacy of the vote obscured the Union's social objectives. 'The working-class women were dropped without hesitation', complained Teresa Billington Greig, leaving the WSPU in protest at Pankhurst autocracy in 1907.[38] Meanwhile the NUWSS's steadily growing membership – its sixteen constituent societies of 1897 had grown into 400 by 1913 – broadened its feminist vision.

Differences between the groups widened after the Liberals came to power in 1905, reflecting their different expectations of the new government. Liberal MPs had been pressed to commit themselves to the female cause since 1902, when the Women's Liberal Federation had resolved not to support anti-suffrage candidates, and the Liberal-dominated 1906 parliament contained nearly 400 pro-suffrage MPs. Most of the sympathisers were indeed Liberals, but support was more evident on the backbenches than in the Cabinet. In any case, an MP's support might mean little: the leading Liberal pro-suffragist W. H. Dickinson admitted that he could not name a dozen MPs willing to go through fire and water for women's suffrage.[39] With few supporters of suffrage convinced of its urgency, and some prominent Liberal leaders, including Asquith and Churchill, hostile, legislation would not spring spontaneously from an ostensibly pro-suffrage parliament.

The responses of the suffrage organisations reflected their attitude towards the Liberal Party. The NUWSS trusted to persuasion and to the sympathy of Liberal backbenchers until 1912, while the WSPU moved towards militancy. Initially Emmeline Pankhurst had envisaged the WSPU as an independent pressure group like the Labour Representation Committee – she had originally intended the organisation to be called the Women's Representation Committee – but she gradually acknowledged that the leverage enjoyed by the LRC derived from its position within the political system. 'You get an eight-hour day for miners. But you get nothing for the sweated women', she complained on the appearance of the 1908 King's Speech.[40] Hence the decision to attack the system from without. The first episode of WSPU militancy was the attempt by Christabel Pankhurst and her devotee Annie Kenney to disrupt one of Edward Grey's election meetings in 1905. Such conduct from women attracted attention denied to male hecklers, and underlined the power of gesture politics. Cabinet ministers' speeches were systematically interrupted from 1907. In 1909 the Union moved to window breaking and other acts of criminal damage, leading to fines, imprisonment for non-payment and hunger strikes in prison. 'Every prisoner brings a harvest of converts', claimed the militant Emmeline Pethick-Lawrence.[41] A lull followed in 1910–12 as suffrage Bills with cross-party support came before parliament, but on their failure sharper forms of militancy were adopted – destruction of the mail in 1912 and an arson campaign from 1913.

The militants' campaign produced examples of striking heroism – Emily Wilding Davidson's suicide at the hooves of the King's horse in the 1913 Derby, and the willingness of several women to risk starvation in prison. Millicent Fawcett, leader of the non-militant NUWSS, acknowledged that 'the physical courage of it all is immensely moving. It stirs people as nothing else can.'[42] But militancy's limitations were also apparent. 'Militancy no good unless on a grand scale', noted the editor of *The Manchester Guardian*, C. P. Scott, in 1913: '100,000 women on the street would mean something'.[43] The destruction of pillar boxes meant little. Even sympathetic politicians could not respond to violence, and the main beneficiaries of militancy were probably the 'respectable' NUWSS, whose influence grew steadily after 1909. The weakness in the NUWSS's position lay less in its commitment to constitutional tactics than in its inability to sell its cause to either of the major parties as a party measure. Suffrage proceeded, in fact, as a cross-party venture with the formation in 1910 of the Conciliation Committee of sympathetic MPs, aiming to produce a Bill acceptable to all shades of suffrage opinion. The results were the three Conciliation Bills of 1910–12, proposing the enfranchisement of female householders. The 1910 and 1911 Bills passed the second reading stage in the Commons with three-figure majorities, but they were not likely to become law without government support. The Liberal Cabinet feared that an independent householder vote would enfranchise Tory spinsters and benefit the Unionists. The Bills' chief proponent, H. N. Brailsford, claimed implausibly that 80 per cent of the beneficiaries would be working-class, but Bonar Law's rumoured support for the measure confirmed ministerial fears. It also helped goad the Cabinet into action. Their preferred strategy was to tie a limited female vote to a Bill removing those features of the male franchise benefiting the Tories, such as the one-year residence requirement and the plural vote for owners of more than one property. This composite measure came to grief early in 1913 when the Speaker ruled that women's suffrage could not be tacked on to a general suffrage Bill.

Even before this failure the NUWSS had abandoned its cross-party strategy in favour of co-operation with Labour, the only unequivocally pro-suffrage party. Labour welcomed the support of an organisation with an income of £35,000 a year, and the Election Fighting Fund created in 1912 underwrote some of Labour's 1912–14 by-election campaigns. Initially the NUWSS did not oppose known Liberal suffragists, but by 1914 it was campaigning against the Liberals in by-elections even when the candidate was an NUWSS member. Liberal NUWSS members were uncomfortable about this strategy, and it might not have survived to the next election, but suffragist resentment of the government ran deep, as the rapid fall in the membership of the Women's Liberal Federation from 1912 showed.

The suffrage question certainly did not show the Asquith régime at its most adept. The NUWSS was essentially a Liberal organisation, committed to Liberal values of citizenship, democracy and internationalism. It was a growing political force by

1913, its standing enhanced by the WSPU's slump. The cause of women's suffrage had achieved such prominence in these years that it was unlikely to have been much further delayed: Catherine Marshall believed the major parties to be bidding against each other for suffragist support by June 1914. Lloyd George was by then already negotiating with Sylvia Pankhurst, who had detached herself from her mother and sister to appeal again to working-class suffragism, forming the East London Federation of Suffragettes as the militant movement declined. By the time the first women did win the vote in 1918, the Liberal Party had been devastated by the events of the war, making it hard to measure the extent of female alienation, but few of those who gained the vote then would have thanked the Liberals for it.

* * *

The period between the Boer War and the First World War had been a pivotal one, in which a political evolution retarded by the Conservative reaction of the 1880s was compressed into fifteen hectic years. Many of the assumptions behind Victorian politics had been discarded, without any comparable consensus emerging in their place. Behind the complexity of Victorian party politics, two objective realities had been accepted by nineteenth-century statesmen: that Britain's dependence upon importing and exporting made her a free-trading nation and that her extensive if scattered possessions made her an imperial power. Both free trade and empire had been strengthened by 'democracy' – the former by the emergence of a working-class consumerism which resisted food taxes, the latter by the growth of the jingo sentiment so evident in the 1890s. It was natural to believe that a consensual popular politics could be constructed by combining an unabashed imperialism with a continued commitment to free trade; this was what the Liberal imperialists and the free traders in the national efficiency movement – notably Rosebery – had aimed to achieve. In reality, though, the political agenda was constructed by the political parties, as Rosebery never ceased to complain, and neither party was content with this attempt to modernise the Victorian fusion of empire and free trade. Many Unionists saw free trade as a Victorian Liberal nostrum ripe for abandonment;

the producer groups within the party sought industrial or agri-cultural protection, while its imperialists sought imperial prefer-ence. Many Liberals, though reconciled to Britain's imperial role, felt uncomfortable with the jingoism, the militarism, the dema-goguery and the amoral diplomacy that empire appeared to have engendered in the late 1890s.

Scarred by the feuds of the 1890s and by their humiliation in 1900, the Liberals of the 1900s proved better at curbing their critics of empire than the Unionists proved at restraining the opponents of free trade. The Unionist civil war over tariffs threatened to allow the Liberals to recapture the centre ground lost in the 1880s while augmenting their working-class support by adventurous social policies and by co-operation with Labour, but as it became clear that free trade implied higher direct taxa-tion, many of the Unionist deserters of 1906 swallowed their doubts about tariffs. By the end of the 1900s voters were being offered not a consensual fusion of empire and free trade but a choice between two 'packages' shaped by the political evolution of the decade. The Liberal defence of free trade came coupled with welfare reform, higher direct taxation and co-operation with the labour movement. The Unionists' refashioning of tariff reform after 1906 had made the policy more Conservative and less Chamberlainite. Economic nationalism was now coupled with regressive taxation, a cautious approach to social reform and a distinct coolness towards organised labour.

The knife-edge results of the two 1910 elections suggest that the choice between these two 'packages' was very evenly balanced before the First World War. Too many uncertainties existed in 1914 to allow worthwhile speculation on the development of British politics had the conflict never occurred. We know that Bonar Law finally pledged himself in January 1913 not to intro-duce food duties without electoral endorsement, but we cannot know whether this would have made protectionism palatable or, by offending the Chamberlainites, merely re-ignited the Unionist civil war. We cannot judge the electoral impact of the new direc-tions in social policy being explored by the Liberals after the disappointing reception of national insurance – the rural land campaign, the urban housing programme, the extension of the minimum wage. We cannot judge Liberal welfarism without knowing how a Liberal government would have tackled the central problem of poverty, following the unhelpful reports of the Poor Law Commission. We can acknowledge that the Lib–Lab relationship forged in 1903 was no longer stable, but we cannot know how damaging its readjustment would have proved to the Progressive alliance. We cannot know what level of female enfranchisement, if any, would have been enacted in peacetime, or its effects upon the 1914 party system. British politics was fluid on the eve of the First World War, with many uncertainties. By 1918 everything had changed.

5 Transformation by War

Stumbling to War

The decision of 2nd August 1914 to send British troops to the Continent if Germany invaded Belgium completed the transformation of British diplomacy since the 1890s. For most of the nineteenth century Britain had considered her vital interests to lie outside Europe, but the expansion of British commitments in the late nineteenth century had made this isolationism more difficult. The colonial ambitions of other European powers underlined the point: 'now that they have ceased quarrelling about provinces in Europe & have turned their eyes to distant places, they find us in the way everywhere', the Liberal Imperialist Edward Grey wrote in 1895.[1] British policy-makers faced the realities that would persist until the 1930s: that Britain possessed a vulnerable empire in a hostile world, and that concentration upon the defence of one territory might invite a predatory attack elsewhere. As Foreign Secretary in 1892–4, Rosebery had acknowledged that unilateral defence of the empire might mean fighting forty wars at once.

Rosebery had aimed to relieve pressure on the empire by maintaining the balance of tension within Europe. In practice this meant supporting the Triple Alliance of Germany, Austria-Hungary and Italy against the Franco-Russian bloc formed in the early 1890s, but at the same time avoiding any commitment to the Alliance which might drag Britain into, for example, the tangled politics of the Balkans. This delicate position became harder for Rosebery's successors to sustain in the late 1890s, as rivalry over Far Eastern markets pitted Britain against Germany. Above all, the embarrassments of the Boer War emphasised the need for a firmer basis to British diplomacy.

Britain had difficulty enough fighting the Boers in 1899–1902; any opportunistic attack upon British possessions elsewhere during those years would have been hard to repel. British embarrassment encouraged those in Berlin who wished to tie Britain more closely to German interests, which in turn encouraged

115

those like Joseph Chamberlain and Cecil Rhodes who dreamed of an Anglo-Saxon alliance of Britain, Germany and the USA. This was a fantasy. Formal alliance with Germany would intensify French and Russian hostility, and deepen colonial rivalry with those powers at a time when the Boer War had underlined how risky colonial engagements could be. Binding alliances were attractive only if they relieved colonial tension and reduced the burden of imperial defence. Such thinking lay behind the Anglo-Japanese Alliance of 1902, by which Britain bound herself to the emerging military power of the Far East, effectively renouncing any ambition for new possessions in the region in return for greater security for those she already had.

Similar motives prompted the Entente with France in 1904. Anglo-French tension in North Africa had persisted since Britain's occupation of Egypt in 1882, and had almost brought the powers to war in 1898. The Entente brought French acknowledgement of Britain's paramountcy in Egypt in return for a free hand in Morocco – a British trading interest but not a strategic one. It was, though, an 'entente' rather than an alliance. While the extent and limits of Britain's commitment to Japan had been spelled out in 1902, the precise nature of her commitment to France would remain unclear until August 1914. 'An Entente is nothing more than a frame of mind', maintained Sir Eyre Crowe, of the Foreign Office's Western Department, 'which may be, or become, so vague as to lose all content.'[2]

The 1904 Entente was welcomed, therefore, both by those Liberals who saw it as a token of peace and by the Germanophobes in the Foreign Office and on the Unionist right who hoped that it would dampen German ambition. It left unclear the extent of any military commitment to France. The Unionist Cabinet did not discuss its military implications when it was concluded, seeing it primarily as a colonial deal, but in the 1900s any arrangement with a European power inevitably had European implications. When Germany sought to revive her claim to a stake in Morocco in the spring of 1905, the British General Staff contemplated British participation in a possible Franco-German war.

The Liberal Foreign Secretary from 1905, Sir Edward Grey, thus inherited an imprecise undertaking. Grey had been a prominent Liberal Imperialist in the 1890s, and shared that group's contempt for the Little Englandism, neutralism or even pacificism that he saw in his party's Radical wing, but where Rosebery had been a Francophobe, Grey distrusted the Germans. He was therefore sympathetic to the Entente and unworried by the possibility of a military commitment to France. He acquiesced in the 'conversations' between British and French General Staffs from 1906 and, crucially, in the decision not to report their deliberations to the Cabinet.

This secrecy reflected Grey's suspicion of Radical Liberalism and its spokesmen in the Cabinet. Foreign policy battles had brought the Liberal Imperialists close to seceding from the party before and during the Boer War, and Grey realised the sensitivity of any military dealings with France. His conviction that Germany was an expansionary menace led him to treat the Anglo-French Entente as non-negotiable and any threat to it as grounds for resignation. He saw the Entente not just as a means of avoiding colonial wars but as the guarantee of British security. Aware that his dealings with the French would be jeopardised by domestic challenges to any military understanding, he kept the military arrangements secret, and the Cabinet did not learn of them until a second Moroccan crisis in 1911 made disclosure necessary.

The result was that foreign policy was shaped to a dangerous degree by the strategic attitudes and rivalries of the Chiefs of Staff. These were resolved between 1908 and 1911 in favour of the Army's view, voiced most belligerently by the Director of Military Operations, General Sir Henry Wilson, that the Entente was worthless without a British commitment to reinforce the French army on its northern flank. In 1908 Grey had still envisaged most of the land fighting being done by the French and Russian armies; by 1911 the Admiralty's failure to produce a plausible naval strategy ensured acceptance of the Army case by the Committee for Imperial Defence. The Army view was shaped by various strategic misconceptions which were denied the scrutiny that they required – Wilson's belief that the Germans would not attack through Belgium, for instance, or the General Staff's assumption that an army of only 120,000 could contain a German advance.

More damagingly, ideas alien to the military mind, such as the concept of economic warfare, were barely discussed, and were not seriously assessed until after the outbreak of war. In fact prewar strategic discussions devoted very little attention to the question of how a liberal superpower could wage war without perverting its political system and destroying its economy – a consequence of leaving military planning to the generals. Grey probably exaggerated the likelihood of Cabinet sabotage. The Liberals, chastened by the traumas of the Boer War years, were more realistic about foreign policy in power than in opposition. A second entente with Russia was realised in 1907 with little Cabinet friction, although many Radicals objected to dealing with a repressive autocracy. The alternative was ever-growing expenditure on policing the Indian frontier: the Cabinet understood that the ententes made pensions affordable, while the failure to agree upon naval limitation with Germany produced the budgetary worries of 1908–9. The Dreadnought controversy brought rows but no resignations: the Cabinet shared Lloyd George's fear of reopening 'all the old controversies which rent the party for years and brought it to impotence and contempt'.[3] Even when the Cabinet decided upon war in 1914 only two of its members resigned; most were determined not to allow the Unionists to militarise Britain. In the short term the Liberals' self-discipline over potentially sensitive foreign policy questions strengthened the party at a time when the Unionists were tearing themselves apart over Chamberlain's imperial vision. In the longer term, though, it meant that no adequate scrutiny was provided, even in Cabinet, for the strategic policies which led Britain into war – the war that would destroy the Liberal Party as a governing force.

Business as Usual

One consequence of pre-war policy-making was inescapable. Grey had presented the military commitment to France as a matter of honour, while leaving the details to the generals. The result was a sharp distinction between purely military planning and the civil support measures that a military commitment required. Fearful that his policy might be savaged in full Cabinet, Grey had played down its implications – a strategy culminating in his notorious claim to the Commons in August 1914 that Britain would suffer little more by entering the war than by standing aside. There was little solid basis for the common assumption that the war would be short: Lord Kitchener, the Boer War commander appointed Secretary of State for War in August 1914, envisaged a three-year conflict. A protracted war would soon underline the lack of planning in those areas which might have been considered had the implications of war been discussed more openly. Alone among the combatant nations Britain had no military conscription. In the event the rush to the colours, which saw 300,000 men volunteer in the first month of war alone, meant that this was not an immediate drawback, but indiscriminate recruiting drained skilled men from key industries, emphasising the inadequacy of industrial planning for war.

Little thought had been given to wartime economic policy – monetary regulation, price control, labour relations or food supply. Policy in these areas was initially made pragmatically, usually in response to crisis. The opening days of the war brought panic in the London money market, which Lloyd George as Chancellor met by effectively abandoning the gold standard – giving banks discretion as to whether or not to redeem paper notes in gold, and issuing Treasury £1 notes to replace the disappearing gold sovereigns. The panic was contained, but the gold standard mechanism was emasculated at a time when public expenditure was being pushed to unprecedented levels by the demands of war and when trade dislocation was creating food and raw-material shortages. The inflationary danger was obvious. By the summer of 1915 retail prices had risen by 40 per cent since the outbreak of war; well before then the government faced unrest on the home front.

The patriotic enthusiasm of August 1914 did not disappear under these pressures, but crystallised into a divisive hunt for the enemy within, for the 'fat cat' exploiting the crisis. In the towns this meant the rentier landlord, already cast as an enemy of society in the pre-war urban land campaign. In industry it meant the opportunistic employer using the crisis to unravel job demarcation – or, in the mines, the eight-hour day – in the interests of higher output. It meant the men who profited from shortages – average profits in coal, shipbuilding, iron and engineering rose by 32 per cent between 1914 and 1916. A rash of 'direct action' responses threatened social crisis. Rent strikes erupted in London, Glasgow, Edinburgh and elsewhere. The industrial truce agreed by the unions three weeks into the war broke down under inflationary pressure. Ten thousand engineers struck on Clydeside and the rank-and-file Clyde Workers' Committee argued that the war in France should be subordinated to class struggle at home. Strikes were threatened on the railways and in the naval dockyards.

Britain did not become ungovernable in the early months of war – the tensions would be much greater in 1917–18 – but she became markedly more difficult to govern. Public opinion and press opinion gained a potency greater than in peacetime and government was forced into *ad hoc* responses to crisis – Lloyd George's 'Treasury Agreement' with the war industry unions in March 1915 limiting strikes and restrictive practices in return for exhortations against profiteering, for instance, or his threats to nationalise the liquor trade to curb drinking at work. The political rewards for such gestures were minimal, though, while military success remained elusive.

It steadily became clear that the stalemate on the Western Front would not be broken easily. The superiority of defensive to offensive tactics in the period between the invention of the machine gun and the development of the tank precluded the knock-out blow that generals sought, though it did not deter them from seeking it. Stalemate could be prolonged because the mechanisation of agriculture and the availability of extra-European food supplies allowed the combatants to keep mass armies in the field and to feed civilian populations for years on end. Once the French army failed to repel the initial German advance, it became clear that Britain's military commitment to France would be much larger than pre-war strategists had hoped.

The troops necessary for this enhanced commitment had already been enlisted. Days after the outbreak of war Kitchener had outlined plans for an army of 700,000 men – much larger than the existing British Expeditionary Force. Where pre-war strategists had assumed a limited military contribution to a short war, Kitchener considered a long war inevitable and a larger British military presence desirable. His proposals were accepted in 'stunned but assenting silence' by Asquith's Cabinet[4] on the assurance that the enlarged army would be a volunteer army. Kitchener envisaged a military force that would strengthen Britain's hand at the eventual peace settlement. To achieve that, his 'New Armies' would have to be largely intact when peace came: his policy differed starkly from the later view of the Western Front generals that victory depended upon sending ever larger numbers of men to their deaths. In practice, though, it was diplomatically impossible to keep what eventually became a million-strong army mothballed while France was fighting for survival. Necessity required its transfer to the Western Front, where Britain's troops were consumed as rapidly as the French.

Kitchener's faith in voluntary recruitment was vindicated by his success in raising the largest volunteer army in history, but mass recruitment conflicted with the government's wish to minimise the impact of war. The government had entered the war with a domestic strategy summarised as 'Business as Usual' – implying minimal disruption to everyday life and economic activity. This proved impossible when, for instance, the first nine months of war saw one-third of the male labour force leave their occupations for the forces or for war industries. The depletion of manufacturing industry weakened Britain's export capacity, which produced balance of payments problems, which weakened sterling against the dollar and made essential war purchases in the USA more expensive. The government's apparent unconcern at the adverse movement of the sterling–dollar exchange annoyed Britain's purchasing agents in the US, but it was only one of many problems caused by the attempt to load a bloated army on to a peacetime economy.

Ultimately 'Business as Usual' would prove inappropriate to the type of conflict that emerged. The government assumed that morale at home could best be maintained by preserving the rhythms and habits of peacetime, but this approach exacerbated the problems of the transition to war. As Gerard DeGroot says, 'Business as Usual' 'militated against emotional mobilisation'.[5] Assured that the impact of war could be minimised, the public reacted sharply to wartime discomforts. In effect the strategy depended upon the war being a short one. The longer the conflict the greater its discomforts, and 'Business as Usual' came to suggest negligence and complacency rather than relaxed control. Worse, the public attributed the lack of a military breakthrough to the government's low-key approach.

During 1915 the charge was made by Unionist politicians and the right-wing press that the war was not being won because it was being conducted half-heartedly. Asquith was a 'dawdling bugger', in the words of the acerbic Unionist polemicist F. S. Oliver, and his government was held responsible for the bottlenecks really caused by the over-rapid expansion of the armed forces – most obviously the shortage of shells on the Western Front which curtailed British operations in the spring. In January 1915 a backbench Unionist ginger group was formed under the portentous title of the Unionist Business Committee. Its aim was to channel criticism of the Liberal government, but it also voiced backbench Unionist concern that their party's leaders had made unnecessary concessions in the name of the war effort. Home Rule and Welsh Disestablishment had been allowed on to the statute book and an electoral truce had been agreed in August 1914. Since the outbreak of war moral pressure had been put on Unionist leaders to support the war effort without any chance to shape policy. In January 1915 Lloyd George privately approached Bonar Law and Austen Chamberlain to air the idea of a coalition. Coalition did not greatly appeal to the Unionist front bench – it 'would tie our hands and close our lips even more effectively than at present', as George Curzon put it[6] – but as the Unionists stepped up their criticism of the government they made it harder for themselves to decline an offer to share power. When a fresh crisis blew up in the spring of 1915 over the resignation of 'Jacky' Fisher as First Sea Lord (in protest at the diversion of ships from the North Sea to the Dardanelles), Asquith sought to avoid another party row by offering leading Unionists posts in the government.

Asquith invited his Cabinet to resign in May 1915 to allow the reconstruction of the ministry as a Coalition. This ended Britain's last Liberal government, but the manoeuvre still benefited the Liberals. The absorption of the Unionist leaders made it possible to defer the election due in December 1915, which the Liberals expected to lose, and to stifle Unionist criticism. Eight Unionists were given posts in the Coalition, and Arthur Henderson became Labour's first Cabinet minister, but the key positions remained in Liberal hands. When Lloyd George was shifted to the newly created Ministry of Munitions, he was replaced as Chancellor by the Asquithian placeman Reginald McKenna. The Liberal majority in the Commons remained, frozen by the electoral truce.

All-Out War

Despite this success, the eighteen troubled months of the Asquith Coalition's life would destroy the Liberal Party as a governing force. Many Liberals asked what were the policy implications of the Coalition and what concessions Law and Balfour had secured in areas of Unionist concern such as tariffs or, above all, compulsory service. The party feared that war would 'Prussianise' Britain and threaten her liberal institutions, and if there was one moment at which these fears began to surface, it was May 1915. 'We shall live under conscription and martial law', C. P. Trevelyan predicted.[7] The new régime reinforced these fears with some *dirigiste* policies. Some were *ad hoc* responses to the failure of earlier *ad hoc* measures: the 1915 Rent Restriction Act, for instance, met the threat of urban rent strikes by fixing rents in existing working-class properties at 1914 levels. This hit the house-owning classes, though as they had few friends in the Liberal Party it proved uncontroversial. More fears were expressed about the Munitions of War Act, passed in July 1915, which replaced the toothless Treasury Agreement with the trade unions with a tighter control of the munitions labour force. The right to strike was abolished in war industries and could be removed elsewhere by Royal Proclamation. Restrictive practices were made illegal, and unions prevented from resisting the replacement of skilled workers by women or the unskilled. 'Leaving certificates' were required by anybody seeking to leave work in a munitions trade.

With these powers Lloyd George, as Minister of Munitions, achieved miracles of output, but his success made the conscription question unavoidable. The skill shortages caused by earlier indiscriminate recruitment threatened the productivity drive. 'Leaving certificates' might halt the drain, but they could not reclaim the skilled men already in the trenches, facing a high risk of death. Only comprehensive powers to direct labour could do that, implying not only industrial but also military conscription: Lloyd George could only reclaim 120,000 skilled men from the front if 120,000 unskilled men could be compulsorily enlisted. He had opposed conscription at the start of the war, when the issue was discussed in terms of numbers alone, but at Munitions he became a conscriptionist. His shift reflected the disenchantment of a natural corner-cutter with the etiquette of 'business as usual': 'instead of "business as usual" we want "victory as usual"'.[8] It brought him closer to the Unionists.

With the failure of the attempted diversionary campaign in the Dardanelles, many Unionists concluded that victory could only be achieved by sheer weight of numbers on the Western Front. Some grim projections emerged: 'if...two million...more of Germans have to be killed,' Curzon mused in June 1915, 'at least a corresponding number of allied soldiers will have to be sacrificed to effect that object.'[9] Kitchener wanted another 1.5 million recruits by the end of the year. 'Business as usual' would not produce these figures. As the realities of trench warfare became understoood, recruitment dropped from the extravagant levels of 1914. It became harder to maintain existing troop levels, let alone increase them, as the 'New Armies' of 1914–15 were depleted by death, disablement and disease. Military conscription appeared inescapable. Few Unionists had qualms about it. Some had supported the pre-war National Service League. Most saw it as a better way of achieving what was being achieved haphazardly by the recruitment drive. Few knew how a still larger army could be afforded, but most felt that the expense should be borne. 'In this war,' Bonar Law wrote to Balfour in October 1915, 'we must risk everything, including national bankruptcy.'[10]

Conscription was anathema to most Liberals. Pre-war New Liberals had seen respect for civil liberty as the most attractive feature of 'old' Liberalism, distinguishing Britain from continental régimes with their national service and standing armies. The growth of state power that they advocated should respect human freedoms; they objected to militarism not merely because war was objectionable but also because it encouraged the repressive state. They would have opposed even 'technical' conscription – controlling the flow of men to the forces and preventing the wastage of skill – had it been introduced in 1914, but by the summer of 1915 it was clear that conscription's purpose was simply to provide more men for slaughter. Ethical objections were reinforced by arguments of utility – since mass sacrifice had achieved so little already, why should greater sacrifice bring better results? Many concluded that earlier mass recruitment had been a mistake. Britain's strength lay in her economy and her financial system: the best chance of victory lay in an attritional conflict, favouring the country with the strongest economic reserves. Victory achieved at the cost of national bankruptcy would be a Pyrrhic victory if it was achieved at all, and all-out warfare would bring bankruptcy before it could bring victory. As Reginald McKenna, Lloyd George's successor as Chancellor, put it: 'there are 100 ways of winning the war and only one way of losing – conscription'.[11]

The anti-conscriptionists in the Cabinet, principally McKenna, Walter Runciman and John Simon, thought Britain capable of fighting for ten years if her economic system was protected, and of emerging from the war with a better chance of winning the peace. In September 1915 McKenna introduced a range of import duties on luxury goods – a revenue measure, but also the first step towards a strategy of economic warfare. The anti-conscriptionist group was developing, belatedly, a Liberal way of warfare, designed to preserve the fabric of the liberal state and the liberal economic order. Arguably they would be vindicated in the long run, as the conscript armies never delivered the knock-out blow and success in 1918 resulted from Germany's internal collapse. By 1915, though, there was no chance of applying their strategy of patience before all-out war had been tried and had failed. Too many lives had been lost, too much dislocation suffered, for the electorate to accept the prospect of a decade of war without tangible success. The public could only conceive of a military victory.

The battle over conscription was therefore loaded in favour of the conscripters. Any decision to perpetuate the voluntary system would have risked the resignations of Lloyd George, the Cabinet Unionists and some service chiefs – damage which no government could have withstood. Asquith sought to delay the decision as long as possible. In October 1915 a semi-voluntary recruiting scheme was promoted by Lord Derby, Director-General of Recruiting, by which unenlisted men were invited to 'attest' their willingness to serve, on the understanding that single men would be called up first. By December, when it was clear that a million single men had ignored Derby's call, Lloyd George threatened to resign and Asquith accepted conscription. The Military Service Act of January 1916 compelled single men to serve, unless they were priests, conscientious objectors or workers in an essential industry. After a predictable rush to the altar, married men were called up by a second Act in April. Ireland was excluded from both measures.

The conscription battle had revealed the unstable foundations of the Coalition. The Cabinet had virtually ceased to function as a forum for discussion, and the debate had been conducted in the lobbies and in the press. Though the anti-conscriptionists had been defeated, all but Simon (who had resigned when the first Military Service Bill was introduced) remained in post. They claimed vindication with the total failure of the Somme offensive in July – the most prodigious wastage of manpower in the entire war, justifying their claim that the 'knock-out blow' would prove elusive. The conscriptionists had won their battle, but Law gained little credit from his backbenchers, who thought him too deferential to the Liberal majority in Cabinet, and backbench criticism of the Unionist ministers became louder during 1916. That summer the parliamentary Unionist party became virtually rebellious, ensuring that the Asquith Coalition's days were numbered.

The palace revolution which deposed Asquith in December 1916 was therefore rooted in the virtual breakdown of Asquith's Coalition. The Coalition had failed politically, in that Liberal and Unionist disagreement on political fundamentals produced profound differences in military policy, but its byzantine system of *ad hoc* committees amplified this lack of common purpose and gave the impression that administrative inefficiency was harming the war effort. In November 1916 the Cabinet Secretary Hankey proposed to Lloyd George the creation of a small War Committee, headed by 'a man of unimpaired energy and great driving power', to relieve Asquith of the day-to-day conduct of the war.[12] This was an administrative solution to an administrative problem, with a 'national efficiency' flavour to it, but Hankey understood its likely appeal to Lloyd George, now openly critical of the conduct of the war, and the sensitivity of any diminution of Asquith's authority. For the proposal to advance at all, it needed to be broached to Bonar Law and kept from Asquith, actions which heightened the impression of conspiracy. Bonar Law's acquiescence was hastened by a memorandum circulated to the Cabinet by his Unionist colleague, the former Foreign Secretary Lord Lansdowne in November, advocating a negotiated peace if victory remained elusive: the unanticipated effect of this document was to drive all the other Unionist ministers closer to Lloyd George in support of all-out war. By late November, when the plan for a War Committee was first presented to Asquith, the Prime Minister had been included as president of a four-man committee, though Asquith remained convinced that the aim of the exercise was to evict him. Lloyd George threatened resignation if the proposal was rejected. After fruitless negotiations, Asquith himself resigned on 5th December. Bonar Law declined to form a government without Asquith's support, but Lloyd George was prepared to govern with Unionist support. When this support was promised by the Unionist leaders, Lloyd George became Prime Minister.

The Lloyd George Coalition

The Coalition of December 1916 rested on the belief that a streamlined War Cabinet and Lloyd George's no-nonsense methods would bring victory. It was a government for all-out war, supported by those who had advocated that strategy during the battles over conscription. It was inescapably a government of the Right. Its heavyweight members, apart from Lloyd George himself, were all Unionists: Law at the Exchequer, Balfour as Foreign Secretary, Carson, Curzon, Derby and Milner. Three of them, Law, Curzon and Milner, served in the new War Cabinet. This preponderance meant that Lloyd George was working with colleagues who had once been his bitter political enemies. He hoped to offset this by drawing a substantial number of Liberals over to him, and had attempted to use the Home Office as bait to detach a major Asquithian, but had failed. Asquith himself declined to serve in a subordinate position. He led his followers into what was envisaged as 'a responsible and sober opposition . . . steadily supporting the Government in the conduct of the war, criticising where necessary, and in the last resort offering an alternative administration'.[13] Many expected this last resort to be imminent.

In fact Lloyd George had greater backbench Liberal support than Asquith had anticipated, but most of it came from the party's right – not Lloyd George's closest allies before 1914. Individual social Radicals like Christopher Addison, who became Lloyd George's Minister of Munitions, joined the new Coalition, and later recruits would include Winston Churchill in 1917, but most 'Lloyd George Liberals' came from the Liberal right – members of the Liberal War Committee, whose commitment to all-out war was comparable to that of the Unionists. The Unionist backbenchers included many who had previously execrated

Lloyd George; most had been wary of dealing with him when Law first aired the possibility in November 1916.

Lloyd George therefore had a mandate, but an uncertain political base. He could control the Commons with little difficulty, but few of those who voted for him were his natural supporters. He came to identify himself most closely with the group of social imperialists around Alfred Milner – the 'Kindergarten' of young Unionists formed during Milner's South African days, who resurfaced now at the centre of power. In South Africa Milner and his apostles had practised efficiency-oriented executive methods which were easier to apply in the empire than in Whitehall. They admired the red-tape-cutting approach that Lloyd George had brought to the Ministry of Munitions and approved of the small executive War Cabinet. One of them, Philip Kerr, became Lloyd George's closest adviser. Milner himself, with no ministerial experience in Britain, went straight into the War Cabinet on its formation. He had, of course, been touted for putative 'national efficiency' ministries during the Boer War, and there was a flavour of 'national efficiency' to the new régime. Many of the administrative prescriptions of the Boer War years, unrealistic then, were implemented in 1916–18: a cross-party government, a small inner cabinet, 'purpose-built' departments for shipping, air, food and national service, the introduction of businessmen into government – Lord Cowdray at Air, Viscount Devonport at Food Control, Sir Joseph Maclay at Shipping – and of non-political 'experts' like Herbert Fisher, Vice-Chancellor of the University of Sheffield, who became President of the Board of Education. The 'Garden Suburb' of private advisers operated from huts in the garden of 10 Downing Street, providing the Prime Minister with independent policy advice.

How far these arrangements were really conducive to efficiency is questionable. Most of the businessmen failed as administrators, and the proliferation of ministers 'grow[ing] like blackberries on a hedge, all around Whitehall',[14] was not self-evidently business-like. The chaotic operations of the Ministry of National Service were instructive. The Ministry had been created to direct civilian manpower in the war industries, under Austen Chamberlain's half-brother Neville. He understood his brief to entail 'vast and revolutionary notions of turning the whole war industry of the country into a state-owned concern', but had no idea of the precise extent of his powers.[15] In fact Lloyd George denied him powers of industrial conscription, in deference to the Labour Party. Chamberlain's voluntary National Service scheme of February 1917 produced well-meaning recruits of limited value, including three dukes, two admirals and a Director of the Bank of England. In the short term, though, the question of efficiency was academic, as the wartime Lloyd George Coalition was forced, much as the Asquith régimes had been, into *extempore* solutions to immediate crises.

Endurance

During 1916–17 the fear grew that Britain's military effort might simply collapse. The failed Somme offensive brought the first significant desertions, provoking an unprecedented tally of executions for disobedience and cowardice. In 1917 the tragedy was repeated in Flanders. At the end of that year Victor Cazalet, of the British Expeditionary Force, reported to Austen Chamberlain that

> the ordinary Tommy & junior officer has no idea at all why we are fighting & no ultimate aim or achievement is put before him. He has absolutely nothing to look forward to except Death, if lucky a wound. He knows that if he survives one battle he is due for the next.[16]

The monthly recruiting returns fell by 50 per cent between June and September 1917. An army uncertain of its war aims and disenchanted with its high command operated on the edge of mutiny for the last eighteen months of the war. Actual mutiny broke out in September 1917 at the base at Étaples, a reception unit devoted to the brutalisation of new recruits. The Western Front became a Hobbesian world in which the maintenance of order depended upon the balance of fear – upon the understanding that death was a certain consequence of disobedience but only a probable consequence of obeying orders. The promises to build 'a land fit for heroes to live in' after the war, which flowed from the Lloyd George Coalition, aimed to provide an incentive to survive. In the short term the tension on the front convinced even the Cabinet Unionists that the generals' appetite for men should be curbed. After the pointless losses at Passchendaele in the autumn of 1917, the government attempted to change the generals' tactics by denying them troops. A new War Priorities Committee assessed the army's manpower claims in the light of the needs of the other services and of civilian production.

The home front was scarcely calmer. The failure of the 1916 harvest and the pressure on domestic food supplies caused by the German U-Boat campaign from February 1917 brought further unrest. The government launched a food production drive, supplemented by a Corn Production Act, which guaranteed arable prices and set minimum wages for agricultural labourers. In fact the interventionist aspirations of the War Cabinet proved unrealistic, as tillage *diktats* were frustrated by the non-co-operation of the farmers (including those in the Cabinet) and by the War Office's wish for more men for the forces. From April 1917 food shortages and rising prices produced tension in the cities: in December *The Times* described 3,000 people queueing for margarine in London.[17] Fuel queues became routine in the winters, and in February 1917 parts of East London were said to be virtually without coal.[18] Direct intervention was the state's response, as with the housing crisis in 1915. Essential food prices were fixed in July 1917; coal was rationed from the autumn of 1917, food from November 1917.

Meanwhile industrial militancy was being fuelled by inflation, profiteering and the government's attempts to enlist skilled men for the army. In April 1916 Lloyd George warned the Cabinet of 'a very considerable and highly organised labour movement', organised by 'violent anarchists' operating in the engineering trades.[19] In fact the strikes in the engineering industry in May 1917, the most serious of the entire war, involving 200,000 men, were orchestrated not by anarchists but by skilled workers in a craft union, but they were none the less militant. Though the government survived this crisis and adopted stronger powers to regulate wages in the summer of 1917, the strength of war industry unions at a time of full employment could not be dispelled by statute. In September the Cabinet accepted the miners' demands for an extra ten shillings a week when threatened with a strike which would have paralysed munitions output.

During 1917 Britain faced the possible breakdown of social order for the first time in the war. The lessons of the collapse of Tsarism in Russia in February 1917 were evident to ministers and public alike. In the event the winter of 1917–18 proved to be the low point of morale, and the interventionist measures introduced during the crisis – particularly food rationing – defused the worst of the problems. One important effect of the events of 1917 would, however, prove irreversible: the emergence of the Labour Party as the focal point for popular opposition to the Coalition.

From 1914 *ad hoc* working-class organisations such as the War Emergency Workers' National Committee, the War Rents League and, in Glasgow, the Clyde Workers' Committee had voiced urban workers' grievances over inflation, profiteering and the other discomforts of war. These organisations advocated direct action to achieve their aims, campaigning to rectify such grievances as rent rises or the inadequate provision for soldiers' wives and widows. The 'official' labour movement, in the Labour Party and the trade unions, distanced itself from this grass-roots action. Most union leaders rejected the anti-war sentiments expressed by many grass-roots activists, as did most of the parliamentary Labour Party. Ramsay MacDonald had resigned the Chairmanship of the party in 1914 in opposition to the war, but Labour served in the Asquith Coalition and served again under Lloyd George. Arthur Henderson, MacDonald's successor as Chairman, had joined the five-man War Cabinet in 1916.

During 1917, though, the Coalition's relationship with the labour movement worsened. Some previously loyal unions, notably the Engineers, were alienated by its attempts to renounce agreements protecting skilled labour from military service. The Trade Union Congress and individual union leaders had to acknowledge the reality of rank-and-file power in 1917 if they wished to retain their influence. The government's increasingly frequent resort to controls over wages and the deployment of labour limited the scope for the unions to deal with Whitehall, reducing their role to the defensive – and potentially confrontational – protection of members' living standards. Where Asquith's Liberal government had excluded employers from the Treasury negotiations in March 1915, Lloyd George had taken employers into government. Some of his business recruits, notably Lord

Devonport at Food Control, had been outspokenly anti-union during the strike-ridden pre-war years. During 1917 both the union movement and the Labour Party identified themselves more openly with the protests over food prices and profiteering, and the gap between grass-roots and official movements narrowed.

Labour was further alienated by the eviction of Henderson from the government. He had been sent to Russia in the summer of 1917 to hold the new Provisional government to the allied cause, but on observing the weakness of the new régime he had concluded that a Bolshevik coup, leading to Russia's unconditional surrender, was a real danger. This inclined him towards a negotiated peace, and he supported a projected international socialist peace conference in Stockholm. The fierce reaction to the Stockholm proposal in the Commons and the Cabinet forced Henderson's resignation in August. Labour did not leave the Coalition, but it did not disown Henderson. The Party's continuing commitment to the government reflected its reluctance to rock the boat further rather than enthusiasm for Lloyd George. Henderson devoted his leisure to designing the new constitution which would allow Labour to operate as an independent party after the war.

He was replaced in the Cabinet – though not in the War Cabinet – by George Barnes of the Engineers, a lesser figure, tainted as Lloyd George's nominee. Labour would not move to full-blooded opposition while the war continued, but it had little sympathy for Lloyd George or his government. In November 1917 Lord Lansdowne aired in the press his arguments to Cabinet a year earlier for a negotiated peace, and as political debate polarised around his proposals, Labour moved further from its earlier 'patriotic' stance. The spokesmen within its ranks for the Union of Democratic Control – a pacifist lobby which would convey many Radicals from Liberal to Labour during the war – found a receptive audience. As Labour and Lloyd George drifted apart, the government sought to build a rival 'patriotic' workers' organisation, the British Workers' National League, created by Milner in 1916 and led by a former British Socialist Party member, Victor Fisher. Ultimately, though, if Lloyd George wished to occupy the space left by the Liberals' disintegration, he would have to fight Labour for that ground. The Liberal collapse had removed Labour's pre-war dilemma: how to expand without destroying the Progressive Alliance. In London, West Lancashire, the West Midlands and the south coast ports, working-class Liberalism was dying by 1918. In the 1920s Labour would add these areas to its blue-collar industrial base, making it, if not a national party, at least sufficiently broadly based to form minority governments.

The constitution approved in 1918 gave the parliamentary party a national organisational base, embracing the trade unions, the Independent Labour Party (ILP) and affiliated socialist societies. It established constituency Labour parties across the United Kingdom to recruit individual members, the task previously performed by the ILP, and it prescribed the form of a National Executive Committee. All affiliated groups would be represented on the NEC (with five places out of twenty-three reserved for representatives of constituency parties and four for women), but it would be elected by the annual party conference, at which affiliated unions and societies would vote in proportion to their paid-up membership. As the unions were much larger organisations than the ILP and the other socialist societies, and as their voting strength included the 'passive' payers of the political levy, the unions in practice dominated the conference and controlled the party. This was perhaps the reason why the socialist objective prescribed in Clause IV ('to reserve for the producers by hand or brain the full fruits of their industry...upon the basis of the common ownership of the means of production and the best attainable system of popular administration and control of each industry or service'), which was unpalatable to many right-wing trade unionists, was ring-fenced in the constitution. As with the formation of the ILP twenty-five years earlier, it was necessary to balance class objectives and ideological ones. Clause IV was the party's only explicit statement of purpose in 1918. It placed Labour visibly to the left of the Liberals, but in practice the socialist objective would mean as much or as little as the union leadership wished it to mean. The Labour Executive – and ultimately the unions who funded Labour – were happier than they might once have been to endorse a socialist objective for the reformed party, but they were also determined to control the forces of syndicalism and militancy so evident in the last year of the war.

Losing Ireland

The greatest threat to Britain's stability lay in Ireland. World war had deferred the civil war threatened in Ulster. Home Rule had been passed in 1914 but its operation had been suspended. Carson and other Ulster Unionists were encouraged to hope that it would never be implemented, but the fact of a Home Rule Bill achieving Royal Assent persuaded the Nationalist leader John Redmond to support the war. He equated Ireland's cause with that of those small nations for whom the Allies were ostensibly fighting, and urged the nationalist private army, the Irish Volunteers, to join the British forces. Some 90 per cent of them did, calling themselves National Volunteers and leaving the Irish Volunteer title to the dissenters. As in mainland Britain, however, public disenchantment grew in Ireland during 1915, fuelled by heavy Irish casualties at Gallipoli and by fears of conscription. The formation of the Asquith Coalition in May 1915 further alarmed nationalist Ireland by bringing Unionists into the Cabinet. The inclusion of Carson, the exponent of resistance to Home Rule in 1912, implied an Ulster veto over future Irish policy and appeared to reward his pre-war militancy. Redmond's consequent decision not to join the Coalition was logical, but it limited his party's role in Irish affairs.

Nationalist fears were reinforced after the failure of the Easter Rising in Dublin in April 1916. Though the Rising itself, staged by the dissident secton of the Irish Volunteers who had refused to enlist in 1914, was easily suppressed, the episode prompted the resignation of Augustine Birrell, the Liberal Chief Secretary identified with pre-war attempts to conciliate nationalism. In the 'interregnum' between Chief Secretaries order was restored by the military authorities under General Maxwell, who, with martial subtlety, executed fifteen of the Rising's leaders and deported a thousand prisoners to Britain. Attempting to defuse the crisis by negotiation with Carson and Redmond, Lloyd George secured agreement to immediate Home Rule accompanied by a temporary exclusion for the six Ulster counties, with the possibility of permanent exclusion after the war. This deal, though acceptable to Carson, was blocked by English Unionists in the Cabinet, who objected to any permanent settlement while the war continued. Bonar Law's attempts to defend it merely fuelled Conservative backbench criticism of his leadership. Redmond was weakened, too, having gained nothing in return for the addition of Fermanagh and Tyrone to the four counties scheduled for temporary exclusion in 1914. During 1916 his constitutional nationalists began to lose ground to the republican Sinn Fein movement, aided by funds from the American Irish community.

The American dimension to the Irish problem assumed greater significance as the USA contemplated joining the war on the allied side during 1917. By instinct the new Coalition, with its Unionist bias, favoured a hard line towards Irish insubordination, but the need to propitiate the US led Lloyd George to continue to seek a settlement. A new talking-shop, the Irish Convention met in Dublin from July 1917, its deliberations bedevilled by the abstention of Sinn Fein and the reluctance of the Ulster Unionists to make binding commitments. In the event the Convention simply advertised the differences between those parties which did attend. When it eventually reported in April 1918 its work had been overtaken by events. The German offensive in March led the Cabinet finally to approve military conscription for Ireland, sweetened by a renewed commitment to a negotiated Home Rule settlement. Conscription proved a potent recruiting officer for Sinn Fein, which co-ordinated the anti-conscription campaign. Sheer military necessity had prompted the measure, and with it the decision to subject Ireland to virtual military rule. In May 1918 the former Western Front commander Sir John French accepted the Lord-Lieutenancy of Ireland on the understanding that he would head a 'quasi-military government'.[20] Ironically, the failure to find a Home Rule settlement acceptable to English and Ulster Unionists led to the abandonment of Irish conscription in June, but by then civil order was deteriorating. Sinn Fein, the Irish Volunteers and the nationalist Gaelic League were proscribed in July. Britain's presence in Ireland now rested upon force.

Reconstruction

The responses to crisis on the home front, in Flanders and in Ireland suggest a government living on its wits, an impression strengthened by Lloyd George's pragmatism, but in the midst of these crises plans were being laid for the peace. The need for post-war planning had been accepted almost as soon as it became clear that there would be no rapid victory. If stalemate necessitated a military truce, leaving Germany's economy largely intact, it was assumed that a lengthy period of economic warfare would follow, requiring continued state control of the economy. The Reconstruction Committee established by the Asquith Coalition in March 1916 was initially concerned with this narrow economic definition of reconstruction, though it first considered social policy during 1916. The Lloyd George Coalition reinforced the shift towards social policy. The Milnerite social imperialists surrounding Lloyd George believed the war to have created a blank slate onto which could be chalked ambitious exercises in social organisation. Conditions in 1917 strengthened their hands.

It was essential to provide both soldiers and civilians with a reason to continue fighting. Reporting on the industrial troubles of May 1917 in south Wales, the pro-war trade unionist Vernon Hartshorn called for a clear commitment to post-war social reform to defuse social tension. The overthrow of Tsarism in the February Revolution weighed on everybody. 'The feeling of the general public is not the same since the Russian Revolution', the Labour Party's assistant secretary J. S. Middleton wrote to his parents in June 1917: 'There is a great chance for a new world after this.'[21] Lloyd George was obsessed with the revolutionary threat, particularly after the Bolshevik coup in October, and he considered social reform pledges essential to contain revolutionary pressure. They also provided the Coalition with a defence against the emergent Labour Party as Labour detached itself from Lloyd George. This mattered all the more as it became clear that the next election would be fought on a greatly extended franchise.

Asquith had deferred that election in 1915. When the issue resurfaced in the summer of 1916 the Unionists were determined to secure the vote for serving troops, fearing that otherwise conscientious objectors and other 'shirkers' would vote while those at the Front were disfranchised for being out of the country. Conscription in 1916 made it difficult to deny the vote to men compelled to risk their lives for the state. The Asquith Cabinet had delegated the issue to a Speaker's Conference – a cross-party committee of Commons backbenchers chaired by the Commons

Speaker. Their report of March 1917 recommended that the existing one-year qualifying period should be reduced to six months (one month for servicemen), and that other technical barriers to male registration should be lifted. A majority supported women's suffrage (subject to a tenurial qualification and an age limit) and the adoption of the Alternative Vote system (a bastard variant of proportional representation). The recommendations would need parliamentary approval, but the eventual measure was bound at least to bring near-universal male suffrage. Future British politicians would have to note the wishes of the enfranchised working class.

The new electorate was assumed to want social reform, and the Reconstruction Committee was encouraged to consider social projects. 'The nation now is in a molten condition', Lloyd George told the first meeting of the new Committee. 'It is malleable now...but not for long.' At his most evangelistic on this topic, he depicted the crises of 1917 as an opportunity, never 'given to any nation before – not even by the French Revolution'.[22] The Reconstruction Committee became a full ministry in July 1917, headed by Christopher Addison – one of the few 'New Liberals' to follow Lloyd George – and charged with rebuilding post-war Britain. Though the Ministry remained primarily a co-ordinating agency, it did seek to systematise reform and to promote the reconstruction programme with the zeal demanded by Lloyd George. It concluded that the principal task of reconstruction would be to minimise the disturbance of the transition from war to peace. Demobilisation and the running down of war industries were expected to produce an unprecedented total of 3.3 million unemployed, with associated distress and labour unrest. The Board of Trade had recommended 'a free policy against unemployment, valid for one year': a housing programme, reforestation schemes and the overhaul of the Poor Law were advanced as palliatives. By the summer of 1917 the government's financial position was perilous, but heightened fears for public morale encouraged the new Ministry to be adventurous.

During 1918 the Ministry produced schemes for Poor Law reform (along the lines of the 1909 Minority Report), a new Ministry of Health, extended secondary and technical education and universal unemployment insurance (replacing the limited 1911 scheme). It aimed to build 300,000 working-class houses within a year of the peace. By 1920 each item in this catalogue, apart from Poor Law reform, had been fully or partially realised. The optimistic statism of the reconstruction programme reflected a one-sided view of the state's record during the war; in the view of the Lloyd George Liberal J.L. Hammond, 'there is no such word as impossible'.[23]

The Return of Social Imperialism

'The very machinery of a new social order is being created hour by hour in the struggle', trumpeted the Milnerite journal *Round Table* in December 1917.[24] In fact the Milnerites had little to do with domestic reconstruction; their principal concern was with the consolidation and development of the empire. Lloyd George, once a Pro-Boer, remained closer to what John Turner calls the 'prophetic wing' of the Milnerite group – Lionel Curtis, Robert Brand, Philip Kerr – coupling imperial federation with extended self-government, than to imperial centralisers like Leopold Amery or Milner himself. The most substantial imperial statement made during the Lloyd George wartime Coalition was in this mould: the Montagu–Chelmsford Report of 1918, enacted a year later, which gave limited self-government to new provincial assemblies in India while retaining for the Viceroy matters of strategic concern to the empire as a whole. This was possible, though, because the India Secretary, Edwin Montagu, was a Liberal. Elsewhere it was the centralisers, and particularly Amery, who made imperial policy.

Amery thought Britain's decision to join in a European war in 1914 a sign of weakness rather than strength, reflecting Britain's dependence upon European allies. The war had emphasised the vulnerability of imperial communications, but it also offered the chance to change the map. Milner wanted 'a really consolidated Empire' to emerge from the war.[25] Amery spoke ambitiously of linking South Africa to Egypt and Britain's Eastern possessions, implying taking over Germany's African territories and those of her Ottoman allies in the Middle East. This apparently fantastic conjecture would largely materialise in the peace settlement. Already in 1916 the most egregious of imperial carve-ups, the secret Sykes–Picot agreement between Britain and France, had

parcelled out the Ottoman Middle East between the two countries. More subtly, the Balfour Declaration of November 1917
had indicated Britain's support for a Jewish homeland in Palestine. The short-term objective was to win support amongst Jewry
in Germany and the USA, the optimistic long-term one to establish a client community in the region more dependable than the
Egyptians. Amery's crescent, a zone of British influence stretch-
ing from Cape Town to Singapore, was beginning to take shape.
In imperial as in domestic policy there was apparently no such
word as impossible.

Social imperialism – the fusion of social reform and empire
development – had been modish since the 1900s but had previously appeared unrealisable. Its strident imperialism had alienated Liberals, while most Unionists rejected its state socialism. In
the hothouse conditions of the First World War, though, social
imperialism resurfaced, more ambitious than ever.

In August 1918 Lloyd George, Addison and the Round Table
group of Milner, Amery and Kerr met at Criccieth to devise a
Coalition platform for the general election that was becoming
inescapable. They emphasised domestic and imperial reconstruction – health, housing, empire development – and envisaged
perpetuating the Lloyd George Coalition into the peace. In
November, with peace approaching, parliament was dissolved
to avoid campaigning against a background of demobilisation.
The problem of defining a Coalition candidate was solved by
the 'Coupon': an open letter of endorsement from Lloyd George
and Bonar Law to those – from any party – identified as government supporters. Lloyd George had hoped to use the Coupon
to create a broad national party, but Asquith's refusal to serve
under him and Labour's withdrawal from the Coalition after the
Armistice limited his ideological range. Instead he used the Coupon principally to shelter Liberals loyal to him. Lack of funds
meant that his *ad hoc* organisation could support only 150 of
them. As a result the peacetime Lloyd George Coalition, like its
wartime predecessor, became a centre-right grouping with a
Tory bias.

Not all Unionists were happy to prolong the affair. Local Conservative associations sometimes refused to support couponed
Liberals: eighteen uncouponed Tories ran in the 1918 election,
four of them successfully. Bonar Law's eagerness to press

continued coalition upon his party might indeed appear pusillanimous, but Tory strength remained uncertain in 1918, in the wake of the franchise extension and the growth of Labour. The Unionists had failed to win the demotic contests of 1910 even under the old system, before inflation and industrial militancy had radicalised the working class. Law believed that 'our Party, on the old lines, will never have any future again in this country'.[26] An association with Lloyd George certainly amounted to a departure from the 'old lines', and with military victory a month before the election, Lloyd George became 'the man who won the war'.

Less clear in 1918 was the Unionists' commitment to the social programme which Lloyd George brought with him. Unionists valued their paternalist tradition and accepted that the case for social reform had been strengthened by the war. They were concerned for returning servicemen and their dependants: even the Diehard Lord Salisbury, son of the former Prime Minister, advocated a housing drive to produce 'homes for heroes'. It is unlikely, though, that most Unionists shared Amery's determination to avoid recreating 'a party of vested interests and strict economy – the anti-Socialist party if you like'.[27] Economy and anti-Socialism came naturally to Unionists. Before the war they had combined an imprecise sympathy for social reform with a specific enthusiasm for the tariff; on offer from Lloyd George was a large dose of state socialism coupled with equivocation about the tariff, which most Coalition Liberals opposed. Without tariff revenues, reconstruction implied higher direct taxation, following the massive tax rises during the war. The same applied to imperial policy: Unionists loved the empire and instinctively approved of its extension, but knew that such extension carried costs. 'Where are they going to find the men and the money for these things?', asked Balfour in 1918.[28] Such questions, persistently asked, would eventually undermine Lloyd George's peacetime coalition.

6 Losing the Peace: Coalition Politics, 1918–22

If it was obvious that war had transformed the political landscape, it was less clear what that transformation implied. The war had accelerated the growth of the state. It had brought interventionist responses to pressing social problems – rent control, fuel and food rationing – along with the public control of key services and punitive taxation of war-inflated profits. It had drawn politicians into uninhibited promises of a better post-war world, to retain the loyalty of the troops at the front and civilians at home. It had brought the extension of the franchise and the liberation of the Labour Party. It had created a mass army waiting to be demobilised. Returning conscripts with votes could not be left at the mercy of the market in an unpredictable post-war economy. J. A. Hobson's belief that the war 'had advanced state socialism by half a century'[1] appeared justified.

Such assumptions were commonplace, but they ignored the complexity of the post-war situation. Though there obviously was a demand for 'state socialism' to ease post-war problems, there were also groups eager for decontrol, for rolling back the state, for disinflation and tax reductions. The landed and salaried classes had themselves suffered in wartime, and did not wish to suffer further in order to appease the working class. Many of them resented the gains made by organised labour and feared the Labour Party, which they equated with the Bolsheviks. They looked to the Tories, who had emerged from the war the strongest of the pre-war parties, to resist state socialism, and feared that the coalition arrangements would inhibit such resistance. They had potential allies in those members of the skilled working class who had been dragged into the tax net for the first time during the war, as the income tax threshhold was lowered, both by policy and by the debasing effects of inflation. The number of income-tax payers trebled between 1913 and 1919. All taxpayers faced the deferred bill for all-out war: by 1920 interest payments on the public debt accounted for nearly a quarter of budget receipts, against less than a tenth in 1913. The cost of ambitious programmes of social and imperial reconstruction would fall on top of a burden of debt repayment which already strained taxpayer tolerance.

When coalition enthusiasts like Leopold Amery dreamed of ending the party dogfights of the past they assumed an underlying consensus about policy, previously obscured by the ersatz conflicts of party politics. In fact the resentments and divisions generated by the strains of war were real enough; what was artificial was the device of the Coupon, invented to conceal party distinctions. The Coupon succeeded in giving the Lloyd George Coalition an overwhelming majority in the new parliament, but this meant only that real political debates would be conducted within the Coalition. Within four years they would pull it apart.

Virtual Democracy

The new electorate was the most obvious political legacy of the war. The recommendations of the 1917 Speaker's Conference report passed largely unscathed into law in 1918, though the proposal for the alternative vote was dropped. The vote was given to virtually all men above the age of 21, as well as to those over 19 who had seen active service. Women were enfranchised at the age of 30 if they were local government electors or married to local government electors. The measure was at least as speculative as the 1867 Reform Act: in the event it almost trebled the electorate, which totalled 21 million in 1918. Unionist politicians who had pressed two years earlier for universal male suffrage to reward servicemen now began to wonder what sort of genie they had released. Their uncertainty about their party's future in the post-war world owed much to the scale of the franchise increase.

It was natural to assume that this democratic electorate would be more radical than its predecessor, but two aspects of the reform made this questionable. First the largest single bloc of new voters, the women, were filtered by the age requirement and by the need to satisfy the local government franchise. The latter provision was not enormously stringent, and probably made little difference, but the age threshold almost certainly benefited the Unionists. Women voters were said to have voted disproportionately for Coalition candidates in 1918 out of enthusiasm for punitive treatment of the Kaiser and his subjects, and there are signs of a Tory bias amongst female voters throughout the 1920s.

The second consideration was the boundary redistribution which had accompanied the franchise reform. This was the first redistribution since 1885 and the first ever to attempt to equalise the size of constituencies. As a result it reflected the rapid growth of suburban Britain since the late-Victorian period, carving out new seats in suburban London, Liverpool, Birmingham and Glasgow. Apart from the Glasgow seats, these were natural Tory strongholds, and it is estimated that the Unionists made a net gain of 34 seats from the 1918 redistribution.

In the 1918 election these changes were disguised by the distortive effects of the Coupon. It required a very strong political base for any uncouponed candidate to defeat an opponent endorsed by Lloyd George and Bonar Law only a month after the Armistice. No fewer than 483 out of 550 couponed candidates were returned. The importance of being couponed was demonstrated most pointedly by the fate of the Asquithian Liberals, of whom McKenna, Runciman, Simon and Asquith himself were evicted from the Commons, leaving only twenty-nine non-couponed Liberals in the new House. It was also demonstrated by the fate of Labour, which failed to make the breakthrough some had anticipated. With 60 seats out of 707 in the enlarged House, it had improved upon its share in December 1910, but 22 per cent of the vote had yielded only 8 per cent of the seats. Thus while the Asquithian Liberals suffered electoral retribution for their leader's wartime reputation and the party split, the containment of Labour owed more to the manipulation of the electorate through the Coupon arrangements. Certainly the patriotic tide in 1918 brought the defeat of the anti-war MPs Fred Jowett, Philip Snowden and Ramsay MacDonald and contributed to that of Arthur Henderson, but the denial of the Coupon damaged many 'patriotic' Labour candidates who might have succeeded in a conventional party contest. Since the Coupon also consolidated the non-Labour vote, its effect in retarding Labour's emergence was substantial. If the 1918 election saw, as

John Turner puts it, 'a deliberate and largely successful effort to hold back the advance of the Labour Party',[2] the Coupon was central to that effort.

In fact the complexion of the new parliament and the balance of power within the post-war Coalition largely reflected the Coupon negotiations of the summer of 1918. Lloyd George had demanded then only the 158 candidates that his party could afford; 25 of them were defeated, so that his followers accounted for fewer than a third of the Coalition's MPs. With Labour already proscribed, the Lloyd George peacetime coalition displayed a marked right-wing leaning.

Social Unrest

Immediately after the Armistice the threat of social disturbance was pressing. Industrial unrest, barely contained during the war years, erupted after the peace, as organised labour sought to protect or extend wartime gains. Union density had risen markedly under the favourable conditions of wartime: from a level of 16 per cent of the labour force in 1910 it would peak at 48 per cent in 1920. Inflation and the extension of working hours had obliterated the benchmarks which had guided pre-war bargaining, and both sides of industry understood that precedents set in the post-war months would be hard to erase. Unions became more inclined to test their bargaining strength by strikes or threats of strikes, employers more determined to resist. The industrial temperature rose as a result. The first half of 1919 saw strikes in the mines, the cotton industry, among the London ship-repairers, amongst the engineers of Glasgow and Belfast, on the London Underground, on the Southern Railway and amongst the police of London and Liverpool. Many of these disputes were tainted by violence; the Glasgow engineers' strike brought rioting in St George's Square.

Armoured cars and cavalry appeared on the streets of Glasgow; four months later the *Daily Herald*, the Labour Party newspaper, published a secret military circular asking commanding officers whether their troops would serve as strike-breakers. Lloyd George believed that concessions to strikers would 'inevitably lead to a Soviet Republic'[3] and was prepared to resist direct action. Stick came with carrot, though: Lloyd George's exhortations to Cabinet were laced with the repeated claim that welfare measures would offer a hedge against the spread of Bolshevism. At a time of mounting social tension, therefore, the Cabinet embarked upon its social programme.

The government concentrated upon the two most pressing concerns of the returning troops – housing and unemployment. There had been an incipient housing crisis before the war, as investors avoided the low returns to working-class house-building. During the war the diversion of labour from the building trades had paralysed residential building, while rent-control had deterred landlords from repairing older property. Christopher Addison's Housing Act of 1919 addressed the problem as one of urgency. Where Victorian legislation had sought to facilitate local housing initiatives, the 1919 Act, in the spirit of its time, *obliged* local authorities to draw up plans for rehousing. Where Lloyd George's plans of 1914 had depended upon prior local taxation reform, the 1919 Act relied on ample central funding. The government would subsidise costs above the amount which could be raised by a penny in the pound on the local rate. This was not the blank cheque for municipal extravagance that Addison's critics would later allege – all schemes required central government approval before the subsidies could be authorised – but the exchequer became vulnerable to the inevitable escalation of costs in an industry experiencing skill and raw material shortages.

Unemployment was the other principal concern. An *ad hoc* response to the problem of returning ex-servicemen was rushed through parliament in November 1918. The Out-of-Work Donation was designed to save ex-servicemen from the Poor Law, but it covered virtually all adult men registering as unemployed and, for the first time, their wives and children. The scheme was inevitably non-contributory: 'the "dole" had arrived'.[4] If anything underlines the shift in attitude from the pre-war years, it is this expedient. Before 1914 all solutions to the problem of the able-bodied unemployed had avoided giving something for nothing. The abandonment of the actuarial caution which had governed the 1911 scheme was inevitable: war veterans were organised in the Discharged Soldiers' and Sailors' Federation and enjoyed wide public support. Such men could not be thrown onto the Poor Law, especially when they had the vote. If the Housing Act was not a blank cheque the Out-of-Work Donation certainly was. Costed at £38 million, it absorbed £62 million before it was wound up in 1921.

The cost of the non-contributory Donation convinced the Treasury that even a near-universal contributory insurance system would be preferable. The decision to extend the 1911 system to cover nearly twelve million people in 1920 was taken in the knowledge that doles and relief works would be still more expensive. The effect of the 1920 Act, though, was to insure sections of the labour force far more vulnerable to unemployment than the groups covered in 1911: only agricultural labourers, domestic servants and professional groups such as civil servants considered invulnerable to unemployment were excluded. Weekly benefit of 15s for men and 12s for women was payable for up to fifteen weeks, on the basis of one week's benefit for every six weeks' contributions. This measure stretched the insurance principle to its limits and enhanced the government's potential liability. It extended coverage to workers who were poor insurance risks, many of whom found the obligation of regular weekly payments unwelcome. It removed any incentive for employers of casual labour to regularise their workforce, as they knew that they could discharge workers in slack times on to the unemployment fund. Above all the increase in benefit levels from the 7s of 1911 outpaced the increase in contributions, so that while the 1911 scheme was solvent up to an unemployment rate of 8.5 per cent of the insured population, the break-even point for the 1920 system was 5.3 per cent. As the groups now insured were more susceptible to unemployment than those covered in 1911, the government now depended upon its own ability to maintain full employment by economic manipulation.

Already in March 1919 the government had met the danger of post-war slump by formally taking Britain off the gold standard. The decision, though taken in the face of Treasury advice, was probably unavoidable. The gold standard had enjoyed only a nominal existence since the outbreak of war, as the impossibility of moving bullion around the world in wartime had weakened the power of gold withdrawals to inhibit inflationary finance. With the return of peace the government had to decide whether to return to gold, risking deflating the economy at a time when returning troops were looking for work, or to prolong the war-time boom at the risk of stoking inflation. Against the alarming background of industrial and social unrest in the spring of 1919 reflation seemed preferable.

The departure from gold generated a speculative boom in commodities, securities and real estate. Even the relatively high Bank Rate (the base rate at which the Bank of England lent to other banks) of 5 per cent, which prevailed until November 1919, failed to check the demand for money or to inhibit lenders: 'we ladled out money', a Lloyd's Bank director recalled in 1930, 'we did it because everybody said they were making and were going to make large profits'.[5] Unemployment, which had begun to rise from its minimal wartime level, once again ceased to be a problem. The government still considered unemployment a greater political threat than inflation, and Bonar Law actually urged the Bank of England to lower Bank Rate in September 1919. The Bank's refusal, and its attempts to convert the Chancellor of the Exchequer, Austen Chamberlain, to deflation, presaged the end of the post-war boom. Chamberlain warned his cabinet colleagues in October of an impending deficit of £95 million; in November the government pledged to return to the gold standard as soon as feasible, and Bank Rate was raised to 6 per cent. Over the winter of 1919–20 the argument in Cabinet was delicately poised between the expansionary instincts of Lloyd George and spending ministers and the caution of Chamberlain. With Law and Milner reluctant to curb spending, and the Treasury seeking only gradual deflation, the advantage still lay with the spenders, but in the spring the capital markets tilted the balance by failing to take up new Treasury Bills. A fresh interest rate increase became necessary to fund the public debt, and in April 1920 Bank Rate was raised to the historically alarming level of 7 per cent.

Under the pre-war gold standard the level of interest rates had been a technical matter, determined by the need to maintain adequate gold reserves to back the currency, and 'no more regarded as the business of the Treasury than the colour which the Bank painted its front door', as one Treasury official later recalled.[6] With the departure from gold, however, interest rates became the only safeguard against inflationary finance and therefore very much the Treasury's business. Neither Treasury officials nor ministers had experience, though, in their use as a tool of economic management, with the result that policy was reactive and, in this case, badly mistimed. By the spring of 1920 the domestic boom was already slackening and the post-war boom on the continent had burst. The 1920 rate increase therefore served less to restrain the boom than to aggravate the slump. Dear money damaged particularly the traditional export trades – coal, textiles, shipbuilding – which were already feeling the contraction of overseas markets and which had often over-extended themselves during the boom. They responded by laying off workers in unprecedented numbers. The unemployment rate among trade unionists rose startlingly from 2.4 per cent to 14.8 per cent in 1920–1. By 1921, 1.8 million insured workers were unemployed. The total would fall again, but not below one million until men were absorbed into the forces in 1940. The dominant domestic problem of the inter-war years had been defined.

The Onset of Unemployment

The dear-money policy would not be maintained for very long – by 1922–3 rates were close to pre-war levels – but the collapse of Western European markets meant that the shake-out of labour in the export trades was not reversed. The rising unemployment level brought one obvious advantage to the government, in that it curbed the labour militancy that had so alarmed ministers in 1919. More accurately, it altered the terms of industrial conflict, making union action more defensive, aimed at protecting wartime gains in an unfavourable climate. The experience of the coal industry was instructive. At the height of union militancy in 1919 the government had appointed a Royal Commission to investigate the return of the industry, in public control during the war, to its unloved private owners. In separate reports the Sankey Commission had recommended an increase in miners' wages and permanent public control of the pits. The government had accepted the wage increase, and a 20 per cent rise was negotiated in March 1920, but it rejected nationalisation. Anticipating a return to private ownership, the miners struck for a further increase in October 1920, gaining what was in effect a productivity deal. When the export market for coal collapsed early in 1921 the government found itself underwriting the industry's growing losses. In March it ended the subsidy and returned the mines to their owners, who announced wage cuts of up to 40 per cent. On 1st April the miners called a national strike, but they failed to secure more than sympathy from their partners in the 'Triple Alliance' of coal, rail and transport workers. The refusal of their Alliance partners to launch futile sympathy strikes on 'Black Friday', 15th April 1921, showed the limits of industrial militancy at a time of high unemployment.

In a pattern which would be repeated in 1926, the miners continued their own struggle, which now became an employers' lock-out; 650,000 people, mostly strikers' families, were thrown onto the Poor Law before a fresh goverment subsidy made a settlement possible in July. The episode demonstrated to the union movement that a powerful union in a key industry could neither single-handedly bring the country to its knees nor depend upon other unions to precipitate a general strike if the circumstances were unfavourable: 'one of our most cherished theories has had a very severe shock', wrote George Hicks of the bricklayers' union in July 1921.[7] The retreat from wartime levels of wages and hours was effected in several industries in 1921–2, often after strikes conducted against the backdrop of soaring unemployment levels.

Trade unionism had grown so rapidly during the wartime years of full employment, with membership peaking at 8.25 million in 1920, that it could not be killed in the post-war depression; there was little employer interest in 'breaking' unions in this period. The union movement did, though, change its nature. While direct action and inter-union solidarity were being discredited in 1921, a wave of union amalgamations produced larger, centralised national unions, most prominently the Transport and General Workers' Union, consolidated in 1922 under its general secretary Ernest Bevin. After a decade in which union leaders had been stigmatised by rank-and-file militants for being out of touch, the union movement was becoming increasingly hierarchical and bureaucratic, relying more upon improved organisation than Quixotic industrial action. 'Direct action' was not dead, as the events of 1926 would show, but in the early 1920s the unions were beginning to restrain their militants, just as the union-dominated Labour Party had reined in its left wing in 1918.

The dear-money policy had not been designed to tame the unions, but that effect was not unwelcome to ministers. In every other respect, though, the rapid rise in unemployment brought problems for the government. Unemployment was coming to be seen as a government responsibility – a welfare problem – to a greater extent than before 1914, partly because monetary policy had contributed to the crisis, partly because the majority of the unemployed were clearly not responsible for their plight. The unemployed in the traditionally buoyant export industries which collapsed after 1920 were 'not the usual type of unskilled or work-shy men, but are largely people who all their lives have been used to regular work at good wages'.[8] Many of them had also been original contributors to the unemployment fund. After seven or eight years of contributions they resented the discovery that their benefit entitlement was exhausted after fifteen weeks. Rigid application of the insurance rules was politically difficult: 'no government,' Lloyd George told the Cabinet in October 1921, 'could hope to face the opprobrium which would fall upon it if extreme measures had to be taken against starving men who had fought for their country'.[9] The result was a succession of attempts to tinker with unemployment insurance. No fewer than fifteen Insurance Acts were passed between 1920 and 1926, two of them reversing legislation still to come into force. This robbed the insurance system of the simplicity which had characterised the 1911 scheme. Its purpose was changed, in Rodney Lowe's words, from 'a task it could perform (the relief of short-term cyclical unemployment) to one it could not (the relief of long-term structural unemployment)'.[10] The Coalition and its successors acknowledged that they could not solve the unemployment problem but also that the unemployed could not be subjected *en masse* to the degradation of the Poor Law. They accepted an enlarged responsibility for maintaining the unemployed in order to preserve civil peace, while realising that the long-term support of men with diminishing employment prospects threatened to wreck the budget.

Thus real benefits were allowed to rise to levels at which long-term subsistence became feasible, and the period over which they could be paid was stretched, but the abandonment of the self-regulating mechanism of the original insurance scheme meant that the system needed strict policing. Between 1920 and 1924 the real value of unemployment benefit for a single man rose by 70 per cent, while the introduction of dependants' benefit in 1921 meant that for a married man with two children the benefit level improved by 155 per cent. From 1921 claimants were allowed two periods of up to sixteen weeks of uncovenanted benefit (that is benefit not related to previous contributions), if they could prove that they were 'genuinely seeking work'. Where there was no work to seek, the test became in practice an assessment of 'the state of the applicant's mind' towards work. From 1922 claimants were subjected to tests of their possessions as well as their minds, as the Means Test – the most durable image of inter-war social policy – was introduced for uncovenanted benefits. The Minister of Labour was given discretionary power to refuse uncovenanted benefit, and various groups – single persons living with relatives, claimants whose spouses were in work, aliens – suffered almost automatic refusal.

These changes distorted the unemployment benefit system almost beyond recognition. In 1911 the system had been largely non-discretionary, with benefits closely related to contributions; limited coverage and limited benefits had ensured the scheme's solvency. By 1922 wider coverage, higher benefits and the emergence of mass unemployment made solvency unattainable – the unemployment fund was constantly in the red after July 1921 – and the Treasury paid the bill. Reluctant to limit that bill by reducing real benefits, it resorted to more irksome scrutiny of claimants and to discretionary refusals. This made the system appear arbitrary in claimants' eyes and turned benefit offices into battlegrounds. The majority of the unemployed were enabled to subsist, and civil disorder was avoided, at the cost of alienating thousands of individual claimants.

However irksome, the 'genuinely seeking work' requirement and the means test were little more than gestures in the face of a growing bill for unemployment relief, which doubled between 1920 and 1922. By 1922, with a million and a half workers unemployed, the state was spending £6 million from taxation on unemployment benefit, along with another £14 million in loans and a windfall £22 million of accumulated reserves from the 1911 scheme. Such Micawberish funding could not be continued indefinitely, and the Coalition sought a policy to dispel mass unemployment.

Neither current theory nor past practice offered much guidance. The Coalition's attempts to deal with the problem were varied and eclectic, and often incompatible with one another. Despite the attention paid to casual unemployment, pre-war analysis of structural unemployment had been limited, and largely confined to the heretics in the tariff reform movement. After the war mainstream opinion clung to the truism that the problems of Britain's export industries derived from impediments to the flow of world trade, and advocated the removal of protective barriers, the re-establishment of international monetary stability and, above all, the assurance of future peace. Lloyd George spent much of his energy in 1921–2 on political and economic diplomacy. This proved to be a game in which prizes were hard won. Though increasingly anxious to secure a diplomatic coup to distract attention from domestic problems, Lloyd George's only tangible success was the ten-year moratorium in warship construction negotiated at the Washington Naval Conference of 1922. Even this achievement was largely a reflection of the growing diplomatic strength of the USA; it was only made possible by Britain's agreement, under American pressure, not to renew the Anglo-Japanese alliance, thus inviting future problems in the Far East. Much hope was invested in trade with the newly independent Baltic republics, and even with Bolshevik Russia ('after all, we trade with cannibals in the Solomon Islands', Lloyd George argued)[11] – though the agreement reached with the USSR in 1921 angered some Conservatives.

Lloyd George sank much political capital in the search for a general European settlement at the Genoa Conference of 1922. Britain's objectives at Genoa were both diplomatic – a European settlement conducive to the revival of European trade – and financial – an ambitious plan for the stabilisation of European currencies on the basis of sterling or dollar reserves, increasing sterling's influence in Europe, reducing the international demand for gold and thus allowing Britain to return to the gold standard without the need for high interest rates to attract the metal. Neither was achieved. The diplomatic objective was wrecked by the pre-emptive Russo-German agreement at Rapallo, which offended the French, while the currency proposals were blocked by the United States, afraid that they would prove inflationary and reluctant to give artificial support to sterling.

Failure at Genoa revived doubts about the feasibility of economic internationalism in the post-war world, and consequently about the Coalition's loyalty to free trade. Protectionism – at least so far as it involved food duties – had not been practical politics during the inflationary period of the boom, but the Coalition's many tariff reformers asked whether the goverment's aims were compatible in principle with free trade. Some argued that the government's expansive welfare objectives left Britain vulnerable to competition from countries with lower overheads; Auckland Geddes, President of the Board of Trade, warned in 1919 that trade would necessarily be reduced by tying up large amounts of capital in the housing programme. The export slump from 1920 intensified such concerns. Amery saw the slump as vindication of his defeatist belief that 'we are no longer the sort of country that can compete industrially in the open market'.[12] He saw unemployment as a structural problem rooted in Britain's previous concentration upon her export industries: 'when...we have over 90 per cent of city workers here and fewer white agriculturalists in the British Empire than there are in France, is there any wonder that unemployment is an ever-haunting spectre?'[13] In response he promoted the 1922 Empire Settlement Act, by which government provided £3 million p.a. to support emigration to the Dominions. The limited success of the measure probably did not surprise Amery, who had always believed that emigration depended upon tariff reform – men would only go to grow crops in the Empire if they could rely upon a sheltered imperial market. This remained contentious. Austen Chamberlain's 1919 budget had taken a step towards imperial preference by reducing the wartime McKenna Duties on luxury imports by one-third for Empire producers only, and the 1921 Safeguarding of Industries Act had exempted the Empire from the 33 per cent duty that it imposed to protect 'key' industries. These steps gave an imperial twist to measures principally designed to satisfy the industrial protection lobby. They nevertheless ducked the question of food duties, which were unacceptable to the Coalition Liberals, sixteen of whom supported an opposition attempt to repeal the Safeguarding Act in 1922. The issue demonstrated the limits of Coalitionism. The Coalition had been intended to transcend traditional party divisions, but was paralysed by the most contentious of pre-war party quarrels, obliging the Cabinet to avoid what was arguably the principal economic question of the day.

With European recovery thwarted and imperial protectionism off the agenda, the government's only remaining response to unemployment was the limited one of public works. In December 1920 the Unemployment Grants Committee (UGC) was created, with a £3 million annual budget to subsidise wages on local authority projects; by 1922 its pump-priming had induced local bodies to undertake £26 million worth of schemes. In October 1921 Lloyd George announced a new employment package including £10 million for relief works, along with export credits and cheap loans for job-creation schemes.[14] The Coalition's public works projects were dogged by the problems which would hamper such proposals throughout the inter-war period: large outlays benefited only small numbers of people, and came on top of already high levels of benefit expenditure. The 40,000 individuals found work by the UGC in the winter of 1920–1 were a tiny fraction of the unemployed total, and as long as the benefit bill was not significantly reduced, public works expenditure would appear questionable.

Anti-Waste

In fact all public expenditure appeared questionable in the early 1920s. Peace had not brought a return to pre-war tax levels, as debt repayments continued to burden the budget. Throughout the Coalition years the standard rate of income tax, at 6s (30p) in the pound, stood higher than during the war. Middle-class individuals had gained or suffered from the war according to the source of their income and the nature of their investments, but those who had seen their savings debased by inflation or had drawn on capital to get through the war were sensitive to continuing heavy taxation. They noted that trade union pressure had persuaded the government to move quickly in 1919–20 to remove many working-class wage-earners from the tax net, into which they had fallen during the war. National middle-class organisations sprang up in the post-war years, more broadly based than pre-1914 ratepayers' associations. Where the pre-war bodies had generally targeted local government, the post-war groups attacked central government's 'extravagance' – reflecting the growth of the income tax during the war.

During 1919 a press campaign against government waste was mounted by the Harmsworth brothers, Lords Northcliffe and Rothermere, who owned respectively *The Times* and *Daily Mail* and the *Daily Mirror*. It was, though, the onset of the slump in 1920, when taxes failed to fall as far as incomes, which galvanised the crusade against extravagance. That year saw the formation of Lord Askwith's Middle Class Union and the renewed enthusiasm for 'Economy without Exception' in the middlebrow press.[15] In 1921 the middle-class revolt took political form. In January an 'economy' candidate defeated the Conservative Coalitionist in the Dover by-election; soon afterwards the 'Anti-Waste League' was formed to maintain this politicial initiative, supported by the Harmsworth press. Two Anti-Waste candidates were successful in parliamentary by-elections in Hertford and St George's, Westminster, in June. Anti-Waste would eventually prove as evanescent as most such groups, but not before it had claimed the head of Christopher Addison, author of the housing programme, who was hounded from office during 1921. Conservative Coalitionists noted that large numbers of their natural supporters were voting for a ginger group hostile to the Coalition. Dover and St George's had previously been safe Unionist seats. After June 1921 most Conservative by-election candidates declined to describe themselves as Coalitionists. For the moment they accepted that the Conservatives would be weaker outside the Coalition than within it, but the roots of the Tory secession of October 1922 are evident in the retrenchment politics of 1921.

'We must take counsel,' Lloyd George warned Austen Chamberlain in June 1921, 'lest we find ourselves caught between labour in the North and anti-waste in the South'.[16] The government was already being forced to prune the social programme by its own deflationary policy, as the real debt burden rose and the rate of interest upon it increased. In December 1920 it had restricted new grants to education authorities, while in May 1921 the Treasury called for a 20 per cent cut in expenditure from all spending departments. But the Anti-Waste victories underlined the need for a more conspicuous response, which came in August 1921 with the appointment of a committee on national expenditure chaired by Sir Eric Geddes, the Minister of Transport.

Geddes was a Lloyd George creation, a railway director turned politician, the kind of businessman that Lloyd George habitually sought to lure into government. His committee consisted of four like-minded men, selected for their views on 'such questions of policy as cutting down Unemployment Benefit'.[17] The appointment of the committee was a political move, initiated by the Prime Minister, which showed how far the Coalition had moved from its earlier ambitious conception of the state. In fact the committee assumed that the expansion of the state since 1914 was the evil that it had been appointed to remedy. As 1914 represented a midpoint, rather than the starting point, of government growth, it effectively prevented itself from considering the shape of the welfare state as a whole or its intellectual basis. Pre-war innovations such as free education, old age pensions and social insurance were treated as legitimate, while post-war extensions, notably in education and housing, were attacked. Still more puzzling was the fact that the committee did not attempt to correct the post-war distortion of the benefit system, despite the predilections of its members, and avoided recommending any reduction in unemployment benefits.

The result was that the 'Geddes Axe' fell disproportionately upon the 'land fit for heroes' elements of the reconstruction policy. Two million pounds p.a. was taken from the housing programme. Education was targeted for cuts of £16.5 million, which would have meant sacking 43,000 teachers, though Fisher's defence of his service in Cabinet reduced the cuts to £5.7 million. This still implied smaller central grants for free places in secondary schools and the ending of state university scholarships. Thus while Geddes did not destroy Britain's welfare system, he pruned its principal political selling points. The bloated unemployment budget, along with pensions, now formed the bulk of welfare expenditure. The attempt to rationalise public expenditure had placed the emphasis on social security at the expense of social services. Though unplanned, this did offer politicians a means of absorbing the effects of deflation: the inter-war years as a whole suggest that unemployment was politically containable so long as the state accepted the responsibility of keeping the unemployed alive. Nevertheless, it meant that by 1922 the welfare state that Lloyd George presided over was less ambitious and less politically attractive than that promised in 1918, let alone that which he had envisaged before 1914.

Imperial Problems

The Geddes Axe cut most deeply into defence costs. Geddes recommended £21 million cuts in both the Army and the Navy estimates, effectively stopping the unthinking assumption of new military burdens which had begun before the armistice.

The post-war settlement had extended British influence in the Near and Middle East, an area considered vital for the security of India but potentially unstable after the collapse of Ottoman and Tsarist authority. Britain had gained a mandate from the newly created League of Nations to govern Mesopotamia (Iraq) and Palestine, and had, in 1919, negotiated the Anglo-Persian agreement to prolong her presence in oil-soaked Persia (Iran). This extension of influence had been designed to protect British interests in a volatile part of the world, but stability usually required a military presence. Palestine was a powder-keg, where the ambiguous promises of the Balfour Declaration had fanned the mutual hostility of the Arab and Jewish communities. From 1917 to 1920 the territory was under direct military control. Once the mandate was granted in 1920 the High Commissioner, the Jewish Liberal Herbert Samuel, sought to create stable political institutions, but he was thwarted by the refusal of the majority Arab population to co-operate in any way which implied acceptance of the Declaration. Throughout the span of the Palestine mandate British authority took the form of the direct rule of the High Commissioner, backed by a military garrison to protect the authorities and to quell communal conflicts. In the ethnically and religiously diverse territory of Mesopotamia British attempts to impose centralised government provoked rebellion in the summer of 1920 which cost 10,000 lives and £40 million to suppress. Even in Egypt, where British authority was firmly established, the war had galvanised native resistance. The outbreak of war had ended the notional Ottoman sovereignty over Egypt and brought a full British Protectorate. War itself had brought inflation, food shortages and the conscription of

Egyptian civilians to provide forced labour for the British army. This did little for the imperial cause in Egypt, and when peace came in November 1918 the British authorities encountered a nationalist delegation (*Wafd*) advocating complete independence. Refusal was followed by the formation of a Wafd party under Sa'd Zaghlul, campaigning against the Protectorate. Zaghlul's arrest and exile in March 1919 brought an explosion of nationalist unrest across the country, which again needed to be suppressed by force.

India too was in turmoil by the end of the war, for similar reasons – the economic disruption, shortages and inflation caused by war – with the added grievance of India's forced military support for the British cause. To relieve the tension the India Secretary Edwin Montagu had committed Britain in 1917 to eventual self-government in India; in 1918 the report of Montagu and the Viceroy Lord Chelmsford proposed qualified self-government for the provinces and a new central legislative assembly, the majority of whose members would be elected on a property franchise. By the time that these proposals became law in 1919 the public order problem had worsened. British actions in the Middle East had the unanticipated effect of encouraging pan-Islamic sentiment amongst India's minority Muslim community. The result was the *Khilafat* (Caliphate) movement of 1919, which was in turn harnessed by the emerging nationalist leader Mahatma Gandhi in his attempts to develop an all-Indian nationalism. These developments occurred in a climate already embittered by Britain's adoption of repressive powers to deal with disturbances, and by the repercussions of the Amritsar massacre in April 1919, when British troops under General Dyer fired on an unarmed demonstration, killing almost 400. This grim exercise in imperial butchery, and the indulgent attitude of the British public towards Dyer, led Gandhi to reject Montagu's constitutional experiments and to co-ordinate a non-co-operation campaign. Had a full-blooded nationalist insurrection emerged in India the authorities could not have hoped to suppress it by force: India was not a military problem in the manner of Palestine or Iraq. It was clear, though, that Britain could no longer treat the Indian army – 85 per cent native by 1918 – as a deferential imperial police force available to suppress insurrection elsewhere, a point made to the British Cabinet by Chelmsford during the war and by the Commander-in-Chief Rawlinson after it.

With British troops tied down in Constantinople, Egypt, Persia, Palestine and India, it was becoming clear that the 'military empire' could not be sustained. 'The policy for England is quite simple', the Chief of the Imperial General Staff briefed his diary in March 1921:'get out of those places which do not belong to you and cling on like hell to those which do'.[18] In fact Britain 'got out' of virtually nowhere voluntarily in this period, but embarked upon an energetic search for devolutionary devices by which power could be maintained with local co-operation rather than through an insupportable military presence. In Egypt and Iraq this was achieved by conferring qualified independence under native leaders who would owe their positions to the British: King Faud in Egypt and Amir Faisal in Mesopotamia (Iraq). Faud agreed that British troops should be allowed to enter his country to protect imperial communications and British residents; Faisal guaranteed British paramountcy and had 'God Save the King' played at his coronation.[19] Elsewhere in the region, Britain cultivated the nationalist movement under Reza Khan in Persia, abandoning in the process the Shah whom it had previously sponsored, and subsidised Faisal's brother Abdallah, a 'very agreeable and civilised Arab prince' in Churchill's view,[20] as ruler of the new British mandate of Transjordan (Jordan). A new version of the Victorian informal empire was emerging.

This indirect rule allowed British influence to be maintained in pivotal areas without a full civil and military presence. In Mesopotamia the garrison costing £25 million p.a. was abandoned, and Britain relied upon air power to chasten dissident tribes – 'a form of terrorism which would involve the death by bombing of women and children',[21] but an economical one. But reliance upon client régimes assumed the availability of dependable clients. It proved irrelevant to Palestine, where a continued military presence was necessary to contain communal tension. Palestine would continue to absorb large numbers of British troops until the abandonment of the mandate in 1947.

The impossibility of simultaneous military defence of all Britain's global interests forced a reappraisal of the expansionist ambitions nurtured during the war. The Near East demonstrated the dangers of empire by proxy when the proxy proved too weak to serve Britain's interests. Lloyd George's Near Eastern policy, animated by Turcophobia, envisaged an enlarged Greece as

Britain's agent in the region, although Greek military weakness became evident in successive conflicts with the Turks from January 1921. This weakness threatened to draw Britain into the region during 1921–2, and produced the stand-off between British and Turkish troops at Chanak, on the Dardanelles, in September 1922. The prospect of a new Near Eastern war disturbed many British Tories, traditionally pro-Turk, and alarmed the Dominions, who feared further demands for money and men. The negotiations at Chanak in fact ended the Turkish advance, but the episode demonstrated the obstacles to military action for anything less than a vital national interest.

Ireland: Towards Partition

Ireland was a microcosm of post-war imperial problems. The Irish question had changed so markedly since 1914 that the implementation of the third Home Rule Bill, passed in 1914 but suspended during the war, was impossible. John Redmond's constitutional Nationalist party had been largely driven from the stage, punished for participation in the failed Convention, and weakened by Redmond's death in March 1918. In the 1918 general election they were routed by the republicans of Sinn Fein, winning only two of the seventy-two seats in southern Ireland.[22]

The Sinn Feiners won the remaining seats but boycotted Westminster, renouncing the thirty-year search for constitutional devolution through Home Rule. In January 1919 they formed their own Dublin parliament and announced the establishment of an Irish Republic. Their gesture was given teeth by an increasingly effective guerilla campaign waged against the Crown's forces during 1919. Although the early coups were carried out by the Irish Volunteers without the knowledge of Sinn Fein, by August the Volunteers had become the Irish Republican Army (IRA), swearing allegiance to the Republic and effectively forming Sinn Fein's military arm. At this time the IRA could mobilise no more than three thousand men, but it gained passive support from the population in its own strongholds, making successful police action against the insurgents virtually impossible.

It also benefited from British eagerness to be shot of the Irish problem. This owed much to sheer war-weariness and something to American impatience with Britain's stance: few in government loved the Union enough to risk poisoning relations with Britain's largest creditor. The Cabinet's Unionist majority did not dispute the conclusion of Walter Long's Cabinet Committee of November 1919 that neither the repeal nor the postponement of the 1914 Home Rule Act was possible. It was clear, though, that the Act could not be forced on Ulster. Few had much time for the Ulster Unionists, but most accepted that Ulster had gained moral credit by its loyalty during the war, and acknowledged Carson's claim that those in Ulster who had lost relatives at the Front would see Home Rule as treachery.[23] Long's Committee proposed a hybrid form of Home Rule with something for everyone – devolved parliaments for southern Ireland and for a nine-county Ulster, a Council of Ireland to consider questions affecting the whole island, and 64 Irish MPs at Westminster. The adoption of the historical nine-county province of Ulster meant swamping the Protestant core with the Catholic population of Donegal, Monaghan and Cavan and implied that the Ulster parliament would soon vote itself out of existence. This was a bait for Sinn Fein, but it was acceptable to those Unionists – in southern Ireland and in England – who opposed partition. The battle for a smaller Protestant Ulster was waged in Cabinet by Balfour,[24] and the eventual Government of Ireland Act of 1920, with a six-county Ulster, reflected his success. The six counties – Antrim, Armagh, Derry, Down, Fermanagh and Tyrone – would become a Protestant redoubt, ensuring the permanence of partition. The Dublin parliament consequently rejected the measure, rendering meaningless the proposals for a Council of Ireland and for continued southern Irish representation at Westminster.

In fact the whole Act was meaningless outside Ulster: the time for limited devolution under a Home Rule scheme had long passed, as most British opinion now recognised, and partition only made the 1920 Act more offensive to nationalists. The IRA campaign continued; the government responded by recruiting a gendarmerie of ex-servicemen, nicknamed 'Black-and-Tans' after their two-tone uniforms. Their notorious brutality was tacitly encouraged by a government which knew no other way to counter a guerilla campaign. Aware that the military defeat of the IRA was unlikely, though, the government had entered into secret talks with Sinn Fein as early as the summer of 1920. Four months of open negotiations from August 1921 produced the Anglo-Irish Treaty of December. The government felt that if Ulster's position was secured the British public would accept an Irish Free State, with dominion status, in the south; the Sinn Fein leaders accepted partition – perhaps hoping that Ulster would be too small to survive – rather than re-ignite the war.

British Unionists had always maintained that there was more to Unionism than the protection of Ulster. Those who had once opposed Home Rule now had to swallow the concession of dominion status to the Free State – placing it on a par with Australia, Canada, New Zealand and South Africa – knowing that the loyalty of the other Dominions to the Empire derived from bonds of sentiment which had never been strong in nationalist Ireland and which were now virtually extinguished. The Treaty was a capitulation to terrorism and meant the abandonment of the southern Irish Unionists: Carson reproached mainland Unionists for yielding 'with a revolver pointed at your head.'[25] By this stage, though, few British Tories listened to lectures from Ulster, which had retained in the Treaty the advantages conferred by the 1920 Act. The forty Tories who voted against the Treaty won their colleagues' respect but could not revive enthusiasm for a dreary conflict.

By 1922, therefore, the post-war expansion of British influence could be seen to have created new liabilities rather than the strategic security that Amery and Milner had promised, and Britain was tacitly lightening the burden of imperial defence. Although the Geddes Committee's recommended cuts in the services were double those in social programmes, they attracted far less criticism. After 1922 imperial policy would aim less at painting the map red and more at strengthening established ties with the white dominions.

The End of the Coalition

After 1920, then, the grander objects of social imperialism had faded from view, and the principal reason inducing Coalition Liberals and, especially, Conservatives to continue supporting the Coalition had become resistance to the rise of Labour. The Labour Party made fourteen by-election gains between 1919 and

1922. The implications of these gains for the Coalition's future were unclear: to some – notably Austen Chamberlain, who had succeeded the ailing Bonar Law as Tory Leader in March 1921 – they warned against any division of the anti-socialist vote, but others inferred that the Coalition was no longer a reliable bulwark against socialism. Continued Tory support for the Coalition depended upon this tactical calculation. Around forty MPs on the Diehard right were already unequivocally hostile to Lloyd George, blaming him for the loss of Ireland, his dealings with Bolsheviks and other crimes. During 1921–2 mainstream Tory opinion discounted any possibility of a second Coupon election. Lloyd George's attempt to bounce his Conservative followers into one in December 1921 produced clear Tory disquiet.

During 1922 the Coalition's hold upon its Tory supporters weakened. The government responded complacently to the public outcry which broke out over the sale of honours in July 1922. The sale of honours had become rather too firmly established as a means of raising funds for the party in power since the 1890s; Lloyd George, lacking a real party, was particularly reliant upon this trade to maintain his own political machine. During 1920 and 1921 twenty-seven peers and eighty-five baronets were created, usually in return for a donation to Lloyd George's private political fund, which stood at around £1.5 million by October 1922. King George V disliked ennobling a succession of undeserving status-seekers; peers objected to the flood of undistinguished *parvenus* into the Upper House; the Labour Party, irritated by attacks upon its own trade union funding, criticised this 'rich man's political levy', and Conservative party managers resented the diversion of funds from their business supporters into Lloyd George's coffers. All the Prime Minister's opponents considered this gravy train characteristic of his notoriously flexible sense of political propriety. The hostile reaction to the announcement of a peerage for J. B. Robinson, a financier once fined £500,000 for fraud in his native South Africa, forced Lloyd George to concede a Royal Commission on Honours.[26] The honours scandal was as much symptom as cause of the Coalition's weakening authority – the smell of corruption had surrounded the ministry from its formation without previously weakening it – but it did make Coalitionism harder to defend from Tory backbench criticism.

Thus when Austen Chamberlain sought to force the question of the Coalition's future in September 1922 by urging an early election, he was told that 180 Conservatives would refuse to fight as Coalition candidates. The decision by the Cabinet Coalitionists to proceed with plans for an early election amounted to a gamble that the Conservative dissidents could be drilled into line. In the event the Carlton Club meeting arranged by Chamberlain in October 1922 to gain endorsement for the election provided a platform for dissident Conservatives, including several junior ministers and, after some hesitation, Bonar Law. Gathering immediately after another by-election defeat, the Conservative Party resolved, against Chamberlain's advice, to fight the next election on its own. Lloyd George resigned immediately.

* * *

Stripped of the idealistic policies of 1918, the Coalition became little more than an anti-socialist device. By 1922 most Tories had concluded that their party could resist socialism better on its own, and the six-year experiment with cross-party government ended ingloriously. The ineffectual and squalid appearance of the Coalition in its last few months should not, though, obscure what is perhaps most significant about the events of October 1922 – that the ejection of the Coalition ended Britain's limited experiment with the principles of National Efficiency.

The Lloyd George Coalition amounted to Britain's closest approximation to a National Efficiency régime, and, as such, her greatest departure from the ground rules of liberal democracy. Several continental countries would, of course, travel much further in this direction in the inter-war years under the pressures of economic slump, but the Lloyd George Coalition, created by the war, was destroyed by its very inability to handle the post-war depression. And while Lloyd George's political approach shared some features with the continental totalitarian régimes – its populism, its contempt for the established party system, its vilification of organised labour, its expansionist economics and its corner-cutting approach to administration – the Coalition remained within the parameters of that parliamentary democracy which National Efficiency conventionally scorned. Certainly the

Coupon election was a wilful distortion of the democratic process and the Coalition itself a deliberate abridgement of the party system, but both represented the manipulation of Britain's democratic rules rather than the renunciation of them. Party politics consequently survived to reassert itself when the Coalition could no longer claim popularity or success, and Lloyd George was denied the chance to become Britain's Mussolini. In 1922, when Italy rejected liberal democracy for totalitarianism, Britain returned to conventional party politics, made all the more unpredictable by the existence of three parties.

7 Three-Party Politics, 1922–31

The Coalition's collapse inaugurated a period of three-party competition in conditions of near-universal suffrage. The Conservatives started with several advantages: the fragmentation of the Liberals, the immaturity of Labour and the disappearance of the southern Irish seats from Westminster after the formation of the Irish Free State. They would, indeed, dominate inter-war politics, but to suggest a continuous Tory hegemony is to impose a false unity on the period. After 1931 Britain was virtually a one-party state, under a Tory-dominated National Government with massive majorities and clear policies. In the 1920s the Conservatives were less secure.

This was an unstable polity. With three parties competing in the first-past-the-post Westminster system, elections became lotteries. In the November 1922 general election, with the Liberals split between the supporters of Asquith and Lloyd George, the Conservatives gained an overall majority of seventy with 38 per cent of the poll. In December 1923, after the Liberal factions had reunited, the same percentage poll cost the Tories 87 seats and their majority. In that election Labour's 30 per cent of the vote made it the second largest party and, after post-election horse-trading, put MacDonald in Downing Street; ten months later Labour's poll rose by 3 per cent but it lost forty seats because the Liberals' collapse consolidated Tory support. These years, the only years of unfettered three-party competition in our period, emphasised the illogicality of the electoral system.

This unpredictability was compounded by the greater complexity of political argument in the post-war world. While the pre-war dispute between free traders and tariff reformers gained intensity from Britain's economic difficulties after 1918, the politics of the 1920s were also marked by class hostility to a much greater extent than before 1914. Where the pre-war Progressive Alliance had appealed to pan-class, communitarian ideals, Labour was avowedly a working-class party. In 1922 it made gains from the Liberals in mining and inner-city areas – gains which would not be reversed. Liberal gains in the 1920s were more likely to come from disaffected Tory voters, and it tended to pitch its appeal at these voters rather than the working class. Thus while the tariff question united Labour and the Liberals, as it had before the war, 'class' issues – questions of taxation, of industrial relations, of welfare policy – were more likely to divide them. Parliamentary arithmetic threw Labour and the Liberals together in 1924 and 1929, but at the local level, 'anti-Socialist' (i.e. Liberal–Conservative) alliances were frequent, while Lib–Lab arrangements were very rare.

Underlying all these difficulties was the central dilemma evident from 1920 – that while the need to appeal to the new electors might imply a generous measure of social reform, the deflationary orthodoxy which had taken hold then made such policies hard to realise. Both the Conservative government of 1924–9 and the Labour government of 1929–31 sought to reconcile social reform with deflation. In both cases the result was an incoherence of policy, damaging to both governments and almost fatal to Labour.

'Suicide during a Temporary Fit of Insanity'

Unemployment was the inescapable central issue of social policy. By the time of the Coalition's fall it was becoming clear that the problem could no longer be seen as a transient one, to be treated by the expedient distortion of the insurance system. Bonar Law, who returned to the Tory leadership and became Prime Minister on the dissolution of the Coalition, believed that the problem was rooted in the disruption of trade by the war, and soluble only through trade recovery. He was sceptical of the public works initiatives of the Unemployment Grants Committee, which he saw as 'stunts' characteristic of the Coalition.[1] He had a tariff reform past, and sympathised with those who advocated industrial tariffs as a weapon against unemployment, but he understood the electoral risks of protectionism. Though his 1922 manifesto suggested a conference of Empire prime ministers to consider imperial trade and development – a forum likely to call for imperial preference – Law committed his party to make no change in Britain's fiscal system without testing the issue in a second election. Whether he wished to shelve the issue or to promote it from a position of strength will remain unknowable, as he served only 209 days as Prime Minister, resigning in May 1923 with the onset of the throat cancer which killed him in October.

He was succeeded by Stanley Baldwin, Chancellor of the Exchequer in the short-lived Bonar Law ministry but otherwise without Cabinet experience. Baldwin owed his promotion to the disgrace of those leaders identified with the Coalition, notably Austen Chamberlain, and to the unpopularity of Lord Curzon with the Tory grandees. The circumstances of his accession might have made Baldwin anxious to assert himself in office; his commitment to a protective tariff within months of taking office was certainly uncharacteristically impulsive.

By the autumn of 1923 protectionist noises were audible not only in those sections of British industry which had always been favourable, such as iron and steel, but even in the traditionally free-trading woollen industry. Baldwin understood the popularity of tariff reform with anti-Coalition Tories, who had wanted a change of policy as well as a change of prime minister in 1922. He had himself entered parliament as a tariff reformer in 1906. Heir to the family iron foundry, Baldwin's protectionism was that of the industrialist fearing unfair foreign competition rather than that of the imperial visionary, but this defensive industrial protectionism was more appropriate to the post-war climate than Chamberlainite idealism. He saw the tariff as a means of reclaiming economic sovereignty at a time when free trade had brought only failure. Whatever the dangers of protectionism, he felt that the miseries of unemployment obliged government to take risks: 'if we go pottering along as we are we shall have grave unemployment with us to the end of time'.[2]

The policy was developed by a group of protectionist ministers in the summer of 1923; Cabinet free traders were deliberately excluded. Ministers hoped that a policy which merely extended the 1915 McKenna Duties and the 1921 safeguarding legislation might not require a second election; the scheme that Baldwin eventually launched in a speech at Plymouth in October 1923 included no food duties and thus almost no imperial preference.

To Austen Chamberlain it was 'father's policy with all that part left out which he cared for most'.[3]

Chamberlain, left sulking on the sidelines since the fall of the Coalition, was none the less drawn back into the Tory fold by the protectionist call. At the same time Baldwin's initiative prevented the opportunistic Lloyd George from adopting his own protectionist platform; instead he sought shelter in his former Liberal home and in November 1923 shared a platform with Asquith – for the first time since 1916 – under the free-trade banner. The return of Austen Chamberlain to the Tory mainstream and the reunion of the Liberal factions helped polarise politics around the tariff question. In practice the debate became a simple one between free trade and protection; the hope that industrial protection without food duties would be uncontroversial proved misplaced, and Bonar Law's pledge of a second election had to be honoured.

The election called for December 1923 was therefore a referendum on Baldwin's protectionist proposals. The results were ambiguous. Free-trading Lancashire punished the Tories, but so did many agricultural voters who wanted food duties. The three major parties' percentages of the poll changed little from twelve months earlier: Liberal reunification was the greatest single reason why a limited percentage swing produced a startling change in the number of seats won. The Tories lost 87 seats and their overall majority. Their losses probably did not demonstrate the electoral revulsion against protection that contemporaries generally inferred – this would have been surprising in the climate of 1923 – but the election had been called to provide a protectionist mandate and had clearly not done so. A government with a substantial majority had committed 'suicide during a temporary fit of insanity'.[4] The comfortable majority gained in the 1922 election had indeed been squandered: the only substantial piece of legislation enacted by either Bonar Law's or Baldwin's government was the Housing Act produced by Neville Chamberlain as Minister of Health in July 1923, making available a capped subsidy of £6 per house to both local authorities and private housebuilders for two years. After the failure of his protectionist gamble Baldwin would take few policy risks in future, relying upon the appeal of 'safety first' and similar placebos.

The First Labour Government, 1924

The unexpected product of the 1923 election was Britain's first Labour goverment. Labour had won 191 seats, 67 fewer than the Tories, and the 159 Liberals were left with the balance of power. Baldwin decided to meet the new parliament as Prime Minister rather than resign immediately, in order to make the Liberals responsible for putting Labour into office. Asquith had little freedom of movement. The dinner-party notion of Tory–Liberal co-operation to keep Labour out was implausible. The election had been fought over free trade rather than socialism and had been characterised by hostility between the Liberals and the Tories at every level. Baldwin was not interested in dealing with Asquith, believing that the Liberals were doomed and that the Tories could inherit their middle-class support without making concessions. The Liberals had unhappy memories of coalition. They therefore voted with Labour to turn Baldwin out in January 1924. Asquith risked alienating middle-class supporters: a week before the vote he had received an open letter from five Liberal businessmen in his Paisley constituency urging him to save business from socialism.[5] The early 1920s were years in which the illiberal demons of protection and socialism enjoyed equal prominence; in a hung parliament a Liberal Party holding the balance of power could not spurn both indefinitely. Many Liberals in the country, not comprehending his dilemma, were none the less surprised by Asquith's choice and did not forgive him for 'putting in the Socialists'.[6] The Liberals never regained the 29 per cent of the vote that they had won in 1923.

In the long run the decision to back Labour in January 1924 therefore hastened Liberal decline. In the short run it obliged the Liberals to sell their support dearly. There was little sign in 1924 of the awareness of shared objectives and a common Tory enemy which had helped keep the pre-war Lib–Lab pact alive. Few Liberals sought anything more than the preservation of free trade. Anxious to demonstrate their continued independence, they made constant sniping the price of their support, beginning with an attempt to blame the government for high-spending Labour boards of guardians only days after MacDonald entered Downing Street.

Labour was none the less eager to take office. A spell in government would have propaganda value, would give the party a responsible image and governmental experience, would embarrass the Liberals and might do some good. Ramsay MacDonald, who had returned to parliament in 1922 and now became Prime Minister, assumed that the experiment would be short-lived and contemplated no adventurous experiments in socialism. Before taking office he promised the King's secretary, Stamfordham, that his government would not promote the capital levy – the wealth tax mooted since the war and included in the party's 1922 manifesto. In fact his Chancellor of the Exchequer, Philip Snowden, was more orthodox in his fiscal views than his two Conservative predecessors, holding that recovery would best be advanced by tax reductions. Snowden was made Chancellor on the unusual grounds that he was believed to understand economics; constructing the rest of the Cabinet presented many difficulties. To overcome Labour's lack of ministerial experience and its weakness in the House of Lords, MacDonald recruited several peers from outside the Labour movement, with the result that the Cabinet eventually contained two Conservatives, one ex-Tory and four ex-Liberals. Only Arthur Henderson and the former Liberal Imperialist Haldane had Cabinet experience. Few of their colleagues looked like Cabinet ministers: the trade union leader J. H. Thomas was taken for a shell-shock victim by the Colonial Office doorman when he announced himself as the new Secretary of State.[7]

The new government's policies remained within the progressive tradition of social reform combined with free trade. The reforms were not negligible. John Wheatley, at the Ministry of Health, enacted the third and most effective post-war housing Act, providing a subsidy of £9 per house to builders (mostly local authorities) building to rent, and extended the life of Neville Chamberlain's 1923 subsidy until 1939. By 1934 the Chamberlain and Wheatley Acts had between them subsidised 2.2 million new houses, equal to 28 per cent of the 1921 housing stock. At the Ministry of Labour Tom Shaw sought to humanise the benefit system. His Unemployment Insurance Act made uncovenanted benefit available indefinitely to those who had paid 30 insurance contributions in the previous two years and, at the minister's discretion, to those who had paid twelve contributions at any time. As his practice was to apply such discretion, uncovenanted benefit, now retitled extended benefit, provided a safety net for most of those who had ever come within the unemployment insurance system. Moreover, the means test applied to this benefit since 1922 was abolished after a battle with the Treasury, as was the genuinely seeking work test.

Snowden pursued an orthodox budgetary policy. His April 1924 budget removed £14 million in direct taxes and £29 million in indirect taxes (including the wartime McKenna Duties) and was presented by its author as 'the greatest step ever taken towards the Radical idea of the free breakfast table'.[8] It renounced both Baldwin's protectionist heresy and the deflationary surpluses engineered by Chancellors since 1920. Foreign policy, directed by MacDonald himself, was similarly Cobdenite, reflecting the Prime Minister's belief that Labour was heir to the ethical traditions of nineteenth-century Radicalism. The programme of cruiser construction inherited from the previous government was pruned, and work on a projected naval base at Singapore halted, against Admiralty opposition.

Anxious to show itself independent of the trade unions, the government faced down a strike of London's tramwaymen by adopting emergency powers. In 1924, as in 1929–31, the Trades Union Congress would see less of Downing Street under Labour than under the Conservatives. This enhanced the irony that this studiously moderate Labour administration should fall on the strength of two red scares. The government's doom resulted from its mishandling of the relatively trivial Campbell case, in which it appeared to hesitate over the prosecution of John Campbell, editor of a marginal left-wing paper, the *British Worker*, for an article urging soldiers never to fire upon strikers. MacDonald invited his fate by misleading the House of Commons, but the government fell because Baldwin had decided that it should, having declined to assist earlier Liberal censure motions. By October 1924 the Conservatives felt ready for another election, the third in two years.

The campaign was dominated by the second red scare, the Zinoviev Letter, ostensibly an instruction from the President of the Communist International in Moscow to British Communists to cultivate revolutionary sentiment amongst sympathisers in the labour movement and the armed forces, but now believed to have been a forgery concocted by White Russian émigrés. The increase of a million in Labour's vote suggests that Zinoviev made little impact upon the party's core support. His greatest achievement was probably to send the Liberals' middle-class supporters of 1923 back into the Tory camp, in an election fought over socialism rather than free trade. A Liberal slump would have been likely anyway. They were less able than their opponents to stand the cost of a third election in quick succession – the 453 Liberal candidates of 1923 fell to 340 in 1924 – and their actions in the 1924 parliament – putting Labour in and then placing every possible obstacle in their path – had won them few friends. The Tories were the main beneficiaries, their 48 per cent of the vote giving them a majority of 223, the largest for a single party since 1832.

The first Labour government left few memorials. Its main purpose – to establish Labour as a plausible party of government – had been achieved, and it would be harder in future to depict a MacDonald government as an exercise in Bolshevism, but the 1924 experiment had also demonstrated that the three-party system of the 1920s produced dilemmas for Labour just as for the Liberals. To have refused office without an overall majority would have risked consigning the party to a future of perpetual opposition which few outside the far left really sought, but with a majority unlikely in the imminent future, Labour could anticipate only periods of weak government, at the mercy of uncertain Liberal allies. The strain placed upon the party's leaders – MacDonald worked an eighteen-hour day as Prime Minister and Foreign Secretary in 1924 – produced tensions within Cabinet and between the front and back benches. By September the overburdened Prime Minister had lost patience with his party, which he privately considered unfit to govern. This effect, like the attempts to distance the government from the TUC, the liberalisation of unemployment benefit and Lib–Lab tension, would recur in 1929–31, with more serious consequences.

New Conservatism

Baldwin won a massive majority in 1924 without undue scrutiny of his policies. This was just as well. The defeat of tariffs in 1923 had removed the policy closest to the hearts of many Tories; what emerged in its place was the confection known as 'New Conservatism'. What was new about it, after the 1923 disaster, was its avoidance of any initiative which might prove provocative. Baldwin disavowed any 'sectional, narrow, partisan or class policy'[9] in favour of an emphasis on the unity of the nation – always the English nation – in the face of Bolshevism and other alien creeds. His objectives were to refurbish the Tory image and to reduce the identification of Conservatism with the party's Diehards, its imperial visionaries or any other lobby. Though he stressed the Disraelian legacy of judicious social reform, Baldwin's undoctrinaire Conservatism was not designed to entice votes from Labour so much as to weaken the Liberals by attracting their middle-class supporters. Baldwin sought to reclaim those Conservatives alienated by tariffs in 1923 and to gain those Liberals alienated by their party's support for Labour during 1924; his 'national' party was a middle-class coalition.

However attractive, Baldwin's affability, his honesty and his patriotism offered few answers to the questions of the mid-1920s. Nor did he seek to impose coherence upon his 1924 Cabinet, which was almost as broad as Lloyd George's had been. The exiled Conservative Coalitionists Austen Chamberlain and Lord Birkenhead had returned to the fold once the Liberals' reunification and their support for Labour had ended hopes of recreating the Coalition. The new Cabinet included not only them but the Diehard Joynson-Hicks at the Home Office, the imperial visionary Leopold Amery at the Colonial Office, the social reformer Neville Chamberlain at the Ministry of Health and, most surprising of all, the peripatetic Winston Churchill – formerly a Tory, an Asquithian and a Coalition Liberal – at the Treasury. Twenty years after leaving the Tories over tariff reform, Churchill's most visible political conviction was still free trade; his appointment as Chancellor demonstrated the government's resolve never again to be tempted by tariffs. Baldwin supervised this eclectic group with a relaxed style that annoyed some colleagues. Amery believed that he was 'not interested in policy as such but in characters and personality':[10] energetic or determined ministers, including Amery himself, enjoyed much freedom, but strategic direction was lacking, most evidently in economic policy. This would be demonstrated by the conflict between the government's social and monetary policies after 1925.

Social policy derived largely from Neville Chamberlain. Chamberlain had been promoted from Health to the Treasury when

Baldwin became Prime Minister in 1923 but as a politician who liked 'spending money far better than saving it',[11] he chose to return to Health in 1924. Less flamboyant than his father, and with a tidier organisational mind, he nonetheless shared Joseph Chamberlain's belief that social reform was 'what one is in politics for'.[12] He had also inherited Joseph's ability to 'think big', understanding that the widely sought expansion of the pension system implied an overhaul of social insurance, and that this in turn would require the reform of the Poor Law that had been ducked in 1909. 'He saw the whole thing as none of us in the Ministry saw it, as just part of a single great problem', his Principal Private Secretary later recalled.[13] Within days of his appointment, Chamberlain had formulated a four-year programme of social and administrative reform, covering housing, slum clearance, pensions, health insurance, dental provision, hospitals, the Poor Law and local taxation, which was approved by an admiring Cabinet in November 1924. The government's first full session produced the Widows', Orphans' and Old Age Contributory Pensions Act of 1925. The core of this measure was the introduction of a contributory pension at age 65, to last until contributors reached 70, when they would transfer to the existing non-contributory scheme. Cost dictated that the new scheme should be contributory, but the expense of covering those admitted in the early years made the 'start-up' expense considerable – initially £6.3 million p.a.

Another ambitious minister with his own agenda was Leopold Amery at the Colonial Office. More truly Chamberlainite than either of Joseph Chamberlain's sons, Amery doubted the feasibility of an imperial policy without tariffs, but made do with Treasury subsidies to emigration, to colonial development and to the marketing of Empire produce within the UK, The Empire Marketing Board was established in 1926 to promote imperial trade by means of advertising, market research, etc., producing a succession of artistic posters which serve as its modern memorial. Amery also secured a £10 million development loan for British east Africa in 1926 as well as Treasury agreement for up to £3 million p.a. in support of development projects or emigration under the 1922 Empire Settlement Act. Assisted emigration projects bore a charmed life in the 1920s in the hope that they could alleviate British unemployment, though the Dominions remained reluctant to receive Britain's unemployables. Amery privately doubted that men would go to grow crops in the Empire unless guaranteed a protected British market by tariffs, but with tariffs unattainable he returned to the policy of 'developing the estate' that Joseph Chamberlain had pursued before floating tariff reform. His work culminated in the Colonial Development Act, passed shortly before the government left office in 1929. It threatened more demands on the public purse, though in the event only £3 million had been spent by 1935, most of it wasted in encouraging the growth of primary products after world slump had depressed their prices.

Amery rightly blamed his lack of success upon Treasury obstruction, but the principal obstacle that he faced was the one facing all spending ministers – that a large proportion of the budget was tied up in the repayment of war debt and the relief of unemployment. This problem was exacerbated by the government's decision to place fresh deflationary constraints upon itself in 1925 by returning sterling to the gold standard at the pre-war dollar parity.

Gold and the General Strike

Britain had gone off gold in 1919 so that the Coalition could reflate to buy social peace. The inflationary effects of the decision had been offset by the dear-money policy from 1920, but by 1925 Britain's domestic prices remained around 10 per cent too high for her export industries to return comfortably to the pre-war parity. The belief that Britain should eventually return to gold, and at the pre-war rate, had nevertheless prevailed ever since the war and had been reiterated by politicians of all parties since then. In 1925 the issue was forced by the imminent expiry of the 1920 gold export embargo, due at the end of the year.

Even with a flexible exchange rate Britain's foreign trade position was weak in the mid-1920s: her trade balance with virtually every part of the world had deteriorated since 1913, making the dangers of a return to the pre-war parity self-evident. The monetary authorities believed that trade levels would ultimately adjust to any fixed exchange rate, and that the problems anticipated by the export industries were largely problems of transition. In so far as they were more serious they reflected the obsolescence of particular industries, which could not be cured by debasing the pound. Treasury discussion betrays the department's detachment from British industry. Before the war financial services had flourished through the solidity of sterling, which had enabled it to be used as a gold substitute in international transactions; the aim was now 'to make the pound look the dollar in the face' once again.[14] Restoring this solidity, and the confidence that it was held to confer, was intrinsic to the policy of the return to gold, explaining why its advocates accepted its hair-shirt effects so readily and why so little consideration was given to returning at a lower parity. All central bankers watched with trepidation the collapse of Weimar Germany into hyper-inflation in the early 1920s. The City also 'suffered fearfully from the forebodings of Labour and Socialism' when MacDonald took office in 1924.[15] Baldwin's victory in the 1924 election produced a speculative rise in sterling which made the return to gold seem less daunting.

'There is no escape', Reginald McKenna, the former Liberal Chancellor, told Churchill, 'you have to go back, but it will be hell'.[16] McKenna, not an uncritical disciple of gold, acknowledged that the financial consensus behind the gold standard was irresistible. The financial community believed that it was not for politicians to dispute monetary issues with them; hence the *de haut en bas* tone in which the issue was put to Churchill not only by the Governor of the Bank of England but also by the Chancellor's nominal subordinates at the Treasury. They feared that politicians would be moved by electoral rather than financial considerations; in an age of near-universal suffrage and Labour governments, the gold standard was reassuringly 'knave proof'.[17]

Churchill believed that Montagu Norman, Governor of the Bank of England since 1920, would happily see Britain possess 'the finest credit in the world simultaneously with a million and a quarter unemployed'.[18] His private memoranda show as clear an understanding of the dangers of the return to gold as any of the decision's critics, but it was difficult for a new minister with no financial expertise to outweigh the near-unanimous view of his civil servants and the monetary authorities. His subsequent – and characteristically full-blooded – conversion to the Treasury view helped silence opponents in the spending departments. The way was cleared for Britain's return to gold in the spring of 1925, at the pre-war dollar parity of $4.86 to the pound.

To its critics the decision appeared a gratuitous surrender to economic internationalism. Less than two years earlier Baldwin had taken a risky step towards economic autarky with his tariff proposals; now his government renounced not only tariffs but also control of monetary policy, placing the economy at the mercy of international developments. The imperial visionaries, already annoyed by the 'unnecessary' election of 1923, saw the return to gold as another step away from the imperial economic policy that they sought. Alfred Milner, in his influential *Questions of the Hour*, published in 1925, portrayed the decision as a socially damaging surrender to 'plutocracy'.

In the short term the government surrendered control over interest rates. With the pound raised to a level perhaps 10 per cent higher than that dictated by Britain's trading position, high interest rates would be necessary to protect the parity. Though the Bank had recovered its monetary autonomy, its room for manoeuvre was limited in practice by the obligation to protect the pound. The government, though, had still less control. Churchill's angry reaction to the Bank's decision to raise Bank Rate by 1 per cent in December 1925 suggests that he had not fully appreciated that the defence of sterling would require a high rate régime. The next rise, in February 1929, occurred with a general election on the horizon and prompted a still stronger protest from Churchill, to equally little effect. Instead this highly political Chancellor responded to by lowering taxes, beginning with the 6d cut in income tax in the 1925 budget. With high interest rates making any fall in unemployment and its related costs less likely, tax cuts threatened budgetary problems for central government. By the time the Baldwin government left office the large surpluses of the early 1920s had given way to real deficits, concealed by Churchill's creative accounting.

The benign case for the return to gold had been that the British example would induce other nations to return, recreating the stable currency régime under which Britain had prospered before the war. The ascetic case was that depreciation had become addictive and that only a commitment to monetary discipline would make British industry competitive again. Most of the devotees of gold called for cuts in real wages, which they believed to have soared out of control in the salad days of the Coalition. Many employers responded accordingly in the summer of 1925, with wage cuts or longer hours being imposed in the engineering and woollen industries and in railway workshops. It is not clear that the government had anticipated this uncomfortable effect of the return to gold. Its response to the gathering crisis in the coal industry suggests that it had not.

Coal offered a good test for the attack on wage levels. It was an old industry, successful before the war but unsuited for the harsher post-war world. French occupation of the Ruhr in 1923 had neutralised the main continental competition and brought an artificial prosperity, but with the return of Ruhr production following the French withdrawal in 1924, prices had collapsed, and the mine owners had sought to claw back the gains made by their workforce. The union's threat of a strike in the summer of 1925 was designed to deter the owners from demanding wage cuts and a longer working day. A protracted coal stoppage was a daunting prospect for the government, but one to be faced if the gold standard was to work its purgative wonders.

Baldwin none the less approached it hesitantly. He made much of his family firm's reputation as paternalistic employers, and did not see a showdown with organised labour as inescapable. To judge from his words after the defeat of the coal strike – 'if we had protected steel we should not now be faced with the problem of 150,000 unemployable miners' – he still yearned for protection to cure this sort of problem.[19] He chose not to let owners and workers fight it out in 1925, resorting instead to two devices rather inconsistent with the rigours of the gold standard world: a Royal Commission on the coal industry under the Liberal MP Sir Herbert Samuel and a nine-month subsidy to bail out the industry until Samuel reported.

The Samuel Commission contained nobody familiar with the coal industry, and its reorganisation proposals were unconvincing. Its other suggestions, for the nationalisation of mining royalties and the abolition of the 1924 minimum wage, alienated both sides. When the subsidy expired in April 1926 hostilities resumed, with the employers proposing sharp wage cuts. Baldwin then intervened, hoping to induce the miners to accept longer hours in return for maintaining existing wage levels.

Such industrial brokerage did not come easily to Tory ministers; inevitably, as the Deputy Cabinet Secretary Thomas Jones sensed, while ministers were at ease with the owners, 'as friends jointly exploring a situation', they were markedly less relaxed with the union.[20]

The miners anticipated widespread sympathy action in support of a strike. Many trade unionists inferred from 'Black Friday' in 1921 not that joint action was futile but that the looming employer offensive made it all the more essential to maintain union solidarity: 'after 1921 when the miners were defeated, everyone else was attacked', one railwayman warned the TUC in 1925.[21] Most members of the TUC General Council understood the difficulties surrounding sympathy strikes, but they were also aware of the support for the miners within the labour movement, which produced the Industrial Alliance between the miners and the transport, steel and general unions in 1925. They feared being sidelined by syndicalist movements which they would be unable to control but which might bring general retribution for trade unionism. They hoped that the mere threat of sympathy action would avert the strike, but when negotiations broke down at the end of April, the General Council had to choose between another capitulation and a general strike. With 'visions of Black Friday on our minds', as the TUC General Secretary Walter Citrine admitted,[22] they took the latter course, calling a general strike in support of the miners on 3 May 1926.

For nine days in May 1926 key services were paralysed.[23] On the railways, on the trams and amongst dock workers the response to the strike call was impressive: the immobilisation of the docks caused greater anxiety to the authorities than any other aspect of the strike. Such was the appearance of solidarity that many smelled a TUC betrayal when the strike was eventually abandoned: 'there had been more diarrhoea in the headquarters than what there has been outside', the miners' president Herbert Smith explained to his union. But the stoppage had never been comprehensive; in particular it had scarcely affected road transport, electricity supply or food imports. The Seamen's Union resisted the strike call, ensuring that seaborne supplies were secure. In the electricity industry, the General Council decided against disrupting domestic power and had only partial success in its attempts to restrict industrial supply. The road haulage industry, lightly unionised and vulnerable to unemployment, also responsed only patchily, which in turn deterred the railwaymen. Given the TUC's inadequate preparation for a stoppage it had not sought, the strike effort was impressive, but it compared unfavourably with the government's response, planned since the crisis of the previous summer. The Cabinet's Supply and Transport Committee, established during the unrest of 1919, worked through local commissioners to mobilise volunteers, unload vessels in the strike-bound docks, distribute provisions by road and preserve law and order. Some 100,000 volunteers offered to run vital services. Ex-army officers drove trains and students stoked power stations, but the volunteers were not exclusively middle-class. The TUC had no power over the unemployed, many of whom proved ready, from desperation or conviction, to replace striking workers. It became clear that the authorities and society at large could endure a long strike, but that the costs to the unions were escalating. During the strike the National Union of Railwaymen spent nearly half its £2 million assets, mostly in strike pay. Meanwhile the government abandoned its earlier attempts to appear impartial between capital and labour once the strike was generalised. Baldwin saw it as 'a challenge to Parliament and...the road to anarchy and ruin'; Neville Chamberlain believed constitutional government to be 'fighting for its life'.[24] Once the TUC had decided to dabble in syndicalism, the government was interested only in its humiliation. On 12th May the General Council called off the General Strike, leaving the miners to struggle on to inevitable, though protracted, defeat.

The End of New Conservatism

The collapse of the General Strike destroyed the belief, lingering in the minds even of non-militant trade union leaders like Ernest Bevin, in concerted union action as a weapon of last resort. It probably encouraged such corporatist experiments as the 1928 Mond–Turner talks between industrialists and unionists, though few practical consequences emerged from these discussions. It made revision of union law inevitable. Baldwin felt no need to resist backbench demands to change the trade unions' favourable legal position, and the Trade Disputes Act of 1927 outlawed the general sympathy strike. The government held back, however, from most of the punitive proposals aired on the Tory right after the strike. It did not make strike ballots compulsory, it made only marginal changes to the law on picketing and it did not restrict union legal immunities – there would be no return to Taff Vale. The principal effect for trade unions of the 1927 Act was therefore to outlaw a tactic already shown to be ineffective. The Act's greatest victims were the Labour Party, hit by a change in the means by which it drew its political levy from affiliated unions. Union members would be in future be obliged actively to assign a fraction of their union subscription to the Labour Party if they so wished, rather than having to 'contract out' if they did not. The change was intended to damage Labour. Backbench Tories had long found the levy provocative; one of them, F.A. Macquisten, had attempted to introduce 'contracting in' in 1925. In fact the levy was already sufficiently controversial to ensure that few unionists paid it unwittingly – around a quarter of union members already contracted out. The Act advertised the levy and counteracted inertia, and local Labour parties worked strenuously to ensure that the levy was paid. The 18 per cent fall in the party's income after the 1927 Act was an irritant, but not as damaging as had been feared.

Other effects of the strike were more significant. A section of Liberal opinion moved to the right in 1926 and Sir John Simon, their spokesman, questioned the strike's legality in the Commons. The unsolicited opinion of this 'bald-headed old bastard',[25] as Victor Feather called him, cut no ice with the trade unions and was of little legal relevance as the government chose not to fight in the courts, but it illustrated the sensitivity of many Liberals to labour militancy. The Labour Party itself had been made aware that while it could not control the unions it could still be punished for their excesses. MacDonald's contempt for syndicalist militancy was reinforced, convincing him that 'the hot air merchants ... will have to be kept in their places in future'.[26] After 1926 he became more of a party disciplinarian, exacerbating Labour's internal tensions when the party returned to office.

The years after 1926 did not bring the wage falls that the gold standard had been intended to encourage. There was no widespread 'employer counter-attack'; the strike had been bruising enough to deter employers from future conflicts, and wage cuts were less frequent than before 1926. The Treasury blamed wage stickiness for continuing high unemployment; even in 1929, when the collapse of the New York stock market devastated British trade, the impact would be measured in soaring unemployment rather than falling wages. Before 1929 the revival of the world economy protected Britain from the deflationary effects of the gold standard. Rather than enduring painful adjustment, the British economy was frozen for four years in roughly its 1925 condition. Bank Rate remained stable, at between 4 and 5 per cent, high enough, in the economist Keynes's words, 'to hamper without hitting, to injure without killing and so to get the worst of both possible worlds'.[27] The high exchange rate made Britain vulnerable to import penetration, as the recovery of the European economies made them competitors rather than customers. British exporters responded by turning increasingly to imperial markets, so that the threat to the balance of payments was contained. In fact 1929 brought the best export performance of the inter-war period, but export volume remained 19 per cent lower than in 1913. Unemployment remained stubbornly high, never falling below 1.05 million.

Unable to use interest rates as a weapon against unemployment, Churchill kept taxes low, using creative accounting to conceal incipient deficits while bullying the spending departments. In 1926–8 there was a running battle with the service chiefs over defence spending. In 1926 the government reduced its contributions to the health and unemployment insurance funds. In 1927 Chamberlain agreed to a cut in state subsidies under the 1923 and 1924 Housing Acts; in 1928 the 1923 subsidy was abolished altogether. But the core of the expenditure problem remained the high cost of unemployment benefit.

In 1925 there had been a press campaign against dole scroungers, and a new investigation into unemployment benefit under the chairmanship of Lord Blanesborough.[28] By the time it reported in 1927 the system faced a crisis, exacerbated by the coal strike. The departure from the strict insurance principles of 1911 had placed heavy pressure on the Unemployment Fund (formed by insurance contributions), and costs had been contained only by stricter scrutiny of claimants. The 'genuinely seeking work' test was reintroduced in 1925, and between 1921 and

1927 the proportion of claimants denied benefit trebled. Where there was no work, the procedure became a rough and ready test of a claimant's motivation, administered by Local Employment Committees of retired businessmen and magistrates in, on average, three minutes per claimant. Married women who had entered the system through war work were weeded out by the means test, with 15 per cent of women claimants disallowed in 1925–8 against 4 per cent of men.

Those refused benefit had to go somewhere. Some claimed sickness benefit: in 1930 almost half the working-class households in Britain used sickness benefit to supplement family income. 'Sickness caused unemployment, and unemployment caused sickness',[29] but the insurance industry feared that health insurance was becoming a surrogate dole. Those denied sickness benefit fell upon the Poor Law, but Guardians' finances in many high unemployment areas had been deranged by the cost of supporting strikers' families during the General Strike. Poor Law offices became battlegrounds, where claimants vented their bitterness towards officialdom ('I was fighting for the likes of such fuckers as you in the trenches when I was fifteen, while you sat behind a desk'[30]). Some authorities sought to pay above the centrally determined relief levels to soften the blow to claimants forced off the unemployment system. The fear that working-class guardians would be elected by 'pauper votes' to pick ratepayers' pockets exercised Tory England in these years, and particularly alarmed Neville Chamberlain, who introduced legislation in 1926–8 to control local guardians. But the real problem lay not with those guardians who broke the law, but with the much larger number who found their tax base strained even by legal relief payments. In Newcastle poor relief for those refused unemployment benefit cost £3,700 per week. The Poor Law had not been designed to provide long-term unemployment relief. The Ministry of Health's inspectors, watching the system collapse, recommended logically if naïvely a return to the strict application of the workhouse test. Instead Chamberlain, characteristically, opted for large-scale administrative reform, abolishing the boards of guardians in 1929 and transferring their powers to county councils. The measure spread costs across whole counties, most of which were under Tory control, but even at county level the local taxation system could not carry indefinitely the burden of out-of-benefit unemployed. They would remain the concern of the state.

Blanesborough offered a partial solution to the problem, proposing a cut in the benefit rate for men and removal of the ministerial discretion over payment of extended benefit. The 1927 legislation based on the Blanesborough proposals brought the most widespread protests of the decade, but even these proposals would leave the system insolvent at prevailing unemployment rates. Like other policy-makers, Blanesborough was betting on a fall in unemployment levels which showed no sign of materialising.

By the late 1920s, therefore, the welfare system had become alarmingly distorted. The Unemployment Fund was losing £250,000 a week by the winter of 1928–9. Transitional benefit had become a kind of national out-relief, and was seen as such by claimants.[31] Unemployment benefit had ceased to be a supplement to private savings and had become a tax-supported safety net. It was, moreover, a safety net with holes, and those who fell through the holes fell upon the other relief agencies. Health insurance had become a substitute dole, while the numbers forced onto the Poor Law meant that poor relief lost much of its stigma.[32] Some slipped through the welfare system entirely, relying upon families, friends or landladies.

In April 1929 the government dodged the threat of 150,000 more claimants being turned off the benefit system a month before the election by extending the temporary transitional benefit for another year. This was, though, a defensive measure. By the spring of 1929 political debate revolved around more ambitious solutions to unemployment. The initiative had been taken by the Liberals, with the publication in February 1928 of the 'Liberal Yellow Book', *Britain's Industrial Future*. Its ideas were given wider exposure in Lloyd George's electioneering *We Can Conquer Unemployment* of March 1929, advocating a £250 million public works programme to employ 600,000 men per annum. The idea of public works was not new but the expenditure proposed was unprecedented, equivalent to 6 per cent of gross domestic product in 1929. The proposals had a carefree tone, as the Liberals were unlikely to have to implement them. They were in fact so ambitious that Labour, which could plausibly contemplate government, shelved its own public works schemes in order to appear responsible by comparison.

The Tories also called for statesmanship rather than stunts in their unadventurous 'Safety First' campaign of 1929. They emphasised the stalwart strengths of Stanley Baldwin as the embodiment of English virtues, but such soothing properties as the New Conservatism had possessed in 1924 had weakened by 1929. In the eyes of much of the industrial working class Baldwin had humiliated the trade unions, starved the miners, pruned housing subsidies and cut the dole: no amount of emollient waffle could alter this record, and Tory strategists did not anticipate gains among the working class. More disturbing was the discontent in the party's heartlands. As in 1920–1, deflation harmed Tory supporters. Neville Chamberlain acknowledged in October 1925 that the effects of the return to gold had hit many members of the 'middle class who read the *Daily Mail* and grumble about our extravagance and our toleration of sedition'.[33] The Baldwin government never fully satisfied these people, and the tightening of monetary policy in 1928–9 alienated them further. Calls for industrial and agricultural protection epitomised middle England's rejection of gold standard economics: 'what does it matter to the lads and lassies of Lancashire how much gold is in the Bank of England?', asked the Tory MP for Bolton in 1928.[34] Baldwin's continued refusal to introduce tariffs was resented. The response came from Churchill, in the form of his derating proposals of 1928, by which central government subsidised 75 per cent of the local tax bill of industrial undertakings and completely relieved agriculture of local taxation. This massive handout cost £35 million, but the use of national taxation to defray local rates was not as good politics as in Salisbury's day, when income-tax-payers had been fewer and richer: if anything derating contributed to the alienation of natural Tory support.

The 1929 election saw the Conservatives reduced to their bedrock vote of 38 per cent and to their bedrock seats in the southern shires and in the suburbs. They still gained a larger aggregate vote than either of their opponents, but lost over 150 seats. This was largely down to the 500 Liberal candidates, who gained the votes of Tory malcontents, but the Liberal unemployment crusade gained them few seats in high unemployment areas. The Liberals' strategy of targeting disaffected Tory voters and their frequent strident criticism of Labour had prevented them from building upon the working-class base that they had possessed before the war, or, indeed, from recapturing many of the industrial seats lost to Labour in 1918 and 1922: by the late 1920s the working-class Liberal voter was becoming an elderly rarity. Labour continued to conquer industrial seats, emerging as the largest party for the first time. It returned to office, but its 288 seats left it twenty seats short of an overall majority.

The Second Labour Government, 1929–31

If the 1924 Labour government had been a propaganda exercise, that of 1929 was not. The Liberals' attitude remained, though, as crucial as in 1924. MacDonald believed that the Liberals would remain supportive unless asked to support unduly provocative policies. Lloyd George, leader since Asquith's death in 1926, warned that 'the very hour the Ministry becomes a Socialist administration its career ends', but he did not want another election.[35] Once committed to supporting Labour he sought to benefit his party, calling for proportional representation – with 23 per cent of the vote the Liberals had gained 9 per cent of the seats – and involvement in the government's decisions. However, the Liberal right wing was reluctant to co-operate with Labour on any terms. From December 1929 the Liberals split repeatedly on important votes and, as in 1924, the government's perceived inadequacy made it difficult even for sympathetic Liberals to support it.

MacDonald returned to Downing Street in June 1929 with unemployment standing at 1.16 million but with Bank Rate already raised to 6.5 per cent to protect gold reserves. With Churchill's financial stewardship having produced a deficit of £14.5 million in 1929–30, fiscal reflation was not an option, unless the government was prepared to resort to overt deficit financing, which a minority government – particularly a Labour minority government – could not do without alarming the markets. This was the situation before the Wall Street Crash.

The collapse of the New York stock exchange in October 1929 produced shockwaves throughout the world economy which Britain was ill equipped to resist. Britain remained a trading nation, and world trade collapsed after October 1929. In the twelve months from September 1929 Britain's unemployment total soared to 2.5 million. A system strained by the earlier unemployment levels stood no chance of coping with those which followed. The notional surplus of £5 million predicted in Churchill's last budget in April 1929 had become a deficit of £14.5 million by the spring of 1930.[36] Though some of the deficit was down to Churchill's pre-election scams, the slump was the principal cause, diminishing tax revenues and swelling the shortfall in the Unemployment Fund.

Snowden, returning to the Treasury, wished to 'put the Insurance Fund on an insurance basis'[37] once again, but this had become politically unthinkable, particularly for a Labour government. For many people transitional benefit was the last defence against destitution; the TUC spoke for the entire labour movement in urging that the costs of the crisis should not fall exclusively upon the working class.[38] It called for devaluation, but devaluation now carried risks. To float the pound when public finance appeared out of control was to invite a sterling collapse; even a lower fixed parity might prompt a drain of gold. When MacDonald raised devaluation with the Governor of the Bank of England he was slapped down so firmly that he apologised for dabbling in the subject.[39] The government's only macroeconomic response was to double expenditure on public works schemes in 1930, though the 150,000 jobs created made little difference to total unemployment .

'The whole economic system is breaking down', MacDonald observed in the privacy of his diary.[40] He became fatalistic in the face of an unprecedented situation and disinclined to undertake policy adventures. In effect Labour aimed during 1930–1 to manage the crisis by protecting the living standards of the unemployed, and to contain the deficit by increasing the burden upon higher-income taxpayers. Shortly after coming to power it had liberalised the system by which benefit claims were judged: the disallowance rate consequently fell to only 4 per cent, and looser scrutiny encouraged an increase in claims. An Act of 1930 increased benefit rates for juveniles and dependants and abolished the 'genuinely seeking work' clause for the second time. The clause had always been an irritant – 'a mere ritual required by the authorities'[41] – but it had helped to contain the cost of unemployment. Its removal added 160,000 beneficiaries to the scheme, 60,000 of them new claimants, and increased the annual

Unemployment Fund deficit by £5 million. In his April 1930 budget Snowden promised to place these burdens upon 'the shoulders best able to bear the weight'.[42] Income tax, surtax and estate duty were all increased. Snowden anticipated raising £56 million over two years by these steps.

The tendency to see the second Labour government as mired in its own moderation obscures the extent to which its tax and benefit policies alarmed hostile contemporaries. Labour had pushed through gratuitous increases in benefit levels at a time when prices were falling – retail prices fell by around 15 per cent between 1929 and 1932 – and had then sought to fund the real gains of the unemployed by 'confiscatory' taxation. Reaction to these policies during 1930 helped to revive the Conservatives after their 1929 defeat and to steer the Tory leadership back towards protection.

The Revival of Protectionism

In the 1929 election many Tory candidates had ignored their leaders' policy and advocated safeguarding or other protectionist devices. Since then protectionist opinion had been strengthened by the collapse of world trade and the threat of large-scale dumping in the open British market. Agricultural protectionism was boosted by the 25 per cent fall in cereal prices over the winter of 1929–30. Conservative defeats in northern seats in 1929 had strengthened the agrarian protectionists of southern England within the parliamentary party. The caution of the leadership strained rank-and-file patience, bringing calls for greater constituency involvement in policy-making. This provided the opening for Lord Beaverbrook's Empire Crusade and his freelance campaign for 'Empire Free Trade'.

Lord Beaverbrook, proprietor of the *Daily Express*, was a Canadian who had been drawn to Britain by Joseph Chamberlain's imperial vision in the 1900s. He believed the British empire to face a choice between greater integration and complete disintegration, to the benefit of the USA. 'Empire Free Trade' meant what it said – not imperial preference but complete free trade within the empire, implying unrealistically that the Dominions abandon their own tariffs. Beaverbrook's bluff populism made light of this and other difficulties. 'The public is my constituency', he claimed in February 1930: 'whether I get the approval or the hostility of the political leaders never enters my head'.[43] He believed that the owner of a mass circulation newspaper could dictate policy to politicans.

He was an effective campaigner, intervening in by-elections from August 1929 either by attacking Baldwin or by running candidates against the Conservatives. His United Empire Party, founded in 1930 with the hesitant support of the *Daily Mail*'s proprietor Lord Rothermere, attracted 173,000 recruits in its first two weeks. As with Anti-Waste a decade earlier, the Tory leaders were embarrassed by a freelance movement appealing to their natural supporters. They were, though, more profoundly alienated by 'Empire Free Trade' than they had ever been by Anti-Waste, and worked for its humiliation. They loathed the *arriviste* press barons. Baldwin felt that 'to call them swine ... was to libel a very decent, clean animal', comparing them instead to the leaders of the TUC during the General Strike.[44] Neville Chamberlain, after a lifetime in Tory circles, thought Rothermere 'the most repulsive brute I have come across in a long time both physically and mentally'.[45] Significantly, the party's frontbench protectionists like Amery also kept Beaverbrook at arm's length, fearful that a protectionist ginger group could split the Tory vote and reprieve the government. By the autumn of 1930 Chamberlain had decided that Beaverbrook must be crushed. This required an end to the party's equivocation over protection.

Snowden's 1930 budget had made this easier by virtually avoiding increases in indirect taxation, refusing to take from 'the poorest of the land any part of their inadequate means'.[46] Tory protectionists reacted in much the way that their predecessors had reacted in 1909, assuming that Snowden's measures were the last gasp of free trade finance. Unlike then, however, 1930 saw protectionism gain a wider support than at any time since the 1840s. It was already well established in the 'smokestack' industries suffering from the depression, notably iron and steel. The traditionally free-trading textile industry became more sympathetic during 1930. So did many of the new industries of the inter-war period, dependent upon working at full capacity to ensure profitability. More striking was the detachment of much of the financial community from free trade. In July 1930 twenty leading City bankers called for imperial preference. In the Victorian period the City had considered free trade essential to maintain sterling as the dominant world currency, and it had supported the return to gold in 1925 in the hope of restoring sterling's primacy. With growing evidence that the gold standard had failed in this, the City interested itself in the development of a separate sterling bloc, and accepted protection as part of this change. In the 1900s the City's opposition to tariff reform had helped fracture Conservatism; Amery greeted its change of heart as 'the biggest leg up since 1903' for protectionists.[47]

Protectionism was changing from a sectional into a national cause. A Liberal Summer School heard a speaker from Manchester, of all places, urge his party to 'get away from the free trade slush'.[48] The Liberal right, under Simon, now saw protection as a lesser evil than Lloyd George's public works schemes or MacDonald's Socialism. Some on the Labour left had long seen free trade as an outdated fetish, while Ernest Bevin, emerging as the TUC's economic spokesman, concluded that free trade was inconsistent with the managed economy and therefore with the party's public ownership objectives. Within the government J. H. Thomas, the Colonial Secretary, and MacDonald himself had been converted to industrial protection after the Wall Street Crash, and MacDonald flirted with agricultural protection during 1930.[49] 'The day is coming,' he wrote to Thomas in January 1930, 'when we may have to give up orthodox free trade as we inherited it from our fathers.'[50]

Growing support for protection made a Conservative commitment far less dangerous than before. In July 1930 an opposition motion called for safeguarding against 'unfair foreign competition'.[51] In October the Canadian prime minister Bennett offered a 10 per cent increase in the duty on non-imperial goods entering Canada if Britain would tax non-imperial food. The collapse in world food prices had hit the Dominions' agrarian economies with much force, and had indeed aided the election of Bennett himself in 1930. The Canadian offer, endorsed by Australia, New Zealand and South Africa, reflected Dominion anxiety for a secure market for their farm surpluses. The Labour Dominions Secretary, J. H. Thomas, sympathetic himself, was bound by Snowden's resistance to tariffs, and had to stall. This allowed Baldwin to offer Tory support, endorsing a Conservative programme for the next election which included 'the fullest extension of imperial preference'.[52]

This was enough to marginalise Beaverbrook. He fell back upon the support of disaffected English farmers who found dumped Canadian grain no more alluring than dumped American grain. He abandoned the concept of Empire Free Trade (though confusingly not the term) for straightforward agricultural protection, and in January 1931 founded an 'Agricultural Party'. Organised agrarian protest was conspicuous by its absence in inter-war Britain, and Beaverbrook's last crusade proved feeble. When Baldwin delivered his famous put-down of the press barons in March 1931, puzzlingly equating their power with 'the prerogative of the harlot throughout the ages',[53] the Empire Crusade was already waning.

The 1931 Crisis

It dwindled not just because Baldwin trumped it, but because protection itself came to appear less urgent than economy in government. Except for those on the Labour left, virtually all protectionists identified themselves with the economy campaign which began after the direct tax increases in Snowden's 1930 budget. Moreover, the campaign gained recruits among Liberal free traders, which would eventually ensure the isolation of the Labour government. It became a commonplace on the right during 1930 that the burgeoning budget deficit showed the financial incontinence of democracy. Pressure for retrenchment gained a small success in October with the appointment of a Royal Commission on Unemployment Insurance, charged with returning the Unemployment Fund to solvency. The Commission provided an audience for the Treasury's warnings of national bankruptcy if the Fund deficit continued to grow.

In January 1931 Neville Chamberlain, as responsible as anybody for the increase in welfare expenditure during the 1920s, promised that the next Conservative government would stop the extension of social services until the country could afford it. In February the Conservatives tried to censure the government for losing control over public finance. This challenge was deflected by the Liberals, anxious as ever to avoid an election, with an amendment calling for a committee to recommend reductions in public expenditure. The Committee was appointed under Sir

George May, a former chairman of the Prudential Assurance Company.

MacDonald still faced a Cabinet battle over the growing cost of benefits. A week before the economy debate MacDonald, Snowden and Margaret Bondfield, the Minister of Labour, had proposed a 15 per cent cut in benefit rates, only to be blocked by a Cabinet refusal to sanction measures against the unemployed without comparable sacrifices from other groups. This battle was fought again in June, when the interim report of the Royal Commission on Unemployment Insurance recommended an 11.5 per cent cut in the standard benefit: a Cabinet committee rejected changes in benefit levels and sanctioned only the means-testing of 'anomalies' – married women, seasonal workers and the like. These changes were not insubstantial – they meant that married women who had contributed to the Fund when single would be wiped from the benefit system during the 1930s – but they would not restore the Unemployment Fund to surplus.

A savage conjunction of circumstances ensured that the next instalment of this crisis split the Cabinet and brought the government down. The European banking crisis that began with the collapse of the Kreditanstalt bank in Vienna in May 1931 led to the near closure of the German banking system in July. Many investors in German banks responded by withdrawing funds from London. In one week in mid-July the Bank of England lost a quarter of its gold reserves. Britain had thus already suffered severely from a crisis unrelated to its own financial problems when, on 31st July, Sir George May's Committee on National Expenditure reported, advertising those problems in arresting detail.

The May Committee report reflected the panic of the moment. It portrayed imminent national ruin in bold type and in the kind of lurid phrases generally alien to official reports ('there is clearly no time to lose',[54] etc.). Its closing assertion of the profligacy inherent in democracy[55] was a lazy recital of modish views, which apparently prevented the Committee from distinguishing between long-term expenditure problems and those caused by the 1929 Crash. Its projected £120 million deficit for 1932–3 was an exaggeration, as the Treasury recognised. The Committee recommended cuts of £96.5 million p.a., of which £66 million would come from unemployment insurance alone. This emphasis on welfare expenditure undermined the Committee's claim to have acted even-handedly towards all sections of the community and strengthened the impression that the jobless were to be sacrificed to protect the rentier: Keynes considered the May report 'a most gross perversion of social justice'.[56]

Unemployment benefit lay at the heart of the report. Although the Royal Commission on Unemployment Insurance had still to produce its final report, the recommendations of its interim report were rejected in favour of sterner measures – higher contributions to the Unemployment Fund, means-testing for transitional benefit and, above all, a 20 per cent cut in benefit rates only months after the Cabinet had rejected proposals for smaller cuts. In response the Cabinet resolved to maintain existing benefit levels and to resist the reimposition of means-testing, reducing the total savings to £52 million. This implied £100 millions of new taxation, for which a minority government would require the approval of the opposition leaders. MacDonald and Snowden carried these proposals to a conclave comprising the Tories Neville Chamberlain and Samuel Hoare and the Liberals Herbert Samuel and Donald MacLean (Lloyd George was hospitalised throughout the crisis for a prostate operation), to receive an unsurprising refusal.

By 21st August the Cabinet, virtually deadlocked, had succeeded only in edging the economies up to £56 million. By now the drain of gold, serious even before the May report's publication, was becoming catastrophic. The Bank told MacDonald that only four days' reserves remained, that it would be essential to obtain emergency credits from New York and Paris to avert national bankruptcy and that the agreed economies would be inadequate to secure these credits. On the following day the Cabinet was asked to accept a further £20 million of economies, including £12.5 million from benefit rate cuts. Again it refused, but hedged its bets by deputing MacDonald and Snowden to ascertain whether such cuts would satisfy the opposition. The opposition leaders agreed to accept the new cuts if they satisfied the markets. On 23rd August MacDonald told his Cabinet that a £76 million economy programme would satisfy the markets and sought approval for the necessary 10 per cent cut in unemployment benefit rates. His proposal was carried by the narrowest possible margin, eleven to nine – a meaningless victory, as the nine so hated the benefit cut that they would resign rather than implement it. The government could not continue. That evening MacDonald conveyed the resignation of the entire Cabinet to King George V, advising him to convene a conference of the party leaders for the following morning. The conference produced an interim cross-party National Government, along lines already suggested to MacDonald by the King during the crisis. A Cabinet of ten included MacDonald, Snowden and Thomas from Labour, the Tories Baldwin and Neville Chamberlain and the Liberal Samuel.

The idea of a cross-party National Government had gained a certain currency during the last months of 1930 and had never completely subsided. 'The ideal would be to banish party divisions and to unite in a National Government for say five years to deal with India, the Dole, Finance, Tariffs and Empire', the Liberal Lord Reading had written in May 1931.[57] Reading had also admitted that he thought the idea 'Utopian'; it did indeed have a certain dinner-party quality to it, but it was strengthened by the recognition that the three-party system which had emerged in Britain during the 1920s was ill-suited to the current emergency.

MacDonald himself found the idea of coalition attractive at the frequent moments when he lost patience with his party and his colleagues. None the less, for most of 1931 the three-party stalemate had appeared more likely to be resolved by a division of Liberal strength between the two major parties. Relations between MacDonald and Lloyd George and Herbert Samuel had warmed during 1931: joint Lab–Lib committees were established on minor topics, regular meetings initiated between front bench figures and a limited electoral pact agreed for by-elections. In July 1931, just before the crisis broke, Lloyd George, Samuel and MacDonald were negotiating still closer co-operation. Meanwhile, on the Liberal right Sir John Simon had been colluding with Neville Chamberlain, now Tory chairman, since November 1930. There was logic in these developments: Samuel was by temperament a progressive and Lloyd George still thought of himself as a radical. Simon was a social and economic conservative whose principal reason for remaining in the Liberal Party was his Congregationalist faith. With religion diminishing as a determinant of political allegiance, figures like Simon found their way into the Tory ranks. Protection was no longer an impassable barrier: Simon was at best an agnostic free trader by 1930 and would shortly declare his conversion to protection. The secession of the Simonites to the Tories and the Samuelites to Labour might have restored two-party politics, while the National coalition actually produced by the 1931 crisis, yoking both Liberal sections with MacDonald, Snowden, Thomas and the Tory leaders, was too broad to last.

In theory it had not been designed to last. The terms drafted by Samuel after the party leaders' meeting stated that 'the Parties will return to their ordinary position' when the financial emergency had been resolved.[58] The government did indeed attend to the crisis immediately, and Snowden's emergency budget enacted the benefit cuts which Labour had been unable to make. There was, of course, an easy Commons majority for these economies, and their passage calmed the economic storm, though the balance of payments problem – the real threat to sterling – remained.

To imagine, though, that normal political life would resume when the economic storm abated was wishful thinking. The crisis had had a traumatic effect upon both the Liberals and Labour. The incipient split within the Liberal Party was formalised in October, when Simon formed his own Liberal National Party, an indication that the Liberal right would fight the next election separately, whenever it came, and not return to Lloyd George's fold. Labour was not split as profoundly as the Liberals, as Mac-Donald carried only a handful of followers with him into the National Government, but the argument provoked by his actions was bitter. MacDonald feared that Labour was losing its 'sense of principle, of . . . service given with one's whole heart to the community', and had proved itself unfit to govern 'except in the calmest of good weather'.[59] The refusal to cut benefit levels when Britain faced national bankruptcy was irresponsible, implying that Labour was a class party rather than a national party. Snowden believed that financial collapse would have brought 'the destruction of the social services and the reduction of the standard of life for a generation'.[60] Their opponents believed that however real the financial crisis, the May Committee's remedies fell disproportionately upon the most vulnerable and that, in Bevin's words, 'the City must not be saved at the expense of the working class'.[61] MacDonald's apparent surrender to the forces of finance offended many in his party. At the end of September 1931 Labour's National Executive decided, in MacDonald's absence, to expel all supporters of the new National Government from the party.

This decision meant that any return to normalcy in British politics after the crisis would exclude MacDonald and his ex-Labour colleagues, who now felt 'like marooned sailors on a dreary island'.[62] Forced to choose between persevering as Premier and retiring ignominiously, MacDonald decided that his continued presence in office was essential to restore confidence at home and abroad. This decision pointed to the next step of fighting an early election under the National banner. Pressure for an election came from his new Conservative colleagues, anticipating a Tory landslide. They had been cautious about the idea of coalition: Baldwin believed that Labour should govern if it could and resign if it could not. As the crisis deepened Chamberlain accepted that pressure to join an emergency coalition would be hard to resist, but resolved to make tariffs and a Baldwin premiership conditions of support. In the event no commitments were made on tariffs, and royal persuasion ensured that MacDonald remained Prime Minister. A Tory landslide would compensate for these concessions. The main obstacle – the fear that an election campaign might undermine sterling – was removed, ironically, by the renewed pressure upon sterling in September. Harvey, Deputy Governor of the Bank of England, warned that sterling's gold parity could not be maintained for more than a month. The Bank had, in fact, already decided against further attempts to save the gold standard, which was abandoned a week after Harvey's warning. With the pound about to float, the case strengthened for a fresh mandate to bolster the currency.

The election, called for October, took a curious form. The components of the National Government – Conservatives, MacDonald's Labour followers, Simonite Liberals and Samuelite Liberals – campaigned separately, without a shared manifesto but on the understanding that they would co-operate in office if the National candidates secured a collective majority. This arrangement preserved the principle of coalition, but it was clear that any coalition emerging from the election would be lopsided. The NEC's proscription had stated the obvious – that there would be no further National recruits from Labour. The Samuelite Liberals ran under the National banner to avoid annihilation, though Lloyd George, still hospitalised, abjured the National bandwagon. They had secured a theoretical concession in the form of a pledge that the National parties should agree to differ about free trade during the campaign, but the corollary of this was that protectionist Tories could run against Liberal free traders. Conservative protectionists remembered how tariffs had been suffocated in the Coalition of 1918–22; the Tories would tolerate no 'coupon' to shelter endangered Liberals in 1931. In the event 92 of the 111 Samuelite candidates were opposed by Conservatives. Successful non-Tory National candidates in 1931 were effectively elected on Tory sufferance: most of them were the right-wing Simonite Liberals, 35 of their 40 candidates being returned. The National coalition produced by the election would clearly be Tory-controlled to a far greater extent than the Lloyd George Coalition had been: the Conservatives would surrender their dominant position in 1931 on no other terms. MacDonald had put himself at the head of a Tory juggernaut, designed to crush his former followers.

The inevitable massive endorsement of the National Government in October 1931 therefore brought with it a Tory landslide. The combined National forces gained a massive 67 per cent of the vote, of which 55 per cent went to Tory candidates. Electoral distortions meant that the National parliamentary majority was even greater, with 554 of the 615 seats, and that 473 of the successful National candidates were Conservatives. A demoralised Labour Party saw its parliamentary strength fall catastrophically, from 288 to 52. MacDonald believed that the events of 1931 would mean the end of Labour government for 25 years. 'Here is Parliamentary dictatorship', observed Thomas Jones, the Cabinet Secretary, as he watched the results come in.[63] He had just voted Tory for the first time in his life.

Lessons of the Crisis

The politics of the 1920s has a modern look to it, in its emphasis upon welfare and industrial relations, on taxation and monetary policy. Some of the quainter areas of pre-war dispute – Welsh disestablishment, licensing reform or denominational education –

disappear from view after 1920. These changes were accelerated by the decline of the Liberal Party, which had always sheltered enthusiasts for this sort of issue, and Liberal decline also marginalised other concerns less obviously anachronistic, such as local taxation reform, land reform or the agricultural minimum wage. But the underlying reason for the obsolescence of so many 'Victorian' issues was that the growth of the electorate had made it more difficult to promote 'faddist' concerns merely by capturing the party machine. The process had begun before the war: the materialistic debate over tariffs in the 1900s differed in its nature from most Victorian political debate, and Peter Clarke has argued that sectarian and temperance politics was withering in Lancashire by 1910.[64] It was encouraged, though, by the vast enlargement of the electorate in 1918.

The inter-war years saw the emasculation of the kind of small but obsessive pressure group that had proliferated in the late-Victorian period. An organisation like the Anti-Waste League might harness genuine grievances which the parties were slow to take up, but it was becoming virtually impossible to manufacture an issue in the way that, for example, the temperance groups had manufactured the drink problem in the 1890s, and harder for lobbies like the Charity Organisation Society to influence policy.

The women's movement provided a partial exception to this rule, for the obvious reason that almost 40 per cent of the electorate was female after 1918. In the main, male politicians assumed that women would respond to bread-and-butter issues: Austen Chamberlain was even said to have paused before endorsing Baldwin's tariff proposals in 1923, fearing the female reaction to possible cost-of-living increases. Politics remained, of course, a male profession: though Nancy Astor became Britain's first serving woman MP in 1919, only 35 women followed her in the entire inter-war period, and the Commons remained 'a boys' school that had decided to take on a few girls'.[65] None the less, the legislative record of the 1920s suggests that the women's organisations exercised a significant influence. Martin Pugh lists twenty-one women's measures passed between 1918 and 1929,[66] suggesting a greater sensitivity to women's concerns in the 1920s than at any time since. The list is dominated by relatively technical measures unlikely to have been demanded by the woman in the street but advocated by the various women's groups, on such matters as guardianship, adoption and equal divorce rights for men and women The largest single measure, the extension in 1928 of the parliamentary vote to those women excluded in 1918 was presumably included in the Tories' 1924 manifesto because it was the principal demand of the women's groups: it could not benefit existing electors.

One caveat applies, though. Most of the 1920s measures, including the franchise Act, were 'equal rights' measures, extending to women civic rights enjoyed by men. Such legislation was cost-free and generally uncontentious, but by the late 1920s the leaders of the women's movement were looking further. Under the presidency of Eleanor Rathbone, the National Union of Societies for Equal Citizenship (NUSEC), successor to the NUWSS, was steered towards the 'New Feminism' – the pursuit of 'what women need to fulfil the potentialities of their natures', in Rathbone's words,[67] rather than mere civic equality with men. In practice this meant a concern for the welfare of working women and in particular the working-class mother. With the important exception of the widows' pensions included in Neville Chamberlain's 1925 contributory pensions scheme, governments were unmoved by demands for women's economic improvement, and, indeed, went to some lengths to remove women from the benefit system. The influence of the women's lobby remained limited.

As politics came to be dominated by economic issues, the influential voices after the war proved to be those of the organisations speaking for the great economic interests – for the City, for industry (the Federation of British Industries was founded in 1916), for agriculture and for labour. Much of the diversity and pluralism of Victorian and Edwardian politics was lost as a result. A parallel process saw local government, source of so much political innovation in the late-Victorian period, drawn more firmly into the control of Whitehall. Again this process was rooted in the pre-war period. One of the enduring effects of the 'national efficiency' movement had been a lower tolerance of local authorities' freedom to neglect their sanitary and educational duties: the Victorian habit of permissive legislation yielded to an Edwardian habit of compulsion. Meanwhile the machinery of the 'New Liberal' welfare state had largely been constructed without reference to local authorities, whose cash crisis left them reluctant to take on new powers. Lloyd George had attempted in 1914 to confer new taxing powers upon the localities, but the Liberals' decline damaged the only party interested in local taxation reform. Post-war governments instead developed the traditional Conservative policy of central subsidy, which increased Whitehall's control over the localities. The ebb and flow of post-war housing policy – with local bodies being obliged by Addison to produce schemes, encouraged by Wheatley to build and then restrained by the reduction of subsidies in the late 1920s – demonstrates how local authorities were harnessed to central social policy. Neville Chamberlain's war on high-spending boards of guardians in 1927–8, resulting in the replacement of some of them by centrally appointed commissioners, showed central control at its most uncompromising.

These would be the ways in which the growth of the state would prove enduring, once the ephemeral state expansion of wartime had passed into memory. State penetration of the welfare field and the concomitant financial control and direction of local authorities survived the enthusiasm for decontrol and for rolling back the state in the 1920s. The wartime ventures into manufacturing industry and economic planning were forgotten, and even the sort of infrastructural work which the state could have carried out successfully was discouraged by the high cost of the welfare system: inter-war Britain produced few prestige public projects comparable to Hitler's Autobahnen or Roosevelt's Tennessee Valley Authority. There could be no doubt, though, that the central state was more prominent in the 1920s than in the 1900s.

Pre-war Liberal thinkers had welcomed the growth of state power to guarantee minimum standards of social security. Their assumption had been that the enlarged state would be a 'Progressive' state – linking middle-class and working-class radicalism and pursuing policies of social reform. Pre-war political debate had, however, produced two forms of statism: one the embryonic welfare state created by the Asquith government, the other the tariff reform state that put economic nationalism and the protection of jobs in home industries ahead of state welfare. This dichotomy had re-emerged in 1929–31. Obviously MacDonald's government differed enormously from Asquith's: a Labour government dependent upon grudging Liberal support was a far cry from the pre-war Progressive Alliance, while the last-ditch defence of benefit levels hardly compared with the confident pre-war experiments in social policy. Nevertheless, Labour's policy mix – free trade, internationalism, welfarism, higher direct taxation – was the same. Before the war this package had proved more marketable than the rival combination of economic nationalism, imperialism and tariffs. By 1931 this was no longer the case. The dead weight of unemployment relief payments limited the scope for more adventurous welfare policies, and itself became unsustainable without higher taxation. Higher tax levels and a larger number of taxpayers made taxpayer tolerance more limited than before the war. The post-war vulnerability of sterling weakened Labour in office, where the Asquith government had not – even in 1909 – had to face a financial crisis until the outbreak of war. Finally the post-1929 slump, both by lowering the price level and by revealing the bankruptcy of conventional economic policy, made protection less of a bogey than it had appeared even in 1923. In short, the pre-war Progressive mix of free trade and welfare reform was no longer viable. Further, the political circumstances were far less propitious for left-of-centre government. Labour's post-war independence made the Lib–Lab relationship more fractious and Lib–Lab co-operation more difficult than before the war. The erosion of the Liberals' working-class base distanced them from Labour, turning the Liberal Party of the 1920s into a middle-class pressure group. The once quiescent Liberal right gained new force. Innately suspicious of Labour, it eventually showed itself ready to swallow protection in preference to socialism, and was drawn into what would prove a permanent alliance with the Tories. The lesson of 1931 was that Progressivism was dead.

Thus it was a Tory statism which triumphed. The deflationary climate of the years after 1929 was favourable to Toryism and protectionism and inimical to Progressivism and welfare. After almost thirty years the way was open for the Chamberlainite economic nationalism once considered implausible. By the autumn of 1932, when imperial preference was achieved at the Ottawa imperial economic conference and the free traders left the National Goverment, Britain had become a protectionist state.

8 The Thirties

Conservative Hegemony

The National Government dominated the 1931 House of Commons to an extent that threatened to debase the parliamentary process. Despite MacDonald's leadership, the National Government was much more firmly under Conservative control than the Lloyd George Coalition had been, with 473 of the 554 National MPs Tories. Whereas Conservative support of the Lloyd George Coalition in 1918–22 had entailed acquiescence in Lloyd George's social programmes and the renunciation of tariffs, the only significant concession made by the Tories in 1931–40 proved to be the sacrifice of a strong party position to form the National Government in the first place. Indeed 1931 had destroyed Labour's governmental credibility and had deepened Liberal divisions, making it easier for Conservatives to suggest that 'the Tories are the nation', as MacDonald privately complained.[1]

The 'odd lot of colonels and sycophants' in local Conservative associations may not have been more 'national' than trade unionists or Labour councillors,[2] but the National Government did win the two largest electoral victories since the advent of universal suffrage. By 1935 it no longer invoked the rhetoric of crisis or claimed to be above party, and Baldwin's return to the premiership in place of the ailing MacDonald in June emphasised the National Government's Tory nature. In the November general election its share of the vote fell from the artificial peak of 1931, but it rested at 53.7 per cent – a higher share than any government has managed since. The Liberal split contributed more than the Labour split to its strength. With the Simonite third of the old Liberal Party permanently fused to the Conservatives, the Liberal remnants could run only 161 candidates in 1935, limiting the party's power to siphon middle-class protest votes from the Conservatives as it had in the 1920s. The three-party politics of 1922–31 had disappeared. Its disappearance showed how dependent Labour had previously been upon the three-party lottery. Labour's vote resembled 'a house of cards on a concrete base', in David Howell's apt image.[3] Its bedrock support proved remarkably firm, given the circumstances of 1931. That 6.6 million voters stayed loyal to Labour after that disaster was striking: 'you cannot kill the Labour Movement... and the bally animal cannot even commit suicide', as the former Labour minister Tom Shaw observed.[4] But the progress made by the party during the 1920s had reflected the extent to which it had expanded beyond its trade union base, through neighbourhood politics, local constituency recruitment, the mobilisation of the women's vote and so on. In 1929 Labour victories in unlikely places such as Reading, Wellingborough and Enfield reflected the growth of local Labour activity. This expansion had transformed the union-dominated pre-war party, a process furthered by the decline of trade unionism under the pressure of mass unemployment in the 1920s. It had turned Labour from a pressure group into a party capable of holding minority office, but it would need to go further to bring a Labour majority. Labour remained weak in centres of the inter-war 'new industries' – motor cars, electronics, chemicals, etc. – where working-class electorates voted Tory. These industries were characterised by high earnings, low unionisation and, often, a higher proportion of female labour; their employees continued to identify Labour with a traditional blue-collar politics irrelevant to their needs. Labour never won the new motor centre of Oxford, and remained weak in the industrial belt of outer London and in the West Midlands. We cannot know whether Labour's further growth was impeded by the 1931 disaster or whether Labour had just reached a natural plateau in 1929, but it is clear that it was not yet strong enough to withstand the consolidation of the middle-class vote caused by the collapse of Liberalism. In 1935 the party gained almost as many votes and a higher share of the poll than in 1929. The young James Callaghan, working for Labour in south-east London, expected to sweep the country,[5] but eight million votes produced only 154 seats.

'No more MacDonaldite slush', the Labour intellectual Hugh Dalton rejoiced in 1931.[6] The second Labour government's collapse pushed the party leftwards. Even the pragmatic Herbert Morrison urged a move to 'the real Socialist Left';[7] a commitment to nationalise the banking sector – held to have subverted Labour in 1931 – was an early result. The increasing prominence within the party of public sector employees as unemployment weakened the traditional industrial unions strengthened Labour's commitment to statist policies in the 1930s. Labour local authorities supported local industry or experimented with health centres in an often innovative way, but such policies did not appeal to centrist thinking in the 1930s as they would in 1945, and Labour's prospects were further damaged by internal disputes.

The events of 1931 convinced Labour's leaders that discipline and solidarity were indispensable, but they convinced many on the left that socialism was unattainable through parliamentary politics. In 1932 the Independent Labour Party, originally the party's vehicle for individual membership, but a left-wing ginger group since that role had been usurped by the constituency associations in 1918, voted itself into oblivion by disaffiliating from the national party. The minority opposing disaffiliation formed the Socialist League which, under the leadership of the wealthy barrister Sir Stafford Cripps, criticised the leadership's moderation from within. Cripps's colleague H. N. Brailsford saw 'no future along the paths of the "New Deals" and capitalist-minded Liberalism'.[8] Electoral defeat in 1935 appeared to confirm the futility of electoral politics and led the League to support the efforts of the Communist Party of Great Britain to affiliate to Labour. The Communist affiliation bid reflected the eagerness of the Moscow-controlled Comintern after 1933 that national Communist parties should work with constitutional socialist parties to create a united front against Fascism. After years of abuse from British Communists, the Labour leadership was unmoved by its entreaties, but the Socialist League identified itself with the Communists and with the remnants of the Independent Labour Party in campaigning for working-class unity 'in common struggle against Fascism, Reaction and War'.[9] The publication of their Unity Manifesto in January 1937 led the Labour executive committee to disaffiliate the Socialist League, the only one of the signatories it was in a position to discipline. This did not prevent Cripps from campaigning for a British Popular Front, embracing the Liberals as well as the Left, as the Fascist threat grew during 1938. Cripps's call in January 1939 for Labour to combine with Liberals, Communists and the ILP led the Labour executive to expel him and sixteen of his followers from the party. These were public squabbles, publicised further by a hostile press. Though the details of the debates made little impact upon voters, the impression of division was dangerous, while Cripps's insistence that Labour on its own was incapable of defeating the National Government contained a worrying germ of truth. Whilst it is impossible to know how the state of international affairs would have affected a general election held in 1939 or 1940, Labour's underlying electoral position was no stronger by then than in 1935.

It was none the less never so weak as to threaten substantial losses to the extreme left. Three years after disaffiliating from Labour the ILP had lost half its membership; outside Glasgow its popular support was negligible.[10] The Communist Party had always suffered from Labour's close relationship with the trade unions, which deprived it of independent industrial bases, and was forced to seek a foothold within Labour, by repeated requests for affiliation, or by clandestine attempts to permeate local party or union branches. Affiliation was routinely denied. Permeation brought little success and guaranteed the enmity of union leaders: the hostility of a political unionist like Ernest Bevin reflected long experience of communist activity within the Transport and General Workers' Union.

The Communist Party of Great Britain (CPGB) worked instead to mobilise the unemployed, a group responsive to the Party's rejection of capitalism and one which often felt itself neglected by Labour. Local Communist branches helped claimants in dealing with benefit authorities and organised resistance to the reductions in benefit levels in 1935. The 'trade union' of the unemployed, the National Unemployed Workers' Movement, orchestrated by the Communist Wal Hannington, organised seven marches against unemployment between 1922 and 1936. The new Labour leader, Clement Attlee, thought it worthwhile to join the reception for the last of these marches, from south Wales, in 1936, though that protest was dwarfed by the simultaneous march from the devastated shipbuilding town of Jarrow, which had not been organised by the Communists. The rise in long-term unemployment from 1929 and the spread of European Fascism encouraged the growth of CPGB membership, which stood at 18,000 by the outbreak of war. This would not, though, confer much power without a stronger hold upon the political élite than the party ever possessed. It enjoyed some success among the guilt-ridden *jeunesse dorée* of Oxbridge, as is now well known: the anti-communism of the future MI5 agent Peter Wright reflected his resentment of those who spent their university careers majoring in treachery when he had been denied higher education by his father's unemployment.[11] Nevertheless, the party's membership consisted largely of the most marginal and politically weakest sections of the working class, and its influence remained limited.

The same is true of British Fascism. The central idea of the totalitarian Right – that liberal democracy was obsolete – had been in vogue since the 1900s, and many had seen the fate of the second Labour government as a demonstration of democracy's failings. Such views, however, generally reflected a patrician concern that the mass electorate was irresponsible. This 'country-gentleman, English Fascism', as Cripps called it,[12] did not crave the demagogy of a British Hitler. How different matters would have been had the 1931 election produced a crushing victory for Labour (as MacDonald initially feared), rather than a crushing defeat, is unknowable, but the National Government landslide quelled worries about democracy. Conservative recruits to the 'New Party' of the former Labour Minister Sir Oswald Mosley, which became the British Union of Fascists (BUF) in 1932, were limited to those who shared Mosley's enthusiasm for corporatist economics or his worries about national decline. Deprived of much élite support, the BUF moved towards populism.

Mosley, impatient and intolerant, was a poor operator but a fine orator, which encouraged his movement's lurch into demagoguery and violence. BUF meetings from March 1933 were marked by violence, culminating with the Olympia meeting of June 1934, when Mosley spoke for two hours while fascist stewards assaulted communist hecklers. Baldwin's parliamentary private secretary, who was present, concluded 'that Mosley [is] a political maniac, and that decent English people must combine to kill his movement'.[13] Olympia underlined the disreputable nature of the BUF and alienated Mosley's only substantial press ally, Lord Rothermere's *Daily Mail*. From 1935 the BBC was urged informally by government not to provide a platform for the BUF. Behind the state's disavowal of Mosley was the growing awareness of the nature of Hitler's régime; Mosley responded by becoming more like Hitler and less like Mussolini, emphasising an anti-semitism not previously prominent. In 1936 the BUF mounted rallies designed to provoke the Jewish community first in Leeds and then in east London. The latter was met by a Communist counter-march, resulting in 'the battle of Cable Street', in which seventy people were injured. The government responded with the Public Order Act of 1936, banning political uniforms and paramilitary organisations and giving the Home Secretary power to regulate public processions. Mosley, fastidiously respectful of the letter of the law, ordered the cessation of the rallies. The BUF even toyed with democracy in 1937, when unsuccessful attempts to contest east London seats in the London County Council elections advertised the feebleness of Fascism. In reality 'Mosley's men looked and felt very different in ordinary clothes';[14] they gained their strength from processions, violence and publicity, and were easily curbed once Mosley crossed the limits of political legitimacy. A successful British Fascist movement required a weak Conservative Party or a strong Communist Party, and neither existed.

The unstable three-party politics of the 1920s had given way after 1931 to a situation in which a coalition government dominated by the Conservatives enjoyed an absolute supremacy. Labour's support was substantial but concentrated, with little sign of further growth. The Liberals were split and virtually dead as an electoral force. The extremists, though noisy, were marginal. Throughout the decade the Conservatives suffered few constraints upon their freedom of movement. This was clear from their fatalistic acceptance of high levels of unemployment, from their hard-nosed remodelling of the benefit system and, above all, from their readiness to bulldoze through a new tariff system.

Economic Nationalism

MacDonald warned his Cabinet in December 1931 that the tariff question would 'present us with the greatest difficulties of our co-operation',[15] though his warning did not deter the protectionists. By 1931 protection was practical politics. The price fall since 1929 had muted consumer opposition to food duties. An £86 million trade deficit was forecast for 1931, increasing demands for import curbs. Currency devaluation after the departure from gold might reduce that deficit, but the monetary authorities still feared an inflationary currency collapse of the sort experienced in the European inflations of the 1920s, and looked to tariffs to regulate trade and control sterling's fall. The Cobdenite belief that free trade produced international harmony sounded hollow in a world of trade rivalry and competitive devaluation. The free trade bloc had been devastated by the events of 1931, with a third of the Liberal Party embracing protection in splitting from their former colleagues, with Snowden's departure from the Treasury in November 1931 (he accepted a peerage and became Lord Privy Seal) and with the return of an overwhelming majority of Tory protectionists in the 1931 election. They could certainly claim a mandate: 1931 had been a crisis election, but real issues were canvassed and protection was among the most prominent of them.

All this facilitated Britain's abandonment of her century-long commitment to free trade in 1931–2. In November 1931 the Board of Trade was empowered to impose punitive duties on goods assumed to have been 'dumped', and the Cabinet approved a quota on imported wheat. In December a Cabinet Committee under Neville Chamberlain recommended a 10 per cent duty on all imports except basic food and raw materials and the establishment of an Import Duties Advisory Committee to suggest higher duties where appropriate; these proposals formed the basis of the Import Duties Bill introduced in February 1932. Goods from the dependent Empire were exempted from these duties, while goods from the Dominions and India gained temporary exemption pending more permanent arrangements for imperial imports. These proposals angered Snowden and the Samuelite Liberals. Their resignations were averted only by the strange expedient of allowing them to speak and vote against the measures without resigning. Only the avoidance of food duties justified their remaining in the Cabinet, and that would not survive the Imperial Economic Conference to be held in Ottawa in 1932.

The British delegation to Ottawa, under Baldwin and Neville Chamberlain, consisted of hardened protectionists, excepting only Walter Runciman, a Simonite Liberal who had renounced free trade. Their mission was to substantiate the dreams of imperial economic integration which had tempted Tories since 1903 – to vindicate 'my father's ghost', in Neville Chamberlain's words.[16] This task was not straightforward. They could offer preference to imports from the Dominions, but a genuine imperial trade bloc would require some reciprocation from the Dominions themselves. All Dominions already gave preference to British goods and hesitated to extend that preference while their farmers and industrialists were suffering from the world depression. Consequently the British negotiators were unable to win reductions in Dominion tariffs on British goods: their hope to establish 'scientific' tariff levels on British exports, allowing efficient Dominion industries to compete but not protecting the inefficient, cut little ice with Dominion ministers who had their own unemployment problems. The negotiations were unsentimental and lacking in imperial warmth. After a century's commitment to free trade, no British minister had experience of tariff negotiations, but having fought for thirty years to establish the principle of imperial preference at home, the British protectionists could not allow the conference to fail. Consequently the deals done at Ottawa tended to benefit the Dominions. They increased British preference in Dominion markets by raising duties on non-British imports but did not improve British exporters' position *vis-à-vis* Dominion producers. On the import side, Britain resisted Australian demands for a meat duty but conceded a five-year restriction on foreign meat imports which may have been more damaging to the British consumer. To dissuade the Dominions from protecting their own farmers, free entry was granted to their eggs, poultry and dairy products for three years, encouraging Australia and New Zealand to dump in Britain.

Snowden resigned, taking the free trade Liberal ministers with him and leaving MacDonald 'not a Prime Minister, but the Chairman of a Tory Cabinet'.[17] In resigning over Ottawa rather than over the earlier Import Duties Act, Snowden was responding to the symbolic significance of imperial preference. In material terms it must be questionable whether Britain gained enough from the Dominions at Ottawa to justify their exemption from the 1932 tariff, while the historian of Commonwealth relations in the period has suggested that the often fractious negotiations at Ottawa weakened the habit of co-operation that had characterised imperial conferences in the 1920s.[18]

British ministers had made these sacrifices in the belief that Empire markets offered long-term growth: 'the future possibilities of Empire trade', Neville Chamberlain believed, 'must be infinitely greater than anything we can hope for from foreigners'.[19] Ottawa provided some encouragement for intra-Empire trade – British imports from the Empire have been estimated at 3 per cent above trend during 1932–5 – but did not reverse the decline in Britain's share of imports into imperial countries, as the Dominions diversified their trade and developed local markets; 33 per cent of Empire imports were British in 1938, compared with 44 per cent in 1913.[20] The real value of Ottawa lay in its providing a safety-net for British exports which would otherwise have been fully exposed to the collapse of world trade after 1929. The value of British exports to the Dominions fell by 22 per cent between 1925–9 and 1934–8, which says little for Ottawa until one realises that the overall fall in British export values in that period was 38 per cent.[21] The rise in the imperial share of British exports from 42 per cent in 1925–9 to 49 per cent in 1935–9[22] demonstrates the 'safe haven' that the Empire still provided in a hostile world. Baldwin saw Ottawa as part of 'the natural process of evolution' towards larger economic blocs.[23]

The 1930s would show, though, that Britain's economic bloc was not so much the imperial unit as the sterling area – the group of countries which habitually conducted international trade in sterling or maintained a steady parity between their own currencies and the pound. The idea of building a currency area of sterling users had been promoted by the Treasury once Britain was forced off the gold standard. It reflected Whitehall's conviction that this disaster had less to do British economic weakness than with the actions of the USA and France in sterilising world gold stocks. Sterling might become 'an effective rival of gold' – 'an invaluable rock', in the Foreign Office's view.[24] London's control of 'an Empire Sterling Standard' might obviate much trade bargaining with the obdurate Dominions.[25] This proved broadly correct: all the Dominions except Canada traded in sterling and had an incentive to trade with other sterling countries once the gold standard system collapsed. The sterling area would shape the pattern of Britain's overseas trade until the 1970s. It was not exclusively imperial, but included non-imperial trading partners in Scandinavia, the Baltic states, Portugal and Argentina. Many of these countries had run up trade surpluses with Britain, making them better export prospects than the Dominions; it is arguable that the deals struck with these nations during 1932–3 represented the high point of British economic diplomacy in these years, but the prominence of the Dominions within Britain's trading arrangements ensured that Ottawa received more attention. Britain appeared, in 1932, at last to have created the imperial economy envisaged in 1903.

The Limits to Recovery

Most Conservative MPs welcomed the Ottawa achievement. Sir Charles Petrie, scribe to the Chamberlain family, recalled the response of 'an old Tariff Reformer' in 1933 to criticism of the National Government: 'that's all very well, but don't forget they gave us the tariff'. There was, as Petrie observed, 'a generation of British history in the words'.[26] The tariff reformers of the 1930s were, on the whole, less visionary than Joseph Chamberlain and his first-generation followers had been: they placed less emphasis upon constructive social reform and imperial development, more on economic autarky and imperial security in a dangerous world, but the doctrine's appeal was still strong. Neville Chamberlain wrote privately of the Import Duties Act that 'this policy and this alone could have saved the empire'.[27]

Social reform remained desirable. Tariff reformers considered *laisser faire* a liberal delusion – 'as dead as the slave trade', in Baldwin's view – but as the tariff evolved into a primarily defensive weapon to halt the decline in Britain's trade balance, it became harder to envisage it generating cash for welfare measures. The promise that tariffs could fund social reform had not won votes in 1906 or, so far as it was made then, in 1923, and was not the reason for protection's popularity in 1931. The retreat from social reform in 1924–9 indicated the difficulty of expanding welfare provision. The fact was that the government had inherited very high unemployment levels which absorbed much of the welfare budget. The growth in the unemployment total after 1929 did not cease until January 1932, when 2.96 million were receiving benefit – around 23 per cent of those insured – and the actual number of unemployed was well over three million.[28] Ministers hoped that a tariff-induced recovery would reduce unemployment, but none expected a rapid improvement. By March 1935 the total had fallen only to 2.25 million. Such figures necessitated a tight rein on the costs of the insurance scheme to avoid a repeat of 1931. Thus not only was there little Tory interest in new social programmes after 1931, but social policy was dominated by the battle to contain the cost of unemployment insurance.

A visible but modest increase in employment can be attributed to the tariff, but protection was only one of several economic measures made possible by the departure from gold. It probably had less impact than cheap money: with no need to support an overvalued pound, British interest rates fell to the levels which had prevailed elsewhere since the crash. By June 1932 Bank Rate stood at 2 per cent. Cheap money enabled the 'sunrise' industries – cars, electrical engineering, chemicals, etc. – to invest more cheaply and facilitated borrowing for house-purchase, which benefited the building industry. House sales in turn generated demand for the accoutrements of the new home, such as cookers, vacuum cleaners and radios – a reminder that the real engine of the 1930s recovery was the improved purchasing power given by the post-1929 price fall to those still in work. The drawback was that a consumer-led recovery tended to make rich areas richer. The building boom was centred in London and the South East. Although the demand for consumer goods generated jobs for many who could not buy houses, the consumer goods industries followed demand and gravitated to the prosperous areas – chiefly outer London and the West Midlands.

The decline of the old industrial centres therefore continued. Few of them had prospered at any point since the war, but the contraction of world trade after 1929 worsened their position, and the chronic but predominantly short-term unemployment of the 1920s yielded to deep-seated and long-term unemployment in the 1930s. Whereas in 1929 only 4.6 per cent of the unemployed had been out of work for a year or more, by 1935 the figure was 26 per cent; it actually rose during the post-1932 recovery.[29] In northern England, in February 1938, 35 per cent of all benefit claimants had been out of work for a year or more.[30] The contemporary Pilgrim Trust survey estimated that 40 per cent of long-term unemployment was concentrated in coal, ship-building, iron and steel and textiles. These industries produced alarming concentrations of unemployment – 71 per cent of the workforce in Crook, in the Durham coalfield, had been jobless for five years by 1936. 'Once in the queue, ever in the queue', the Trust concluded.[31] For much of the 1920s, industrialists, like politicians, had hesitated to accept the permanence of mass unemployment; in the 1930s they gradually did so, and defined that section of the workforce which was surplus to requirements – predominantly unskilled, unfit and old.[32] The material effects of unemployment had almost certainly been worse in the 1920s than in the 1930s, when falling prices after 1929 raised real benefit levels,[33] but the long-term unemployment of the 1930s generated a culture of unemployment and encouraged investigation of the phenomenon. The thirties are still seen as the decade of the dole.

Government acknowledged tacitly that no end to the problem was visible. In 1935 a Cabinet Sub-Committee predicted average unemployment of 16 per cent over the next ten years, while the Committtee on Economic Information forecast a downturn in 1937 on the scale of 1931. Such predictions warned against the *ad hoc* distortions of the benefit system adopted in the 1920s. Instead the system was recast in the early 1930s. Neville Chamberlain, as Chancellor from 1931, did what Snowden had wished to do and restored the insurance basis of benefits, making insurance-funded benefits more attractive and building disincentives – above all the means test – into uncovenanted systems.

As early as October 1931 the government had restricted eligibility for unemployment benefit and limited the payment period. As always, though, the weakness of the local tax base in many high unemployment areas dissuaded Whitehall from throwing the rest of the unemployed on to the local authorities. Instead 'Transitional Payments' replaced Transitional Benefit for insurable workers who had exhausted their entitlement. Central government met the cost of these payments and local employment offices determined the eligibility of applicants and their needs. The dangers of building local discretion into a national system should have been obvious. Inevitable discrepancies in local practice produced alarming anomalies: in Leicester and Manchester claimants were required to have virtually exhausted their savings before they became eligible, while in Edinburgh a claimant could have £500 in the bank. Some Committees simply sought to be as generous as possible. The means test was prominent in the 1932 local elections, and relief authorities feared electoral retribution for undue stringency in applying the test. Spending Treasury money rather than their own, they had little incentive to economise: in Rotherham and in Merthyr Tydfil 98 per cent of claimants were paid at the full rate, against a national average of 50.8 per cent.[34]

Local Committees had hesitated to take on needs assessment because of the unpopularity that it entailed. The most frequent reason for generous payments was authorities' reluctance to make deductions for earnings by other members of the claimant's family: the strongest working-class objection to the means test was that it threatened to break up families by forcing earning teenagers to leave home. In addition, the relief authorities were not used to dealing with the able-bodied unemployed, and tended to assume that the Ministry's regulations had not been intended to be applied to such people with the strictest rigour. These considerations cut little ice, though, with a government which suspected that its regulations were being distorted by local authorities for political reasons. Neville Chamberlain, as Chancellor, was largely responsible for the further revision of benefit law introduced in 1934. That year's Unemployment Act accepted that if central government was to pay for the uninsured unemployed it would have to establish a national administration. A two-tier machinery was created, by which a restored insurance system looked after the insured at a reasonably generous level, while a safety net was produced for those who had exhausted their cover. Two new quangos operated the system: the Unemployment Insurance Statutory Committee, under Sir William Beveridge, looking after the insured, and the Unemployment Assistance Board (UAB), looking after the rest.

Since the onset of mass unemployment in 1920 an individual's chance of finding work before his insurance cover was exhausted had depended more upon the local economy than upon the claimant's merits, and governments in the 1920s had hesitated to turn deserving individuals off the system once their entitlement was exhausted. This had largely been because the alternative was the Poor Law, which was both unpopular and unable to support large numbers of men with limited employment prospects. As a result, the insurance system had been bankrupted in the 1920s in order to support as many as possible of the uninsured. The new system restored the insurance principle, giving a year's benefit to those with sufficient previous contributions, at the higher pre-1931 levels and without demeaning scrutiny. Those whose insurance was exhausted, however, were left to the UAB, 'a new kind of centralized Poor Law' authority,[35] dealing with poverty arising specifically from unemployment. If it lacked the stigma of the Poor Law, the UAB was scarcely welcoming to its clients. The inauguration of the UAB and of new standard benefit scales in 1935 brought mass protests in areas where benefit rates were reduced, and the government acted with striking haste to ensure that claimants whose previous payments had been higher continued to be paid at the old rate.

The means test remained, though, to symbolise the flinty-heartedness of unemployment assistance in the 1930s. With a high proportion of UAB applicants being long-term unemployed who were unlikely to work again, the means test became an indispensable way of containing costs, rather as the 'genuinely seeking work' test had been in the 1920s. It combined the arbitrary administration which had been characterised the 'genuinely seeking work' regulations with an intrusive scrutiny of claimants' possessions. It obliged formerly provident savers to sell their homes.[36] It carried public functionaries into the houses of the unemployed, seeking signs of unacknowledged affluence. It forced families to conceal working teenagers whose earnings would be deducted from the father's benefit: fifty years later one Middlesbrough man still remembered 'scurrying into a back kitchen and gritting my teeth' at the sound of an officiously loud knock on the door.[37] Fewer than a third of claimants had their benefit reduced by means-testing, but the test was a worry to all: 'not that I'm doing anything wrong', an unemployed man in Leicester told the Pilgrim Trust investigators, 'but I feel they're always spying'.[38]

The means test was hated for its intrusiveness, its mistakes and its intrinsic scepticism but above all because it persecuted life's victims. The Unemployment Assistance system was a safety net for the long-term unemployed and, by extension, for older workers, many of whom would never find work. The test intensified the frustrations of their condition. Some of the unemployed were admittedly 'better off on the dole': 'I don't want work while the dole is paying me £2.1s.6d', one Leicester man told the Pilgrim

Trust researchers, 'I can manage just nice with that and get plenty of beer.'[39] Unskilled men with large families could claim dependants' allowances, taking their benefit level far above the low wages that they would earn in work – 'I could get a job tomorow if I could work for a single man's wage', a Liverpool man with nine children admitted[40] – but most of the unemployed resented their lot. The Pilgrim Trust described one Leicester man, who was 'obviously a thoroughgoing individualist' but had been converted by the experience of unemployment into 'one of the most violent adherents of the National Unemployed Workers' Movement'.[41] Extremism, however, like crime and benefit fraud, tended to be the young man's response to unemployment, and the long-term unemployed in the depressed areas tended to be the older members of the workforce. The skilled tended to react more bitterly than the unskilled. A resigned stoicism was the more frequent response of the unskilled – 'bread and cheese is a good meal for anyone when you get used to it'[42] – though the deepest sacrifices were made by their wives, who starved themselves to feed their families and their notional breadwinners. The men themselves were made irritable by the pervasive boredom of their condition – 'time is my worst enemy now'.[43] Time might be passed by devoted reading – from cheap magazines to Tolstoy or Balzac – or by political discussion. Beales and Lambert's 1934 survey found many of the unemployed learning economics in an attempt to understand the system which had failed them.[44] Voluntary unemployed clubs appeared in the depressed areas, sometimes sponsored by prosperous regions (Surrey 'adopted' Jarrow). In general the most blighted areas offered the greatest social protection, as the concentration of unemployed allowed support networks to develop. Perhaps the harshest experience of unemployment was suffered by the workless in prosperous areas where such collective support was lacking, most evidently in London, which flourished in the 1930s but never had fewer than 100,000 unemployed.

The 1930s public was struck by those features reflecting the growth in long-term unemployment after 1929 – the idea that fit men in their forties might be unemployable for the rest of their lives, the emaciation of entire communities for want of work. This accounts for the success of demonstrations like the 1936 Jarrow March, advertising the collapse of a single-industry town with

77 per cent of its workforce unemployed after the closure of Palmer's Shipyard four years earlier. It also accounts for the appearance of freelance surveys and investigations on a scale unknown in the 1920s – *The Times*' 1934 articles on the mining communities, Beales and Lambert's interviews with the unemployed, E.W. Bakke's investigation of unemployment in Greenwich, the radio presentations by individual unemployed men in 1934 under the title of *Time to Spare* and the Pilgrim Trust's survey of six employment blackspots. Most of this work was reasonably objective, but its message was one which the government did not wish the public to hear, and certainly not to hear so frequently. MacDonald even attempted to bully John Reith, the unbending Director General of the BBC, into dropping the *Time to Spare* talks.[45] Efforts by the government's chief medical officer (Sir Ernest Newman) to tamper with evidence concerning the health of the depressed areas epitomise the state's defensiveness on the question.

The government lost the propaganda battle over unemployment, as was probably inevitable as long as it set its face against ostentatious palliatives. The Treasury remained unconvinced by public works schemes, noting that £110 million of public works expenditure in 1929–31 had generated jobs for only 61,000 men;[46] it still believed that recovery could best be induced by the revival of Britain's overseas trade. It cultivated the sterling area and used the funds in its newly created Exchange Equalisation Account to keep sterling stable. It relied upon 'cheap money and plenty of it' to stimulate industry.[47] Although there was a greater readiness to depart from strict budgetary orthodoxy, no attempt was made to make a virtue of deficit financing. The *de facto* deficits of the 1930s were concealed by the same accounting fictions that had concealed the deficits of 1924–9. By the mid-1930s, when the academic case for contra-cyclical public works was becoming respectable, rearmament proved a godsend. The distinction between vicious borrowing to keep men in idleness and virtuous borrowing for national defence was accepted in the Treasury and the City, and rearmament probably prevented unemployment from reaching the 3 million level which balanced budgets would have produced in 1938.

Neither accounting fictions nor rearmament offered, though, much political credit. Sporadic job-creation initiatives such as the subsidy to the shipping line Cunard to complete the *Queen Mary* on Clydeside, or support for extensions of the London Underground, made little impact. The most elaborate response to unemployment was the attempt to stimulate the economies of the depressed regions through the 'special areas' policy, inaugurated in 1934. Two commissioners – one for England and Wales, one for Scotland – were appointed to promote industrial development in four defined depressed areas.[48] In 1935 legislation was passed to facilitate the development of trading estates in these areas. Chamberlain saw the special areas as 'experimental plots or research laboratories in which ideas can be quickly put into operation and tried out without reference to Departments',[49] and there may have been benefits from the cutting of red tape, but in other respects the caution of the scheme ensured very limited results. The Commissioners were forbidden to carry on any profit-making activities themselves or to assist profit-making undertakings financially. After the resignation of both Commissioners in 1936 their successors' powers were liberalised by allowing them to lease factories and to grant tax and rate rebates to industry, and the Special Areas Reconstruction Association was set up to provide loans to new industries. But the areas were, though, so small as to make strategic planning unfeasible, and the Reconstruction Association remained undercapitalised. In the first phase of the policy the inducements and exhortation available did little to offset the disadvantages which had led industry to shun the areas in the first place: they attracted only thirty-four of two thousand new factories established in England and Wales in 1934–7.[50] Rate and tax rebates after 1937 might have proved more enticing, but by 1938 the policy had been implicitly jettisoned, subsumed in the rearmament programme: 'depression and distress are to be bought off by expenditure on guns and battleships', as *The Economist* put it.[51] Neville Chamberlain's private acknowledgement that it was 'not a question of spending a great deal of money, but of showing that the matter had not been pigeonholed'[52] provides the scheme's best epitaph.

The government was more concerned to operate a financially sound system of unemployment relief than to risk speculative job-creation policies. The unemployment of the 1930s was containable. There was no great danger of social breakdown: the age structure of the unemployed population made them unlikely to take to crime or extremism in large numbers. Even the political danger was limited. No government which really feared electoral retribution for unemployment would have introduced the 1935 benefit scale four years into a parliament. Throughout the decade around five-sixths of the labour force were in work, most enjoying improving standards of living. In the gold standard years the Baldwin government had convinced itself that Britain would be a happier place if its international competitiveness could be restored by wage cuts. No such illusion afflicted the National Government, which was well aware of the political advantages of real wage increases for those in work and of a generous tax régime for the middle class. The general election called against a background of recovery in November 1935 cut back the artificial majority of 1931, but left the National forces with 431 of the 615 MPs, bringing the re-election of a sitting government for the only time in the inter-war period.

By the mid-1930s, therefore, the National Government had successfully remodelled social policy along Tory lines. The achievement was less visible and less controversial than the tariff, but no less comprehensive. At its heart was a shift in emphasis away from tax-funded measures, and towards contributory ones. The process had really begun in 1925 with the extension of the pensions scheme on a contributory basis, and had been accelerated under gold-standard pressure in the late 1920s. In 1926 the state contribution to the health insurance scheme was reduced. Housing subsidies were pruned from 1927. In 1932 the National Government sought to introduce the means-testing of secondary school scholarships, though it was forced by local authority pressure to beat a retreat. In 1931 and 1934 it ended the open-handed state support for the unemployment insurance system which had developed during the 1920s. In 1937 it introduced a further, voluntary, contributory pension. The net effect was not to abandon welfare, but to increase the extent to which the individual funded his own security. By 1939 the welfare system, though much larger than it had been in the Victorian period, was almost certainly less redistributive.

The majority of the electorate were happy with this development, or accepted it as inescapable, or expected nothing better from the Opposition. The conditions of the depression induced individuals to protect themselves through insurance. The same search for security that brought a substantial rise in building society savings in the 1930s led the public to insure against the uncertainties of life. By 1935 some 5.25 million people insured themselves against the cost of hospital treatment.[53] In 1936 agricultural labourers, one of the few groups still excluded from the unemployment insurance system, gained a separate contributory scheme of their own, which proved popular though it paid lower benefits than Unemployment Assistance. In 1911 the principle of compulsory insurance had apparently damaged the Liberal government, but by 1937 the think-tank Political and Economic Planning believed that 'the population is becoming insurance-minded'.[54]

When the shift to tariffs is also taken into account, a high proportion of the cost of Britain's comparatively extensive welfare system in the 1930s was borne by the working class. This was, in effect, the middle way which tariff reformers had always sought between *laisser faire* and confiscatory 'socialism'. It satisfied the desire of modern Conservatism to be identified with social reform while preserving the relatively generous tax treatment of their middle-class supporters that had been a feature of the Conservative governments in the 1920s and had been threatened in 1930–1.

The disadvantage was that some features of the welfare system were more suited to insurance funding than others. The reformed unemployment insurance system after 1934 was a success, admired from abroad. On the other hand, services such as council housing, which could only feasibly be developed by direct subsidy, suffered: municipal house-building dwindled during the 1930s and the emphasis shifted to the less expensive option of slum-clearance. The same applied to education: had the government succeeded in means-testing secondary education scholarships there can be little doubt that working-class access to grammar schools would have diminished. The health insurance system was showing clear cracks by the late 1930s. Its curious hybrid nature, as a compulsory public scheme operated by private profit-making agencies, resulted in a steadily widening gap between sick and healthy and between rich approved societies and poor ones. Profitable societies used their profits to attract healthy clients by offering such fringe benefits as optical and dental care, leaving the bad risks to the weaker companies, whose weakness was thus compounded. This process secured the best health care for those who needed it least. It also carried the risk that those who needed care most would lose their cover if their society went bankrupt, which was a genuine danger in the depression. By 1939 the health insurance system was clearly in need of reform.

For all that, the National Government had, by the late 1930s, reshaped domestic policy on its own terms to a degree that no previous Tory government had managed to do. It was the collapse of its foreign policy which destroyed it.

Appeasement

International relations in the 1930s were dominated by the efforts of three expansionist powers – Japan, Italy and Germany – to change the world order to their advantage. The three were, in varying degrees, totalitarian, militaristic and demagogic states, governed by régimes which used international belligerence to win domestic support. Conventional diplomacy was consequently of limited value in dealing with any of them; 'facing the dictators' required negotiation to be combined with at least the threat of force, though the correct balance remained hard to determine.

Britain was involved in virtually all the international crises of the 1930s. At no point before the outbreak of war in 1939 did any of the expansionary powers directly threaten Britain or any part of the British Empire, but the indirect dangers were evident. A resurgent Japan might threaten Britain's Far Eastern possessions, India and even Australia and New Zealand. Italy had long had an interest in North Africa and might threaten British Egypt. Germany posed no threat to any British possession, but German dominance of the continent of Europe would threaten the security of Britain herself. These were all dangers inherent in any breakdown of international stability: the makers of British foreign policy sought to protect that stability in a changing world. The question before them was one not easily answered: whether the demands of the expansionary powers were finite, implying that a new stability could be gained if they were satisfied, or whether yielding to threats would merely encourage further demands. In the absence of an immediate danger to British territory, British diplomats and politicians leaned towards concession rather than resistance, a tendency which became more marked after Neville Chamberlain succeeded Baldwin as Prime Minister in May 1937. What emerged was the policy stigmatised as 'appeasement'.

In September 1931 Japan invaded the Chinese province of Manchuria, which it annexed over the next two years. Though British interests in Manchuria were considerable, Britain could not contemplate a military response except in conjunction with the United States, and when it became clear that the US would not take military action, the British foreign secretary Simon sought to dissuade America from lesser provocations. Japan remained in Manchuria. In 1935 Italy invaded Ethiopia, where her troops had been humiliated forty years earlier. The British government, aware that a vocal section of British opinion sought collective action against aggression through the League of Nations, actually advocated League trade sanctions against Italy, believing that the French and other powers would block them. Sanctions became the ostensible reason for calling a general election ahead of time in November 1935. The election was won but the diplomatic gamble lost as the French assented to limited sanctions. Fearful, once again, that action sufficient to provoke but not to deter might prompt further aggression, the British Cabinet sent Simon's successor, Sir Samuel Hoare, to Paris, to concoct a settlement recognising Italy's conquests in Ethiopia and granting her effective control of most of the country. Public outcry at this emasculation of a sovereign state led the Cabinet to sacrifice Hoare and to contemplate oil sanctions, which might have had some effect. This possibility disappeared when France named as a condition of her participation in the oil sanction a British commitment to protect the Rhineland, German territory demilitarised under the terms of the 1919 Versailles treaty. Britain demurred, the sanction was not applied, Italy remained in Ethiopia and, in March 1936, Germany remilitarised the Rhineland. In principle this action obliged Britain and the other signatories of the 1925 Locarno agreement to take military action to restore the Versailles arrangements. In practice the British instinct was to ignore Locarno, in the belief that an agreement with the Nazi dictator Adolf Hitler offered a better prospect of long-term peace, and British diplomatic energies were devoted to restraining the French. German troops remained in the Rhineland, and her strengthened western frontier allowed Germany to contemplate expansion to the east.

This came in March 1938, when German troops annexed Austria. The likelihood that Hitler's next target would be Czechoslovakia, which France was bound by treaty to support, brought French pressure for British support against Germany in that event. Britain was reluctant to go to war for Czechoslovakia, where she had no vital interests; hence Neville Chamberlain's eagerness, in two private meetings with Hitler and at the notorious four-power Munich conference in September 1938, to negotiate a diplomatic fig-leaf covering the German seizure of the Sudetenland, a part of Czechoslovakia containing three million ethnic Germans. The Sudetenland was duly sacrificed at Munich, subject to the holding of plebiscites which never took place. The hope that Hitler's ambitions were limited to ethnic German areas was destroyed in March 1939 by the German occupation of Prague and the remainder of Czechoslovakia. Chamberlain convinced himself that 'the military occupation was symbolic, more than perhaps appeared on the surface',[55] but Prague marked the point at which most British observers ceased to make allowances for Hitler. It became more difficult either to condone German aggression or to negotiate with Hitler, but Britain remained reluctant to go to war when no direct threat existed to British interests. The British guarantee to Poland, issued shortly after the Prague *démarche*, indicated a diminishing faith in Hitler, but it was really designed to deter a German invasion of Poland and discourage the Poles from coming to terms with Germany. Britain could not unilaterally protect Poland, and Chamberlain had little faith in any collective defence arrangement, particularly as it would involve dealing with the Soviet Union.

Meanwhile aggression continued unchecked. In April 1939 Italy invaded Albania and threatened Greece. In June the Japanese occupation forces in China tightened their control over entry to the British concession at Tientsin, north of Peking, visiting various humiliations upon British residents there. Before the Tientsin affair could be resolved, the pressure was relieved by the largely unexpected pact between Nazi Germany and Soviet Russia in August 1939, which raised the danger for the Japanese that Russia could pursue her own interests in Manchuria without fear of German attack. But whatever relief the pact brought to the British in the Far East was offset by the European implications of this diplomatic monster. The Polish guarantee had been issued in the belief that ideological hostility prevented a Russo-German understanding and that a German attack upon Poland would therefore always be risky. By squaring Stalin, Hitler had gained a free hand in Poland. The British guarantee lost such deterrent value as it had ever possessed, but it could not be renounced without jeopardising what remained of Britain's diplomatic credibility. Poland was no more a vital British interest than Czechoslovakia had been and was no more defensible against German attack. When German troops did invade Poland on 1st September 1939, therefore, Chamberlain hoped to negotiate another sell-out rather than go to war.[56] By now, though, neither parliament nor the majority of the Cabinet would countenance this indignity. On 3rd September 1939 Britain went to war with Germany.

Appeasement was an unedifying policy. It could only be justified if it succeeded in preserving the peace, which it failed to do. It frustrated – and risked alienating – all the major powers on whose alliance Britain's wartime survival would depend. It tarnished permanently Neville Chamberlain's reputation. Why was it pursued?

The decisions behind it were consciously made, and the British government was not constrained by political pressure, as was subsequently claimed. It appears unlikely that the slow pace of rearmament was dictated by public opinion. The government possessed substantial power to influence opinion: though it had its problems with the BBC, it generally got its way with the cinema newsreels. Most of the national press, including *The Times*, endorsed appeasement. The National Government enjoyed unprecedented strength in parliament and is unlikely to have felt inhibited by the public's assumed views on the pace of rearmament. Actually going to war was another matter. At the time of Munich the public remained apprehensive about the prospect of war. Chamberlain's awareness of this mood undoubtedly reinforced his pursuit of a negotiated settlement, but his attitude scarcely needed reinforcement. Indeed it would be hard to cite any point at which public opinion forced the government into a more pacific policy than it had intended; the points at which public opinion might be thought to have deflected policy – the disowning of the Hoare–Laval pact over Ethiopia, or the commitment to the Polish guarantee – were occasions when appeasement was rejected.

Nor was British policy seriously constrained by the views of the Dominions. Britain could not assume unlimited Dominion willingness to sacrifice money and men to any cause: Dominion leaders remained concerned that reckless British involvement in continental disputes might involve them in battles irrelevant to them. They had been wary of the 1925 Locarno agreement, which they feared might drag them into a European war, and opposed any attempt to invoke the treaty during the Rhineland crisis. They welcomed Munich, which appeared to reduce the danger of war. Had the British government shown a greater readiness to use force to resolve European conflicts or to enforce treaty obligations, it is possible that Dominion reluctance might have inhibited them, but Britain needed little encouragement to avoid European commitments which it considered avoidable. In any event, there was a difference between seeking to influence the course of diplomacy in order to prevent war and refusing to participate in a war once it had broken out. In the last resort British policy-makers inferred from the precedents of 1899 and 1914 that Dominion support would generally be forthcoming if Britain went to war. The Irish Free State would not fight for Britain, and there might be problems with South Africa, where Boer War grievances survived amongst the Afrikaaner population and where there were some Nazi sympathisers, but the loyalty of Australia, Canada and New Zealand was guaranteed.

In fact the conviction that a diplomatic solution must be available for any international crisis was so firmly rooted in the minds of British politicians and diplomats in the 1930s that it is unnecessary to seek external influences behind appeasement. The external advice that did influence policy-makers, that of the service chiefs, tended to reinforce their inclinations. The Chiefs of Staff understood the impossibility of protecting all of Britain's extended empire at the same time and urged negotiation to prevent the simultaneous eruption of military crises. With predators proliferating in the 1930s, ready to bring their tanks to the conference table, the logistical problems of imperial defence became a real constraint upon Britain's negotiating freedom, but the vulnerability of Britain's Empire had always been evident, and it had not previously produced a diplomacy aiming at the avoidance of war at all costs. For most of the inter-war period, however, the service chiefs were hostile to military involvement on the Continent, invoking 'the lessons of history' against a continental commitment as late as 1936.[57] They were supported by the Treasury, which argued that an unaffordable defence programme risked precipitating economic collapse and handing Hitler an effortless victory.[58] As late as December 1937 the Cabinet framed the army estimates on the assumption that no British field force would be committed to a European campaign early in a war, creating the impression – borne out in 1940 – that Britain would fight to the last Frenchman.

Minimising the value of any continental land force reflected developing speculation on the role of air power. Initially British politicians had been transfixed by the potency of an apparently irresistible threat: Baldwin's 1932 warning that 'the bomber will always get through' may have been designed to inject urgency into the Geneva disarmament conference, where ministers still hoped to negotiate military aircraft out of existence, but it reflected real unease about this new branch of warfare and concern for the vulnerability of London.[59] When Germany abandoned the Geneva conference in 1933 and embarked upon aerial rearmament, Britain was drawn from disarmament towards a deterrent strategy based on the creation of a bomber force. This decision emanated from the 1934 report of the Defence Requirements Committee calling for rearmament against both Germany and Japan. In Cabinet the report was emasculated on account of its cost and Germany was singled out as the principal foe, because of the damage she could do by air to Britain's cities. An aerial Home Defence Force was to be created to deter Germany and bolster morale at home. In the event this deterrent failed to deter. Britain's bombers were lightweight and needed to operate from continental bases. Increased British output strained the capacity of British industry, but encouraged German aircraft production. In December 1937 the Inskip Report on Defence Expenditure acknowledged the futility of this air race and recommended an emphasis on fighters rather than bombers, to enable Britain to withstand a German knock-out blow. In 1940 this strategy would ensure Britain's survival, but in 1938 the fighters which would repel the Luftwaffe were still unbuilt. Munich occurred during this window of danger. Fighter Command then had 100 Hurricanes and three Spitfires, one of which had broken down; the 1,100 planes of Bomber Command could barely reach Germany. Though he did not hurry to acknowledge the fact, Chamberlain was hampered at Munich by his insistence, as Chancellor of the Exchequer four years earlier, upon a 'cheap' bomber deterrent, cosmetic rather than real.

It is, though, unlikely that Chamberlain's strategy at Munich would have differed greatly even had Britain's fighter strength been as great in 1938 as it would be in 1940. Britain had never stood to gain from war: she was the most satiated power of the inter-war world. As the rearmament of the unsatisfied powers advertised the horrors of modern warfare, British politicians' awareness that war offered no gains and many losses was reinforced by their fear of its physical effects. Chamberlain described the consequences of aerial warfare in the way that we might today envisage the aftermath of a nuclear strike, with 'people burrowing underground, trying to escape from poison gas, knowing that at any hour of the day or night death or mutilation was ready to come upon them'.[60] He would try to evade his own military commitment to Poland in September 1939 and, as a member of Churchill's War Cabinet, advocated a negotiated peace with Germany when the British Expeditionary Force was driven back to the French coast in 1940. British policy-makers' single-minded aversion to conflict throughout the 1930s, hardening as it did under Chamberlain, owes more to this attitude than to any deference to public opinion, Dominion sentiment or even the service chiefs. At the same time it was always appreciated that the ambitions of the hungry powers threatened a state of international anarchy in which war might break out anywhere, jeopardising the security of the empire and even of Britain herself. Isolationism was never an option for Britain; she had to attempt to preserve international stability.

In principle a durable settlement implied accommodating the legitimate demands of the expansionist powers and resisting their unreasonable claims. Much British opinion favoured some revision of the post-war order, believing that the Versailles settlement had been a punitive peace tailored by the French to humiliate Germany, and that German attempts to unravel it were understandable. The taxi driver who told Anthony Eden, British Foreign Secretary during the Rhineland crisis, that 'Jerry can do what he likes in his own back garden'[61] voiced a view which British policy-makers probably shared. There was some feeling – much of it in the Foreign Office – that the abandonment of the Anglo-Japanese alliance to preserve the wartime co-operation with the USA in 1921 had been a mistake, sacrificing a reliable pre-war ally at the request of an economic rival. Such views did not make Japanese attacks upon British interests and British citizens any more welcome, but to many observers they appeared to explain them and reinforced the obvious strategic objections to any military response at such a distance.

This habit of thought – that the demands of the expansionist powers were understandable, however unpleasant their régimes, that the French were paranoid and the Americans self-interested – conditioned the British choice between confrontation and appeasement. It encouraged the two assumptions central to most British thinking during the decade – that the dictators' grievances were comprehensible and therefore were capable of being resolved, and that alliances designed to curb the expansionist powers carried dangers of their own.

It was not difficult to identify potential partners in any combination against the two strongest expansionist powers. The United States had commercial interests in the Far East which were threatened by Japan, and resented German attempts to build a closed economic area on the Continent. France and the Soviet Union both feared German domination of Europe for simple reasons of national security. There is little difficulty in understanding British wariness of dealing with the Soviet Union. Nothing could make Stalin an enticing partner, and his military weight became questionable when he executed many Soviet army and air force leaders after 1936. The case for a Russian alliance became most compelling in the spring of 1939, when it became necessary to give the Polish guarantee teeth in the east, but it was always complicated by the suspicions of the Poles themselves towards the Soviet Union. Polish reservations encouraged an unenthusiastic Chamberlain to stall, falsely confident that a Russo-German agreement was impossible.

Dealings with the French were clouded by the British conviction that France was fixated by memories of 1870 and 1914, that she could not see Germany as anything other than a predator and that she sought a substantial military commitment from Britain to guarantee her security. Such a commitment might in itself provoke Hitler and encourage French diplomatic recklessness. The French had been allowed more than their due revenge at Versailles and the mistake should not be repeated. They had been unreasonably reluctant to ease the reparations imposed on Germany in 1919 and their obsessive distrust of Germany had made it impossible to secure multilateral arms limitation at the 1932 disarmament conference. 'To do a good thing for its own sake is not in accordance with French official nature', MacDonald had noted during the stressful summer of 1931; his successors held similar views.[62]

Anglo-American relations present, to modern eyes, the greatest missed opportunities. Since 1941 the 'special relationship' has been seen as central and indispensable by British policy-makers, whatever the view held of it in Washington, but before that date the relationship between the two English-speaking democracies was more strained. To understand this it is necessary to understand the extreme unease felt by tariff reformers towards the US as an opponent of British imperial preference and as an economic competitor. America was felt to be constructing its own economic empire whilst assaulting the European territorial empires with anti-colonial rhetoric. While preaching economic liberalism the US had destroyed the gold standard experiment by hoarding gold; since 1932 it had sniped at Britain's tariff system, which Cordell Hull, President Roosevelt's Secretary of State, did indeed believe would have to be dismantled for the greater good of the world economy. For all that, the principles that made the US impatient with British protectionism made her even more hostile towards the Nazi closed economy, and American military potential was, unlike that of France, unquestionable. Perversely, British leaders continued to doubt its actual value. They noted the growth of isolationist sentiment, particularly after Congress passed the first Neutrality Act in 1935, and, safe in their own command of parliament, stressed the constitutional restraints upon the American President. Chamberlain believed that whatever honeyed words Roosevelt might offer about the defence of democratic values, Congress would prevent him from backing them by force: 'they would probably come in on our side eventually but they would probably come in too late'.[63] The superior tone in which Baldwin and particularly Chamberlain tended to address the US changed, like so much else, during 1938–9, as Britain's vulnerability became evident. By the summer of 1939 the Treasury doubted Britain's capacity to survive a long war without American economic support.[64] Chamberlain came to accept that a degree of flexibility towards the Americans might soften Congressional criticism of Britain and thus make it easier for Roosevelt to be helpful. The 1938 Anglo-American trade agreement produced reciprocal reductions in protection levels. It was a significant concession to American criticism of Britain's tariff system, but it did not imply that the British experiment in economic nationalism would be wound up to satisfy the Americans. Chamberlain would never shed his suspicion of the US: 'Heaven knows I don't want the Americans to fight for us,' he wrote to his sisters three months into the war, 'we should have to pay too dearly for that if they had a right to be in on the peace terms.'[65]

Reflex views of Britain's potential allies – that the Soviet Union was incorrigible, that France wished to pull Britain into war with Germany and that the USA wished to dismember the British empire – lay behind Britain's preference for direct dealing with the expansionist powers. A delicate strategy emerged during the decade which, while not irrational, depended upon certain critical assumptions. Effective resistance to Japanese aggression in the Far East was acknowledged to be impossible, but it was held that the greatest danger from Japan lay in opportunistic aggression if Britain were to be distracted by European involvements, so that the key to containing Japan lay in containing Germany. Undue faith was placed in the power of the Italian leader Mussolini to restrain Hitler, with the result that Britain avoided tightening the sanctions imposed after the invasion of Ethiopia and ignored the attack on Albania. Britain's dealings with Hitler were determined by the view that his revisionist demands were ultimately rational and satiable, but that he was personally impulsive, liable to be provoked by any insensitive response to his actions and above all by any threatening combination of powers. Chamberlain liked to believe that he possessed a particular ability to do business with Hitler and Mussolini: 'these Dictators are men of moods', he wrote in 1937, 'catch them in the right mood and they will give you anything you ask for'.[66] Such optimism was fed by the success of earlier diplomatic contact with Germany – the Anglo-German trade agreement of 1934 and, particularly, the Anglo-German naval convention of 1935, which limited German naval construction to 35 per cent of the British level. All that the 1935 agreement proved, though, was that it was easy to reach a bilateral agreement where both parties had something to gain from the trade – Hitler the chance to breach the naval limits imposed at Versailles without initiating a naval arms race, Britain the opportunity to concentrate her naval strength in the defence of her Far Eastern empire against Japan. On other occasions bilateral negotiation failed. Hitler spurned the offer of the return of Germany's pre-1918 colonies in 1936 because he rightly saw little economic benefit in Tanganyika or the Cameroons. Where Britain had nothing to offer, her military weakness and her obvious reluctance to go to war meant that negotiation could do little more than legitimise aggression. This was evident both during the Rhineland crisis and at Munich where, on each occasion, British diplomatic efforts were devoted not to restraining Hitler but to persuading France to tolerate German aggression.

Much therefore depended on Britain's faith that Hitler's demands were finite. This view came more easily to the British, who believed that unprovoked German attack on Britain was unlikely, than to the French – twice within living memory invaded by Germany – or to the Russians, ideological targets of Nazism. Their anxieties ensured that Britain's attempts to appease Germany raised new dangers even when they appeared successful. The Anglo-German naval agreement, by indicating that Britain was prepared to deal with Germany directly and to condone a beach of the military limitations imposed at Versailles, led France to secure protective alliances with Russia and with Czechoslovakia. The Russian deal allowed Hitler to claim that the Locarno system (of collective defence of the Versailles terms) was dead, and consequently to remilitarise the Rhineland. The Czech deal would have brought European war over the Sudetenland but for the Munich agreement. Munich deferred war, but convinced Britain's potential allies that she would make any concession to avoid conflict. Roosevelt concluded that British foreign policy was tainted by 'too much Eton and Oxford' and wondered whether anything could be done to save a great power apparently bent on suicide.[67] Stalin inferred that Britain's eagerness to deal with Fascism limited her value as an ally against Hitler, destroying the slender prospect of Anglo-Soviet co-operation and pointing him towards the Nazi–Soviet pact.

After Hitler's absorption of Austria, Orme Sargent of the Foreign Office had accurately defined the choice before Britain as one between tolerating a resurgent Germany and entering into military alliances to resist her. British reactions to Hitler's moves during 1938 and 1939 revealed her inclination to tolerate German expansion to the east, where no British interests were at stake, and Chamberlain sought to abandon the Polish guarantee in September 1939. The assumptions behind his strategy – that Hitler had no necessary quarrel with Britain and that his eastward expansion did Britain far less damage than would a war to prevent it – remain unrefuted, but by September 1939 the policy was unsustainable. The other powers would not endorse a second Munich to solve the Polish problem, and such a solution was unacceptable to the British Cabinet, to parliament and to a public now resigned to war. Thus Britain went to war for the sake of a guarantee which she could not honour, unable to defend her Far Eastern possessions, incapable of winning a lightning war with Germany but economically vulnerable in a long one, and uncertain of the military resilience of France or the extent of US support. The failure of appeasement exacerbated the dangers of war.

* * *

Neville Chamberlain's father had promoted tariff reform in the 1900s in order to equip Britain to survive in a world of competing empires. During the First World War Joseph Chamberlain's followers had argued that the failure to make the Empire self-sufficient had forced Britain into European commitments of questionable value and ultimately into a damaging war. After 1918 they had sought to build up imperial self-sufficiency, and the diplomatic philosophy of the tariff reformers came close to isolationism. Writing to *The Times* in 1922 Bonar Law had argued that Britain could not afford to act as the world's policeman, and that without active support from her wartime allies she would have to 'restrict [her] attention to the more immediate interests of the empire'.[68]

The problem was that even the most watertight imperial economic system could do nothing to offset the strategic vulnerability of Britain and her empire to attack. Neville Chamberlain understood that a strategically watertight empire was a fantasy, and was prepared to defy the imperial obsessives in his party to conclude the Anglo-American trade agreement. He understood, likewise, that Britain would have to involve herself actively in continental diplomacy if she wished European peace to be preserved. But the tariff reformer's suspicion of entangling alliances remained in him, and was strengthened by economic rivalry with Britain's potential allies during the slump. As Robert Boyce points out, the distrust engendered between Britain, France and the USA by the world economic collapse limited their readiness to co-operate in defence of democracy during the 1930s.[69] Neville Chamberlain certainly displayed a suspicion of the USA that was characteristic of the imperial visionaries; he saw the US less as Britain's strongest potential ally than as the most hostile critic of the imperial economic order that he had done so much to create. His diplomacy was coloured by his disbelief that the Americans could or would offer meaningful support. Averse to commitments to the US, France or Soviet Russia, Chamberlain relied upon unilateral diplomacy to keep the peace, despite Britain's inability to impose stability on Europe or the world. Consequently Chamberlain's dealings with Nazi Germany hinged on his belief that Hitler's demands could eventually be satisfied and that European equilibrium would be attained when they were. That Hitler's demands were finite remains questionable; if they were, they had not been satisfied before appeasement was rejected by the British Cabinet, by parliament and by public opinion.

The world depression had ended attempts to restore free trade internationalism and made possible the National Government's experiment in economic autarky, but it had also brought the dictators to power and embittered international relations. Imperial economic autarky had arguably succeeded, but imperial diplomatic autarky proved unattainable. So extensive and so vulnerable were Britain's overseas interests that she could not hope to defend them all adequately on her own, while simultaneously protecting the home front. She had to choose between involvement in deterrent alliances which would impair her diplomatic independence and a unilateral diplomacy which preserved the facade of independence but which entailed bargaining from a position of weakness. Chamberlain's conviction that alliances might provoke war while diplomacy might avert it loaded the scales heavily in favour of appeasement. At heart he feared that the domestic and imperial order that he had done so much to build would not survive British involvement in another European war. The failure of his diplomacy to prevent that war would, with grim irony, prove him right.

Conclusion: A Conservative State?

This book opened with Gladstone's 1884 analysis of the essentially liberal character of the Victorian state. In recording Gladstone's words in 1903, his biographer John Morley noted that the years since 1884 had seen the reversal of the Liberal ascendancy, 'notwithstanding the enlargement of direct popular power'.[1] By 1939 it would be still clearer that the Tories had done well out of democracy. Conservative governments or Conservative-dominated coalitions had held power for 37 of the 54 years since 1885.

* * *

In the 1880s the Liberals had lost the confidence of the metropolitan establishment that they had enjoyed since the 1840s. They never regained it, except perhaps in the years after 1903 when they could present themselves as defenders of orthodoxy against the tariff menace. Labour, of course, could never aspire to be the establishment party. After 1886 the left-of-centre parties would not be able to regain the kind of consensual approval among opinion-formers and the political establishment that mid-Victorian Liberalism had enjoyed. Left-of-centre government would in future require the 'masses' simply to outvote the 'classes'.

From the point at which 'democracy' first became feasible, in the 1860s, many politicians had instinctively assumed that the working class, once enfranchised, would vote in one bloc, in pursuit of class interest. Men possessing a sophisticated ability to 'read' the old electorate stuck to this crude view of the new voters even after working-class enfranchisement had become a reality. It was a view which gave no political weight to the distinction between the urban and the rural working class, between skilled and unskilled, employed and unemployed, unionised and

236

ununionised or, after 1918, male and female working-class voters. It ignored the significance of status distinctions, regional differences and denominational rivalries within the working class. Class mattered politically, of course, and it mattered more as more of the working class gained the vote, but its impact was never uniform. The working man who believed that his superiors knew best, or who loathed the Irish, or who thought the Liberals unpatriotic or who believed the trade unions would damage the nation, might vote Tory. The employed worker who saw his standard of living rise during the 1930s might credit the Tories: the prosperous 'new industry' areas of outer London and the West Midlands voted Conservative throughout the inter-war years. Working-class Toryism was a significant electoral feature throughout the years covered by this book; historians who witnessed the phenomenon in the 1980s are less likely than their predecessors to dismiss it as a mark of deviancy.

This is not to deny that the forces pulling working-class voters to the Liberals or later Labour were stronger than before, but they were never strong enough to produce the class-based radical hegemony that Salisbury and most of his successors feared. Ironically, the clearest instance of a political development founded upon class, the emergence of a trade union-based Labour Party, benefited the Tories in the short term by dividing the left. This book has not been about the irresistible 'rise' of Labour. The early Labour Party was too narrowly industrial, union-dominated and male to command the allegiance of the entire working class, while being too strong in its strongholds to be obliterated. Between the wars Labour steadily became less exclusive, and colonised many inner-city working-class seats which had previously been Liberal strongholds, but it did not capture the entire working class. Labour rose sufficiently to gain organisational independence, to end its pre-war client relationship with the Liberal Party and to frighten the Liberal right wing, but not sufficiently to govern on its own. A partial 'rise' which destroyed the pre-war Progressive Alliance without producing majority Labour governments merely divided the left and helped the Tories.

Throughout this period left-of-centre government required a weakening of middle-class support for the Tories and the containment of Lib–Lab divisions. Both of these conditions prevailed after 1903, when tariff reform alienated some natural Conservatives and the Macdonald–Gladstone Pact kept Lib–Lab divisions in check, and they did indeed produce the only majority left-of-centre government of the entire period in 1906. But the Progressive Alliance faced an uncertain future even by 1914, and the repercussions of the war made Progressivism unsustainable – by liberating Labour and turning the Liberals into a middle-class pressure group, by burdening the budget with the cost of the unemployed and by lowering taxpayer tolerance of welfare expenditure. Between the wars the always difficult task of establishing a non-Tory government became virtually impossible.

If there was a 'natural party of government' between 1885 and 1939, it was the Conservatives. They enjoyed the normal support of the London press, of metropolitan society and of the Anglican Church. Their electoral support was less regionally concentrated than the Liberals' and less sectional than Labour's, an advantage most evident in the testing three-party conditions of the 1920s. They benefited from several political contingencies: the constituency redistributions of 1885 and 1918, the Liberals' splits in 1886 and 1916, the removal of the southern Irish seats in 1922, the limited female franchise between 1918 and 1928, the Labour and Liberal splits of 1931. Surveying the whole period, it is striking how little the Tory ascendancy owed to the party's actual policies in office.

To some extent the ease with which the Tories could gain power after 1885 diminished the need to 'buy' votes with constructive policies. Salisbury, indeed, never maintained that Toryism was compatible with democracy, though he won three general elections, two of them in landslides. His was essentially an oppositional philosophy: translated into government by the fracturing of the Liberal Party and his own tactical skill, he continued to display a view of the uses of power which seldom rose above the tactical. It is clear, though, that any analysis of modern Conservatism which merely examines the party's ability to gain and retain power is inadequate.

Today's historians of the Conservative Party warn sternly against treating the party as a collection of 'common-sense' pragmatists, stolidly resistant to ideology.[2] They are right to do so: the myth of a traditional Conservatism which spurned the doctrinaire was one propagated by the Tory left in the 1980s to justify their (ideological) attack upon Thatcherism, and should be treated as a debating device. The recent work on the religious beliefs of Salisbury and Baldwin has enabled us to understand better the intellectual basis of their actions.[3] Neville Chamberlain, principally responsible for guiding the inter-war party, was a technician, perhaps, but hardly a mere pragmatist. The imperial visionaries – Milner, Amery and their kind – were as doctrinaire as any politicians of the period.

Of course the Tory Party in this period contained a majority of members whose Conservatism derived from social, denominational or regional influences and whose thought on political issues was shallow or unsophisticated, but that is true of any major party. Even the most bovine Tory backbencher sensed, as Britain became an imperial superpower from the 1880s, that previously dominant liberal doctrines – free trading, internationalist and 'cosmopolitan' – were hard to reconcile with Britain's extended world role. The fear that in a world of competing empires Britain would suffer by sticking to Victorian liberal values was shared by Tories from Salisbury to Neville Chamberlain. Initially the difficulty lay in constructing a synthesis as comprehensive as the liberal orthodoxy that had developed in the mid-Victorian years, linking domestic and international policy. The massive appeal of Joseph Chamberlain's tariff reform proposals to the Unionist rank-and-file reflected Chamberlain's success in doing that.

Tories did not pursue tariff reform because they took perverse pleasure in taxing the people's food or even because they preferred indirect to direct taxation. They did so because they believed that Chamberlain's economic nationalism would strengthen the Empire where free trade and economic liberalism might weaken it. They believed that domestic industry and employment would revive under a tariff régime. They believed that tariff revenues could support legitimate social reform without resort to confiscatory taxation. Imperial preference offered, in other words, a modern and distinctively Conservative programme. Its weakness lay, of course, in the centrality of the proposal for food taxes, the unpopularity of which was demonstrated in 1906 and again, if more equivocally, in 1923. For most of our period, therefore, the Conservatives enjoyed repeated electoral success without gaining the power to implement the policy closest to Tory hearts. The shapelessness of Tory policy during so much of the period derives from this paradox. A party better able to gain power than to use it began to make a virtue of the winning of elections and the thwarting of opponents. This is how the myth of Tory 'pragmatism' took root, to be amplified by historians preoccupied with Salisbury's clever manipulation of the honours system or Baldwin's winning radio manner. But political virtuosity could not conceal the fact that for twenty-five years after the emphatic rejection of tariff reform in 1906 the Tories were uncertain in their policy direction. The party understood that democracy posed challenges which it would have to face, and there was no desire to return to Salisbury's negativism, but it was impossible for Conservatives to outbid their rivals in the social reforms that democracy was assumed to require without risking the alienation of their natural supporters. The evaporation of the various constructive options attempted during this period – the Tory welfarism advocated by the Unionist Social Reform Committee before 1914, the social imperialism of the Lloyd George Coalition Tories, Neville Chamberlain's social programme of 1924 – proved the point.

This changed in 1929–31, when world slump, domestic unemployment, a price fall (which reduced the inflationary dangers of food duties) and splits in both the Labour and Liberal parties made Chamberlainite economic nationalism politically practicable. The pre-war Unionist 'package' – economic nationalism, imperial preference, an emphasis upon indirect rather than direct taxation and a cautious approach to welfare – was implemented without political retribution. A coherent Conservatism had finally emerged. Essentially a Chamberlainite policy, it was largely constructed by Joseph Chamberlain's youngest son.

The irony was, though, that the world economic crisis which had made Chamberlainite policies acceptable to the British electorate had also fuelled the growth of expansionist totalitarianism, underlining the vulnerability of the British Empire and increasing the danger of a second world war. Imperial economic nationalism had been intended to enhance the security of the empire, but it became attainable only in circumstances which simultaneously made the empire more vulnerable than ever before. The fact – not always acknowledged by tariff reformers – that economic autarky would not allow Britain to opt out of international diplomacy, became inescapable. Neville Chamberlain believed that the emerging Conservative state would not survive Britain's involvement in a second international conflict and single-mindedly sought to avoid such a conflict as long as no immediate British interest was at risk.

The resultant appeasement diplomacy was ignoble and unsuccessful, but on his own terms Chamberlain was eventually proved right. The war really did destroy the state that he had done so much, as Chancellor and as Prime Minister, to build. The postwar world would see the first majority Labour government, the universalist welfare state, economic and diplomatic dependence on the USA and, eventually, the dismantling of the British Empire. The Conservative Party survived the conflict, of course, but the Conservative state so laboriously constructed in the half-century after the Home Rule crisis was blown away by the Second World War.

Notes

(The place of publication is London unless otherwise stated.)

Notes to Introduction: A Liberal State

1. J. Morley: *The Life of William Ewart Gladstone*, vol. III (1903), 128–9.
2. T. Farrer: *Free Trade Versus Fair Trade* (1882), 1.
3. S. and B. Webb: *English Local Government. Vol. 8. English Poor Law History. Part II. The Last Hundred Years. I* (1929), 312.
4. H. C. G. Matthew: *Gladstone, 1809–74* (Oxford, 1986), 230.
5. Resolution at an open-air demonstration of Liberals, Salford, 1880, quoted by E. F. Biagini: *Liberty, Retrenchment and Reform. Popular Liberalism in the Age of Gladstone* (Cambridge, 1992), 127.
6. Quoted by D. Brooks: 'Gladstone and Midlothian: The Background to the First Campaign', *Scottish Historical Review*, 64 (1985), 51.
7. A. B. Cooke and J. Vincent: *The Governing Passion. Cabinet Government and Party Politics in Britain, 1885–6* (Brighton, 1974), 3.

Notes to Chapter 1: Liberal Disintegration

1. That is, dedicated to the preservation of the Union between mainland Britain and Ireland in the face of the Home Rule threat.
2. L. M. Springhall: *Labouring Life in Norfolk Villages, 1834–1914* (1936), 97.
3. A. Adonis: *Making Aristocracy Work. The Peerage and the Political System in Britain, 1884–1914* (Oxford, 1993), 243.
4. A. Armstrong: *Farmworkers in England and Wales. A Social and Economic History, 1770–1980* (Ames, 1988), 111.
5. A. Offer: *Property and Politics, 1870–1914* (Cambridge, 1981), 185.
6. M. Freeden: *The New Liberalism* (Oxford, 1978), 27.
7. J. P. D. Dunbabin: *Rural Discontent in Nineteenth-Century Britain* (New York, 1974), 186.
8. S. Warwick-Haller: 'Parnell and William O'Brien', in D. G. Boyce and A. O'Day (eds): *Parnell in Perspective* (1991), 54.
9. J. L. Garvin: *The Life of Joseph Chamberlain, Vol. I, 1836–1885* (1932), 258.
10. W. Lubenow: *Parliamentary Politics and the Home Rule Crisis. The British House of Commons in 1886* (Oxford, 1988), 209.
11. T. A. Jenkins: *Gladstone, Whiggery and the Liberal Party, 1874–1886* (Oxford, 1988), 7, 8.
12. T. A. Jenkins, op.cit., 174.
13. H. C. G. Matthew (ed.): *The Gladstone Diaries*, Introduction to vol. X (Oxford, 1990), xxxiv.

14. H. C. G. Matthew (ed.): *The Gladstone Diaries*, Introduction to vol. XII (Oxford, 1994), xlvi.
15. W. Lubenow, op.cit., 8.
16. T. A. Jenkins, op.cit., 16.
17. D. W. Bebbington: *The Nonconformist Conscience. Chapel and Politics, 1870–1914* (1982), 9.
18. G. C. Brodrick: *The Duty of Moderate Liberals at the Coming Election* (Oxford, 1885), 14.
19. G. W. Smalley, quoted by P. Marshall: 'The Imperial Factor in the Liberal Decline, 1880–1885', in J. E. Flint and G. Williams (eds): *Perspectives of Empire. Essays Presented to Gerald S. Graham* (1973), 134.
20. H. C. G. Matthew (ed.): *The Gladstone Diaries*, Introduction to vol. X (Oxford, 1990), lv.
21. P. Marsh: *Joseph Chamberlain. Entrepreneur in Politics* (New Haven, 1994), 179.
22. M. O'Callaghan: *British High Politics and a Nationalist Ireland. Community, Land and Law under Forster and Balfour* (Cork, 1994), 119.
23. H. C. G. Matthew (ed.): *The Gladstone Diaries*, Introduction to vol. X (Oxford, 1990), clxi, fn.1.
24. W. Lubenow, op.cit., 9.
25. P. Marsh: *The Discipline of Popular Government. Lord Salisbury's Domestic Statecraft, 1881–1902* (Hassocks, 1978), 85.
26. T. A. Jenkins, op.cit., 190.
27. W. Lubenow, op.cit., 83.
28. P. Burroughs: 'Liberal, Paternalist or Cassandra? Earl Grey as a Critic of Colonial Self-Government', *Journal of Imperial and Commonwealth History*, 18 (1990).
29. T. Dunne: 'La Trahison des Clercs. British Intellectuals and the First Home Rule Crisis', *Irish Historical Studies*, 23 (1982), 172.
30. P. Marsh: *Chamberlain*, 233.
31. T. Dunne, op.cit., 146.

Notes to Chapter 2: Unionist Ascendancy

1. Salisbury: 'Disintegration', *Quarterly Review*, 312 (October, 1883).
2. Quoted by E. D. Steele: 'Salisbury and the Church', in Lord Blake and H. Cecil (eds): *Salisbury: The Man and His Policies* (1987), 211.
3. A. Gailey: *Ireland and the Death of Kindness. The Experience of Constructive Unionism, 1890–1905* (Cork, 1987), 30.
4. P. Marsh: *The Discipline of Popular Government. Lord Salisbury's Domestic Statecraft, 1881–1902* (Hassocks, 1978), 165.
5. P. Marsh: *Discipline*, 130.
6. A. Adonis: *Making Aristocracy Work. The Peerage and the Political System in Britain, 1884–1914* (Oxford, 1993), 20.
7. M. Barker: *Gladstone and Radicalism* (Hassocks, 1975), 90.

8. G. I. T. Machin: *Politics and the Churches in Great Britain, 1869–1921* (Oxford, 1987), 199.
9. J. Loughlin: *Gladstone, Home Rule and the Ulster Question, 1882–1893* (Dublin, 1986), 245.
10. M. Barker, op.cit., 73.
11. H. C. G. Matthew (ed.): *The Gladstone Diaries*, Introduction to vol. XII (Oxford, 1994), lxx.
12. S. J. Brown: '"Echoes of Midlothian": Scottish Liberalism and the South African War, 1899–1902', *Scottish Historical Review*, 71 (1992), 161.
13. *Birmingham Daily Post*, quoted by D. Brooks (ed.): *The Destruction of Lord Rosebery. From the Diary of Sir Edward Hamilton* (London, 1986), Introduction, 24.
14. D. Brooks, op.cit., 86.
15. P. F. Clarke: *Lancashire and the New Liberalism* (Cambridge, 1971), 4.
16. P. Marsh: *Discipline*, 189.
17. P. Marsh: *Joseph Chamberlain. Entrepreneur in Politics* (New Haven, 1994), 356–7, 359.
18. P. Marsh: *Discipline*, 269.
19. J. M. Maclean, quoted by P. Marsh: *Discipline*, 192.
20. The Liberal/Radical majority adopted the label Progressive in deference to the convention that national party politics was inappropriate to local bodies, though it was also the case that the Progressive group included some Liberal Unionists and, from 1892, some labour councillors.
21. E. P. Hennock: 'Technological Education in England 1850–1926: The Uses of a German Model', *History of Education*, 19 (1990); N. D. Daglish: 'The Politics of Educational Change: the Case of the English Higher Grade Schools', *Journal of Educational Administration and History*, 19 (1987).
22. See W. H. Fraser and I. Maver: 'Tackling the Problems', in W. H. Fraser and I. Maver (eds): *Glasgow*, vol. 2, 1830 to 1912 (Manchester, 1996), 420–5.
23. J. F. Oakeshott: *The Humanizing of the Poor Law* (1894), 10.
24. T. MacKay: *A History of the English Poor Law, Vol. 3, From 1834 to the Present Time* (1899), 579.
25. J. Harris: *Unemployment and Politics. A Study in English Social Policy, 1886–1914* (Oxford, 1972), 145 and fn.1.
26. P. Hollis: *Ladies Elect. Women in English Local Government, 1865–1914* (Oxford, 1987), 30.
27. B. H. Brown: *The Tariff Reform Movement in Britain, 1880–1895* (Columbia, 1945), 3.
28. G. Stedman Jones: *Outcast London. A Study in the Relationship between Classes in Victorian Society* (Oxford, 1971), 315.
29. D. Howell: *British Workers and the Independent Labour Party, 1888–1906* (Manchester, 1983), 41.
30. D. Howell, op.cit., 146.

31. D. Rubenstein: *Before the Suffragettes. Women's Emancipation in the 1890s* (Brighton, 1986), 112.

Notes to Chapter 3: Tariff Reform

1. A. Offer: *Property and Politics, 1870–1914* (Cambridge, 1981), ch. 14.
2. C. Headlam: *The Milner Papers*, vol. I (1931), 232–5.
3. A. N. Porter: *The Origins of the South African War. Joseph Chamberlain and the Diplomacy of Imperialism, 1895–1899* (Manchester, 1980), 247.
4. J. Wilson: *C. B. A Life of Sir Henry Campbell-Bannerman* (1973), 317.
5. A. Sykes: *Tariff Reform in British Politics, 1903–1913* (Oxford, 1979), 27.
6. G. I. T. Machin: *Politics and the Churches in Great Britain, 1869–1921* (Oxford, 1987) 317.
7. N. Daglish: *Education Policy-Making in England and Wales. The Crucible Years, 1895–1911* (1996), 36.
8. G. A. Lowndes: *The Silent Social Revolution. An Account of the Expansion of Public Education in England and Wales, 1895–1965* (second edition, Oxford, 1969), 61.
9. D. W. R. Bahlman (ed.): *The Diary of Sir Edward Walter Hamilton, 1885–1906* (Hull, 1993), 433.
10. P. T. Marsh: *Joseph Chamberlain: Entrepreneur in Politics* (New Haven, 1994), 293–4.
11. R. M. Kesner: *Economic Control and Colonial Development* (Oxford, 1981), 72.
12. A. Sykes, op.cit., 48.
13. H. A. Clegg, A. Fox and A. F. Thompson: *A History of British Trade Unions since 1889*, vol. I, 1889–1910 (Oxford, 1964), 276.
14. D. Marquand: *Ramsay MacDonald* (1977), 80.
15. D. Howell: *British Workers and the Independent Labour Party, 1888–1906* (Manchester, 1983), 366.
16. D. Howell, op.cit., 66.
17. D. Tanner: *Political Change and the Labour Party, 1906–1922* (Cambridge, 1990), 145, 189, 196.
18. H. V. Emy: *Liberals, Radicals and Social Politics, 1892–1914* (Cambridge, 1973), 91.
19. D. Tanner, op.cit., 23.
20. *Quarterly Review*, April 1906, quoted by A. K. Russell: *Liberal Landslide. The General Election of 1906* (Newton Abbot, 1973), 199–200.
21. A. K. Russell, op.cit., 113.
22. *Preston Guardian*, quoted by M. Savage: *The Dynamics of Working-Class Politics. The Labour Movement in Preston, 1880–1940* (Cambridge, 1987), 148.

23.   H. Pelling: *A Social Geography of British Elections, 1885–1910* (1967), 210, 232.
24.   A. Sykes, op.cit., 51.

Notes to Chapter 4: Liberalism and Welfare

1.   By Trevelyan, quoted A.K.Russell, op.cit., 70.
2.   M. Freeden: *The New Liberalism* (Oxford, 1978), 57, 15.
3.   D. W. R. Bahlman, op.cit., 376.
4.   At the Queen's Hall, July 1908, quoted by B.B.Gilbert: *David Lloyd George. A Political Life, Vol. I: The Architect of Change, 1863–1912* (1987), 349.
5.   A. J. A. Morris: *Radicalism Against War, 1906–1914* (1972), 131.
6.   B. K. Murray: *The People's Budget, 1909–10: Lloyd George and Liberal Politics* (Oxford, 1980), 146.
7.   B. B. Gilbert: *Lloyd George*, I, 355.
8.   B. Mallet: *British Budgets, 1887–1913* (1913), 303.
9.   At Limehouse, quoted B.B. Gilbert: *Lloyd George*, I, 386.
10.   N. Blewett: *The Peers, the Parties and the People: The General Elections of 1910* (1972), 74, 76.
11.   B. K. Murray, op.cit., 153.
12.   P. F. Clarke: *Lancashire and the New Liberalism* (Cambridge, 1971), 99.
13.   N. Blewett, op.cit., 408.
14.   J. D. Fair: *British Inter-Party Conferences. A Study of the Procedure of Conciliation in British Politics, 1867–1921* (Oxford, 1980), 84 and ch.IV.
15.   P. Jalland: *The Liberals and Ireland. The Ulster Question in British Politics to 1914* (1980), 58, 43.
16.   A. Jackson: *The Ulster Party. Irish Unionists in the House of Commons, 1884–1911* (Oxford, 1989), 77.
17.   P. Jalland, op.cit., 103.
18.   M. Laffan: *The Partition of Ireland, 1911–1925* (Dublin, 1987), 23.
19.   P. Jalland, op.cit., 203.
20.   M. Laffan, op.cit., 46.
21.   P. F. Clarke, op.cit., 99; Y. Cassis: *City Bankers, 1890–1914* (Cambridge, 1994), 307.
22.   Quoted by P. Hollis: *Ladies Elect. Women in English Local Government, 1865–1914* (Oxford, 1987), 298.
23.   S. and B. Webb: *English Local Government, Vol. 8: English Poor Law History, Part II. The Last Hundred Years, I* (1929), 456.
24.   J. Harris: *William Beveridge* (Oxford, 1977), 137.
25.   Royal Commission on the Poor Laws, *Parliamentary Papers* 1909 XXXVII, Minority Report, 1196, 1238.
26.   Royal Commission on the Poor Laws, *Parliamentary Papers* 1909 XXXVII, Majority Report, 661, 655.
27.   Quoted by P. Hollis, op.cit., 298.

28. A. Fenton: *The Turra Coo. A Legal Episode in the Popular Culture of North-East Scotland* (Aberdeen, 1989).
29. B. B. Gilbert: *The Evolution of National Insurance in Great Britain* (1966), 446, fn.112.
30. B. B. Gilbert: *Lloyd George*, I, 445.
31. B. B. Gilbert: *David Lloyd George. A Political Life, Vol. II: Organiser of Victory, 1912–16* (1992), 60.
32. A. Offer, op.cit., 392.
33. C. J. Wrigley: 'The Government and Industrial Relations', in C. J. Wrigley (ed.): *A History of British Industrial Relations, 1875–1914* (Brighton, 1982), 153.
34. J. E. Cronin: 'Strikes, 1870–1914', in C. J. Wrigley (ed.), op.cit., 91.
35. P. Thane: 'The Labour Party and State Welfare', in K.D. Brown (ed.): *The First Labour Party, 1906–1914* (1985), 202ff.
36. M. Savage, op.cit., 156.
37. D. Tanner, op.cit., 321.
38. J. Liddington and J. Norris: *One Hand Tied Behind Us. The Rise of the Women's Suffrage Movement* (1978), 207.
39. M. Pugh: *Electoral Reform in War and Peace, 1906–1918* (1978), 35.
40. S. S. Holton: *Feminism and Democracy: Women's Suffrage and Reform Politics, 1900–1918* (Cambridge, 1987), 24.
41. A. Rosen: *Rise Up, Women! The Militant Campaign of the Women's Social and Political Union, 1903–1914* (1974), 109.
42. S. S. Holton, op.cit., 47.
43. S. S. Holton, op.cit., 95.

Notes to Chapter 5: Transformation by War

1. H. C. G. Matthew: *The Liberal Imperialists: The Ideas and Politics of a Post-Gladstonian Elite* (Oxford, 1973), 204–5.
2. K. M. Wilson: *The Policy of the Entente. Essays on the Determinants of British Foreign Policy, 1904–1914* (Cambridge, 1985), 37.
3. A. J. A. Morris: *Radicalism Against War, 1906–1914* (1972), 151.
4. B. B. Gilbert: *David Lloyd George. A Political Life*, Vol. II, *Organiser of Victory, 1912–16* (1992), 124.
5. G. J. DeGroot: *Blighty. British Society in the Era of the Great War* (1996), 70.
6. M. Pugh: *Electoral Reform in War and Peace* (1978), 52–3.
7. J. Turner: *British Politics and the Great War* (New Haven, 1992), 62.
8. Quoted by D. French: *British Economic and Strategic Planning, 1905–1915* (1982), 162.
9. D. French: *British Strategy and War Aims, 1914–16* (1986), 119.
10. D. French: *British Strategy*, 171.
11. D. French: *British Strategy*, 121.
12. B. B. Gilbert: *Lloyd George*, II, 366–7.

13. Lord Crewe: 'Memorandum on the Break-Up of the Coalition Government, December, 1916', reprinted in J.Pope-Hennessy: *Lord Crewe, 1858–1945. The Likeness of a Liberal* (1955), 188.
14. James Bryce, quoted by M.Bentley: *The Liberal Mind, 1914–1929* (Cambridge, 1977), 75.
15. K. Grieves: *The Politics of Manpower, 1914–1918* (Manchester, 1988), 83.
16. J.Turner: *British Politics and the Great War*, 266.
17. T.Bonzon and B.Davis: 'Feeding the Cities', in J.Winter and J.-L.Robert (eds): *Capital Cities at War: London, Paris, Berlin, 1914–1919* (Cambridge, 1997), 330; B.Waites: *A Class Society at War* (Leamington Spa, 1987), 227.
18. A.Triebel: 'Coal and the Metropolis', in J.Winter and J.-L. Robert (eds), op.cit., 359.
19. K. Middlemas: *Politics in Industrial Society. The Experience of the British System since 1911* (1979), 102.
20. J.Turner: *British Politics and the Great War*, 293; E. O'Halpin: *The Decline of the Union. British Government in Ireland, 1892–1920* (Dublin, 1987), 158.
21. D.Tanner: *Political Change and the Labour Party, 1906–1918* (Cambridge, 1992), 396.
22. P.B. Johnson: *Land Fit for Heroes* (Chicago, 1968), 38.
23. P.B.Johnson, op.cit., 222–3.
24. P.B.Johnson, op.cit, 154.
25. P.Guinn: *British Strategy and Politics, 1914 to 1918* (Oxford, 1965), 193.
26. K.O.Morgan: *Consensus and Disunity: The Lloyd George Coalition Government, 1918–1922* (Oxford, 1980), 31.
27. To Worthington-Evans: L.S.Amery: *My Political Life*, Vol. 2, War and Peace, 1914–1929 (1953), 173–4.
28. M. Howard: *The Continental Commitment* (1972), 71.

Notes to Chapter 6: Losing the Peace: Coalition Politics, 1918–22

1. K.O. Morgan: *Consensus and Disunity* (Oxford, 1979), 21.
2. J.Turner: *British Politics and the Great War* (New Haven, 1992), 434, 412, 423.
3. K.O. Morgan, op.cit, 49.
4. W.R. Garside: *British Unemployment, 1919–1939. A Study in Public Policy* (Cambridge, 1990), 35.
5. R.H. Brand, quoted by S.Howson: *Domestic Monetary Management in Britain, 1919–1938* (Cambridge, 1975), 10.
6. Quoted by D.E. Moggridge: *British Monetary Policy, 1924–1931: The Norman Conquest of $4.86* (Cambridge, 1972), 160.

7. H. A. Clegg: *A History of British Trade Unions since 1889*, Vol. II, 1911–1933 (Oxford, 1985), 324.
8. Cabinet Relief of Distress Committee, 1921, quoted by B.Waites: *A Class Society at War* (Leamington Spa, 1987), 169.
9. A. Deacon: *In Search of the Scrounger. The Administration of Unemployment Insurance in Britain, 1920–1931* (1976), 16.
10. R. Lowe: *Adjusting to Democracy. The Role of the Ministry of Labour in British Politics, 1916–1939* (Oxford, 1986), 136.
11. Lloyd George in Cabinet, November 1920, quoted K.O.Morgan, op.cit., 137.
12. P. B.Johnson: *Land Fit for Heroes. The Planning of British Reconstruction, 1916–1919* (Chicago, 1968), 369.
13. I. Drummond: *British Economic Policy and the Empire, 1919–1939* (1972), 41.
14. K. O. Morgan, op.cit., 286.
15. Rothermere, quoted by M. Cowling: *The Impact of Labour* (Cambridge, 1971), 51.
16. A. McDonald: 'The Geddes Committee and the Formulation of Public Expenditure Policy, 1921–1922', *Historical Journal*, 1989, 650.
17. Geddes, quoted by A. McDonald, op.cit., 651.
18. K. Jeffery: *The British Army and the Crisis of Empire* (Manchester, 1984), 50.
19. W. L. Cleveland: *A History of the Modern Middle East* (Boulder, 1994), 193.
20. K. O. Morgan, op.cit.,120.
21. Aylmer Haldane, quoted by K. Jeffery, op.cit., 153.
22. Their grand total of seven was completed by four Catholic Ulster seats and T. P. O'Connor's Liverpool stronghold.
23. J. Turner, op.cit., 282.
24. Carson had resigned from the War Cabinet in January 1918 and did not hold office in the post-war Coalition.
25. D. G. Boyce: *Englishmen and Irish Troubles* (Cambridge, Ma., 1972), 180.
26. This account is taken from G. R. Searle: *Corruption in British Politics, 1895–1930* (Oxford, 1987), ch.15 and p.379.

Notes to Chapter 7: Three-Party Politics, 1922–31

1. R. Blake: *The Unknown Prime Minister. The Life and Times of Andrew Bonar Law, 1858–1923* (1955), 499–500. For the UGC's limited achievement see E. M. Burns: *British Unemployment Programs, 1920–1938* (Washington, 1941), 12.
2. Baldwin at Plymouth, October 1923, quoted by K. Middlemas and J. Barnes: *Baldwin. A Biography* (1969), 229
3. Quoted by R. C. Self: *Tories and Tariffs. The Conservative Party and the Politics of Tariff Reform, 1922–32* (1986), 181.

4. Philip Snowden, quoted by R. C. Self, op.cit., 235.
5. I. G. C. Hutchison: *A Political History of Scotland, 1832–1924* (Edinburgh, 1986), 326.
6. M. Bentley: *The Liberal Mind, 1914–1929* (Cambridge, 1977), 90
7. K. Theakston: *The Labour Party and Whitehall* (1992), 16.
8. Snowden quoted by D. Marquand: *Ramsay MacDonald* (1977), 326.
9. J. Ramsden: *The Age of Balfour and Baldwin, 1902–40* (1978), 211.
10. Quoted by K. Middlemas and J. Barnes, op.cit., 487.
11. Chamberlain to Baldwin, May 1923, quoted by D. Dilks: *Neville Chamberlain. Vol. I: Pioneering and Reform, 1869–1929* (Cambridge, 1984), 369.
12. D. Dilks, op.cit., 405.
13. Sir Douglas Veale, quoted by D. Dilks, op.cit., 413.
14. Sir Charles Addis, quoted by R. D. Boyce: *British Capitalism at the Crossroads. A Study in Politics, Economics and International Relations* (Cambridge, 1987), 58.
15. Norman, quoted by R. D. Boyce, op.cit.,50.
16. Quoted by R. D. Boyce, op.cit.,76.
17. Sir John Bradbury, quoted by P. Clarke: *The Keynesian Revolution in the Making, 1924–1936* (Oxford, 1988), 37.
18. Quoted by D. E. Moggridge: *British Monetary Policy, 1924–1931: The Norman Conquest of $4.86* (Cambridge, 1972), 75–6.
19. To Cabinet, 1927, quoted by D. Dilks, op.cit., 517.
20. K. Middlemas (ed.): T. Jones: *Whitehall Diary*, II (1969), 19.
21. Quoted by G. A. Phillips: *The General Strike. The Politics of Industrial Conflict* (1976), 55.
22. Quoted by G. A. Phillips, op.cit.,128.
23. For this paragraph see G. A. Phillips, op.cit., 206ff, 132, 152ff, 146.
24. K. Middlemas and J. Barnes: *Baldwin. A Biography* (1969), 412; D. Dilks: *Neville Chamberlain, Vol. 1: Pioneering and Reform, 1869–1929* (Cambridge, 1984), 470.
25. Victor Feather, the future TUC General Secretary, quoted by M. Morris: *The General Strike* (1976), 91.
26. MacDonald to George Kerr, 14th May 1926, quoted by D. Marquand, op.cit., 442.
27. D. E. Moggridge, op.cit., 237.
28. R. Lowe: *Adjusting to Democracy. The Role of the Ministry of Labour in British Politics, 1916–1939* (Oxford, 1986), 146; A. Deacon: *In Search of the Scrounger. The Administration of Unemployment Insurance in Great Britain* (1976), 41.
29. N. Whiteside: 'Counting the Cost: Sickess and Disability among Working People in an Era of Industrial Recession, 1920–1939', *Economic History Review* second series 40, 1987, 243.
30. Claimant to relieving officer, late 1920s, quoted by J. Bourke: *Working-Class Cultures in Britain, 1890–1960. Gender, Class and Ethnicity* (1994), 15.
31. E. W. Bakke: *The Unemployed Man. A Social Study* (1933), 88–9.

32. A. Powell and E. C. Blight: 'Poor Law Relief', in H. Llewellyn Smith (ed.): *The New Survey of London Life and Labour* (1930), *Vol. I, Forty Years of Change*, 377–9.
33. D. Dilks, op.cit., 444.
34. R. Boyce, op.cit.,172.
35. A. Thorpe: *The British General Election of 1931* (Oxford, 1991), 50; P. Williamson: *National Crisis and National Government. British Politics, the Economy and the Empire* (Cambridge, 1992), 109ff.
36. B. Mallet and C. O. George: *British Budgets*. Third Series, 1921–2 to 1932–3 (1933), 281, 444–5.
37. Quoted by P.Williamson, op.cit, 78.
38. P. Williamson, op.cit., 65.
39. Quoted by R. Boyce, op.cit., 304–5.
40. August 1930, quoted by D. Marquand, op.cit., 544.
41. Quoted by R. Lowe, op.cit., 147.
42. Quoted by B. Mallet and C. O. George, op.cit., 288.
43. Quoted by A. F. Cooper: *British Agricultural Policy, 1912–1936. A Study in Conservative Politics* (Manchester, 1989), 114.
44. P. Williamson, op.cit., 126; S. Ball: *Baldwin and the Conservative Party. The Crisis of 1929–31* (New Haven, 1988), 91.
45. R. C. Self, op.cit., 510.
46. B. Mallet and C. O. George: *British Budgets*. Third Series, 1921–2 to 1932–3 (1933), 288.
47. R. Boyce, op.cit., 253–4.
48. R. Boyce, op.cit., 255.
49. P. Williamson, op.cit., 97; D. Marquand, op.cit., 557.
50. Quoted by R. C. Self, op.cit., 609.
51. R. Boyce, op.cit., 254.
52. K. Middlemas and J. Barnes, op.cit., 576.
53. K. Middlemas and J. Barnes, op.cit., 599–600.
54. Committee on National Expenditure, 1931 (Cmnd 3920), *Report*, 20.
55. 'The electoral programme of each successive Party... has usually been prepared with more regard to attracting electoral support than to a careful balancing of national interests ... a solution has to be found if democracy is not to suffer shipwreck on the hard rock of finance.' Committee on National Expenditure, 1931 (Cmnd 3920), *Report*, 223.
56. Quoted by D. Marquand, op.cit., 610.
57. To Willingdon, quoted by P. Williamson, op.cit., 229.
58. Quoted by K. Middlemas and J. Barnes, op.cit., 629.
59. Quoted by D. Marquand, op.cit., 609, 653.
60. Quoted by A. Thorpe, op.cit., 102.
61. Quoted by P. Williamson, op.cit., 312.
62. P. Williamson, op.cit., 401; D. Marquand, op.cit., 645.
63. Quoted by K. Middlemas and J. Barnes, op.cit., 653.
64. P. F. Clarke: *Lancashire and the New Liberalism* (Cambridge, 1971), 266, 273.

65. Edith Summerskill, elected Labour MP for West Fulham in 1938, quoted by M. Pugh: *Women and the Women's Movement in Britain, 1914–1959* (1992), 190.
66. M. Pugh, op.cit., 108–9.
67. M. Pugh, op.cit., 238.

Notes to Chapter 8: The Thirties

1. D. Marquand: *Ramsay MacDonald* (1977), 746.
2. Quotation from MacDonald: D. Marquand, op.cit., 677.
3. D. Howell: *Briitsh Social Democracy. A Study in Development and Decay* (1976), 25.
4. P. Williamson: *National Crisis and National Government* (Cambridge, 1992), 460.
5. Personal conversation with Lord Callaghan, 1981.
6. Quoted by P. Williamson, op.cit., 384
7. September 1931, quoted by P. Williamson, op.cit., 462.
8. Quoted by D. Blaazer: *The Popular Front and the Progressive Tradition* (Cambridge, 1992), 168.
9. B. Pimlott: *Labour and the Left in the 1930s* (Cambridge, 1977), 95.
10. D. E. McHenry: *The Labour Party in Transition, 1931–1938* (1938), 246.
11. P. Wright: *Spycatcher. The Candid Autobiography of a Senior Intelligence Officer* (1987), 13.
12. Quoted by B. Pimlott, op.cit., 67.
13. Geoffrey Lloyd, quoted by G. D. Anderson: *Fascists, Communists and the National Government. Civil Liberties in Great Britain, 1931–1937* (Columbia and London, 1983), 103.
14. Sir John Simon, quoted by G. D. Anderson, op.cit., 207.
15. S. Howson and D. Winch: *The Economic Advisory Council, 1930–1939. A Study in Economic Advice During Depression and Recovery* (Cambridge, 1977), 97.
16. Quoted by P. Williamson, op.cit., 507.
17. Snowden, quoted by R. C. Self: *Tories and Tariffs. The Conservative Party and the Politics of Tariff Reform, 1922–32* (1986), 733. The Samuelite Liberals continued to vote with the National Government in the House of Commons until November 1933.
18. R. Holland: *Britain and the Commonwealth Alliance, 1918–1939* (1981), 144.
19. Quoted by R. C. Self, op.cit., 718.
20. I. M. Drummond: *British Economic Policy and the Empire, 1919–1939* (1972), 23.
21. P. J. Cain and A. G. Hopkins: *British Imperialism. Crisis and Deconstruction, 1914–1990* (1993), 84–5.
22. B. Porter: *The Lion's Share. A Short History of British Imperialism, 1850–1983* (2nd edn, 1984), 261.

23. K. Middlemas and J. Barnes: *Baldwin. A Biography* (1969), 668–9.
24. I. M. Drummond: *The Floating Pound and the Sterling Area, 1931–1939* (Cambridge, 1981), 16, 22.
25. I. M. Drummond: *Floating Pound*, 16.
26. Quoted by J. Ramsden: *The Age of Balfour and Baldwin, 1902–1940* (1978), 322.
27. To Lord Lloyd, quoted by P. Williamson, op.cit., 480.
28. E. M. Burns: *British Unemployment Programs, 1920–1938* (Washington, 1941), table p.343.
29. Pilgrim Trust: *Men Without Work* (Cambridge, 1938), 6, 9.
30. N. F. R.Crafts: 'Long-term Unemployment in Britain in the 1930s', *Economic History Review*, second series 40, 1987, 421.
31. Pilgrim Trust, op.cit., 18, 21, 75.
32. The average age of the long-term unemployed in the Pilgrim Trust sample was 44, against an average age of 32 for the employed workforce. 8.1 per cent of unskilled manual workers were long-term unemployed against 2.7 per cent of skilled and semi-skilled workers: Pilgrim Trust, op.cit., 20, 26.
33. K. Nicholas: *The Social Effects of Unemployment on Teesside, 1919–1939* (Manchester, 1986), 58–9, 213.
34. E. M. Burns, op.cit., 130; W. R. Garside: *British Unemployment, 1919–1939. A Study in Public Policy* (Cambridge, 1990), 69; E. Briggs and A. Deacon: 'The Creation of the Unemployment Assistance Board', *Policy and Politics*, 1973–4, 53–8.
35. R. C. Davison: *British Unemployment Policy. The Modern Phase since 1930* (1938), 41.
36. Few of the 1930s unemployed were home-owners, of course, but for an example of a 'staunch Presbyterian' forced to sell his home, who 'vowed never to save anything again', see K. Nicholas, op.cit., 196.
37. K. Nicholas, op.cit., 195.
38. Pilgrim Trust, op.cit., 186; E. M. Burns, op.cit., 243.
39. Pilgrim Trust, op.cit., 170.
40. Pilgrim Trust, op.cit., 167.
41. Pilgrim Trust, op.cit., 56.
42. Pilgrim Trust, op.cit., 71.
43. Pilgrim Trust, op.cit., 150.
44. H. L. Beales and R. S. Lambert: *Memoirs of the Unemployed* (1934), 134–5, 154, 209, 234.
45. P. Scannell and D. Cardiff: *A Social History of Broadcasting* (1991), *Vol. I, 1922–1939, Serving the Nation*, 66. Reith threatened to broadcast twenty minutes of silence and announce that this was being done at the request of the government.
46. R. Middleton: *Towards the Managed Economy* (1985), 165.
47. Phillips, quoted by S. Howson: *Domestic Monetary Management in Britain, 1919–1938* (Cambridge, 1975), 86.

48. The South Welsh coalfield, Tyneside and County Durham, West Cumberland and the Scottish industrial belt outside Glasgow: E. M. Burns, op.cit., 288fn.
49. Quoted by R. Lowe: *Adjusting to Democracy. The Role of the Ministry of Labour in British Politics, 1916–1939* (Oxford, 1986), 225.
50. For precise figures see E. M. Burns, op.cit., 287fn.
51. Quoted by W. R. Garside, op.cit., 264.
52. Quoted by W. R. Garside, op.cit., 255.
53. A. Deacon and J. Bradshaw: *Reserved for the Poor. The Means Test in British Social Policy* (1983), 9.
54. PEP: *Report on the British Social Services* (1937), 160.
55. R. A. C. Parker: *Chamberlain and Appeasement. British Policy and the Coming of the Second World War* (1993), 200.
56. R. A. C. Parker, op.cit., 338ff.
57. M. Howard: *The Continental Commitment* (1972), 103; D.C.Watt: 'The European Civil War', in W.J. Mommsen and L. Ketternacker (eds): *The Fascist Challenge and the Policy of Appeasement* (1983), 15.
58. G. C. Peden: *British Rearmament and the Treasury, 1932–1939* (Edinburgh, 1979), 65.
59. M. Smith: *British Air Strategy Between the Wars* (Oxford, 1984), 114–15.
60. Quoted by M. Smith, op.cit., 215.
61. Quoted by K. Middlemas and J. Barnes: *Baldwin. A Biography* (1969), 916.
62. D. Marquand, op.cit., 605; R.A.C. Parker, op.cit., 14–19.
63. Quoted by D. Reynolds: *The Creation of the Anglo-American Alliance, 1937–1941* (1981), 22.
64. D. Reynolds, op.cit., 73.
65. Quoted by D. Reynolds, op.cit., 78.
66. Quoted by R. A. C. Parker, op.cit., 110.
67. Quoted by D. Reynolds, op.cit., 43.
68. Quoted by G. Schmidt: *The Politics and Economics of Appeasement* (English translation, Leamington Spa, 1986), 380.
69. R. D. Boyce: *British Capitalism at the Crossroads. A Study in Politics, Economics and International Relations* (Cambridge, 1987), 373.

Notes to Conclusion: A Conservative State?

1. J. Morley: *The Life of William Ewart Gladstone*, vol. III (1903), 129.
2. E.g. J. D. Fair and J. A. Hutcheson: 'British Conservatism in the Twentieth Century: An Emerging Ideological Tradition', *Albion* 19, 1987; D. Jarvis: 'British Conservatism and Class Politics in the 1920s', *English Historical Review* 111, 1996.
3. E. D. Steele: 'Salisbury and the Church', in Lord Blake and H. Cecil (eds): *Salisbury: The Man and His Policies* (1987); P. Williamson: 'The

Doctrinal Politics of Stanley Baldwin', in M.Bentley (ed.): *Public and Private Doctrine. Essays in British History Presented to Maurice Cowling* (Cambridge, 1993).

Bibliography

(The place of publication is London unless otherwise stated.)

Introduction

Note: The works by Parry (1986) and Biagini (1992) are indispensable in understanding the Victorian Liberal Party at its zenith, as are Colin Matthew's introductions to the volumes of the Gladstone Diaries, collected as *Gladstone 1809–1874* (Oxford, 1986), and *Gladstone 1875–1898* (Oxford, 1995).

Biagini, E., *Liberty, Retrenchment and Reform: Popular Liberalism in the Age of Gladstone, 1860–1880* (Cambridge, 1992).
Brent, R., *Liberal Anglican Politics: Whiggery, Religion and Reform, 1830–1841* (Oxford, 1987).
Brooks, D., 'Gladstone and Midlothian: The Background to the First Campaign', *Scottish Historical Review*, 64 (1985).
Brown, B. H., *The Tariff Reform Movement in Britain, 1880–1895* (New York, 1943).
Cooke, A. B. and Vincent, J., *The Governing Passion. Cabinet Government and Party Politics in Britain, 1885–6* (Brighton, 1974).
Farrer, Sir T. H., *Free Trade Versus Fair Trade* (1882).
Howell, D., *British Workers and the Independent Labour Party, 1888–1906* (Manchester, 1983).
Mandler, P., *Aristocratic Government in the Age of Reform: Whigs and Liberals, 1830–1852* (Oxford, 1990).
Matthew, H. C. G., *Gladstone, 1809–1874* (Oxford, 1986).
——(ed.), *The Gladstone Diaries*, Introduction to vol. VII (Oxford, 1982).
Morley, J., *The Life of William Ewart Gladstone*, vol. III (1903).
Parry, J., 'Religion and the Collapse of Gladstone's First Government, 1870–74', *Historical Journal*, 25 (1982).
Parry, J., *Democracy and Religion. Gladstone and the Liberal Party, 1867–1875* (Cambridge, 1986).
Robinson, R. and Gallagher, J. with Denny, A., *Africa and the Victorians. The Official Mind of Imperialism* (1961).
Shannon, R. T., *Gladstone and the Bulgarian Agitation* (1963).
Smith, P., *Disraelian Conservatism and Social Reform* (1967).
Webb, S. and B., *English Local Government. Vol. 8: English Poor Law History. Part II. The Last Hundred Years. I* (1929).

Chapter 1: Liberal Disintegration

Note: Colin Matthew's Introduction to volume X of the *Gladstone Diaries*, reprinted in *Gladstone, 1875–1898,* assesses the subtle mental processes of the architect of Home Rule. Lubenow (1988) and Loughlin (1986) provide intelligent modern analyses of the politics of the Home Rule crisis. The closing sections of Parry (1986) relate the crisis to earlier Liberal disputes, while Dunne (1982), Burroughs (1990) and Marshall (1973) examine different aspects of Whig–Liberal disaffection.

Adonis, A., *Making Aristocracy Work. The Peerage and the Political System in Britain, 1884–1914* (Oxford, 1993).

Armstrong, A., *Farmworkers in England and Wales. A Social and Economic History, 1770–1980* (Ames, 1988).

Barker, M., *Gladstone and Radicalism* (Hassocks, 1975).

Bebbington, D.W., *The Nonconformist Conscience. Chapel and Politics, 1870–1914* (1982).

Bew, P., 'Parnell and Davitt', in Boyce, D.G. and O'Day, A. (eds), *Parnell in Perspective* (1991).

Boyce, D. G. and O'Day, A. (eds), *Parnell in Perspective* (1991).

Burroughs, P., 'Liberal, Paternalist or Cassandra? Earl Grey as a Critic of Colonial Self-Government', *Journal of Imperial and Commonwealth History,* 18 (1990).

Davis, J., *Reforming London. The London Government Problem, 1855–1900* (Oxford, 1988).

——, 'Slums and the Vote, 1867–1900', *Historical Research,* 64 (1991).

—— and Tanner, D., 'The Borough Franchise after 1867', *Historical Research,* 69 (1996).

Dunbabin, J. P. D., *Rural Discontent in Nineteenth-Century Britain* (New York, 1974).

Dunne, T., '*La Trahison des Clercs*. British Intellectuals and the First Home Rule Crisis', *Irish Historical Studies,* 23 (1982).

Freeden, M., *The New Liberalism* (Oxford, 1978).

Garvin, J. L., *The Life of Joseph Chamberlain, Vol: I, 1836–1885* (1932).

Harris, J., *Unemployment and Politics. A Study in English Social Policy, 1886–1914* (Oxford, 1972).

Harvie, C., *The Lights of Liberalism. University Liberals and the Challenge of Democracy, 1860–1886* (1976).

Hennock, E. P., 'Poverty and Social Theory in England. The Experience of the 1880s', *Social History,* I (1976).

Hilton, B., 'Gladstone's Theological Politics', in M. Bentley and J. Stevenson (eds), *High and Low Politics in Modern Britain* (Oxford, 1983).

Hoppen, K. T., *Elections, Politics and Society in Ireland, 1832–1885* (Oxford, 1984).

Hunter, J., *The Making of the Crofting Community* (Edinburgh, 1976).

Hutchison, I.G.C., *A Political History of Scotland, 1832–1924* (Edinburgh, 1986).

Jenkins, T. A., *Gladstone, Whiggery and the Liberal Party, 1874–1886* (Oxford, 1988).

Kellas, J. G., 'The Liberal Party in Scotland, 1876–1895', *Scottish Historical Review* (1965).

Kynaston, D., *The City of London, Vol. I: A World of its Own, 1815–1890* (1994).

Lawrence, E. P., *Henry George in the British Isles* (East Lansing, 1957).

Lee, A. J., *The Origins of the Popular Press, 1855–1914* (1980).

Lloyd, T., *The General Election of 1880* (Oxford, 1968).

Loughlin, J., *Gladstone, Home Rule and the Ulster Question, 1882–93* (Dublin, 1986).

Lubenow, W., *Parliamentary Politics and the Home Rule Crisis. The British House of Commons in 1886* (Oxford, 1988).

McCaffrey, J. F., 'The Origins of Liberal Unionism in the West of Scotland', *Scottish Historical Review*, 50 (1971).

Machin, G. I. T., *Politics and the Churches in Great Britain, 1869 to 1921* (Oxford, 1987).

Marsh, P., *The Discipline of Popular Government. Lord Salisbury's Domestic Statecraft, 1881–1902* (Hassocks, 1978).

——, *Joseph Chamberlain. Entrepreneur in Politics* (New Haven, 1994).

Marshall, P., 'The Imperial Factor in the Liberal Decline, 1880–1885', in Flint, J. E. and Williams, G. (eds), *Perspectives of Empire. Essays Presented to Gerald S. Graham* (1973).

Matthew, H. C. G. (ed.), *The Gladstone Diaries*, Introductions to vols X (Oxford, 1990), and XII (Oxford, 1994).

——, *Gladstone, 1875–1898* (Oxford, 1995).

O'Callaghan, M., *British High Politics and a Nationalist Ireland. Community, Land and Law under Forster and Balfour* (Cork, 1994).

O'Day, R. and Englander, D., *Mr Charles Booth's Inquiry. Life and Labour of the People in London Reconsidered* (1993).

O'Day, R. and Englander, D. (eds), *Retrieved Riches; Social Investigation in England 1840–1914* (Aldershot, 1995).

Offer, A., *Property and Politics, 1870–1914* (Cambridge, 1981).

O'Leary, C., *The Elimination of Corrupt Practices in British Elections, 1868–1911* (Oxford, 1962).

Olney, R. J., *Lincolnshire Politics, 1832–1885* (Oxford, 1973).

Orwin, C. S. and Whetham, E., *History of British Agriculture, 1846–1914* (1964).

Parry, J., *Democracy and Religion* (Cambridge, 1986).

Pelling, H., *Social Geography of British Elections, 1885–1910* (1967).

Ramm, A. (ed.), *The Political Correspondence of Mr Gladstone and Lord Granville, 1876–1886*, vol. I (Oxford, 1962).

Robinson, R. and Gallagher, J. with Denny, A., *Africa and the Victorians. The Official Mind of Imperialism* (1961).

Schreuder, D., *Gladstone and Kruger: Liberal Government and Colonial Home Rule, 1880–1885* (1969).

Shannon, R. T., *Gladstone and the Bulgarian Agitation* (1963).

——, *The Age of Salisbury, 1881–1902* (1996).

Southall, H., 'The Origins of the Depressed Areas: Unemployment, Growth and Regional Economic Structure in Britain before 1914', *Economic History Review*, Second Series, 41 (1988).

Springhall, L. M., *Labouring Life in Norfolk Villages, 1834–1914* (1936).

Thompson, F. M. L., *English Landed Society in the Nineteenth Century* (1963).

——, 'Private Property and Public Policy', in Lord Blake and Cecil, H. (eds), *Salisbury: the Man and his Policies* (1987).

Warwick-Haller, S., 'Parnell and William O'Brien', in Boyce, D.G. and O'Day, A. (eds), *Parnell in Perspective* (1991).

Webb, S. and B., *English Local Government, Vol. 8: English Poor Law History, II. The Last Hundred Years* (1929).

Williams, K., *From Pauperism to Poverty* (1981).

Chapter 2: Unionist Ascendancy

Note: The Salisbury phenomenon is very well covered by Shannon (1996), Marsh (1978), Smith (1972) and the Blake and Cecil (1987) collection. On the Liberal side, Matthew's Introduction to volume XII of the Gladstone Diaries, reprinted in *Gladstone, 1875–1898* is indispensable. His *Liberal Imperialists* is an impeccable study of that infuriating group, while David Brooks's introduction to selections from the Hamilton Diaries provides the best analysis of the Rosebery premiership. Barker (1975) gets to the heart of the late-Victorian Liberal Party, while Emy (1973) remains an important study of social Radicalism. The emergence of social politics at national and local levels may be pieced together from Harris (1972), Harris (1993), Hennock (1987), Davis (1988), Hollis (1987) and Thane (1978). Howell's excellent study of the early ILP is essential for an understanding of embryonic labour movement.

Adonis, A., *Making Aristocracy Work. The Peerage and the Political System in Britain, 1884–1914* (Oxford, 1993).

Barker, M., *Gladstone and Radicalism* (Hassocks, 1975).

Blake, Lord and Cecil, H. (eds), *Salisbury: The Man and His Policies* (1987).

Brooks, D. (ed.), *The Destruction of Lord Rosebery. From the Diary of Sir Edward Hamilton* (1986).

Brown, B. H., *The Tariff Reform Movement in Britain, 1880–1895* (New York, 1943).

Brown, S. J., ' "Echoes of Midlothian": Scottish Liberalism and the South African War, 1899–1902', *Scottish Historical Review*, 71 (1992).

Clarke, P. F., *Lancashire and the New Liberalism* (Cambridge, 1971).

Clegg, H. A., Fox, A. and Thompson, A. F., *A History of British Trade Unions since 1889, Vol. I: 1889–1910* (Oxford, 1964).

Crowther, M. A., *The Workhouse System, 1834–1929. The History of an English Social Institution* (1981).

Curtis, L. P., *Coercion and Conciliation in Ireland, 1880–1892. A Study in Conservative Unionism* (Princeton, 1963).

Daglish, N. D., 'The Politics of Educational Change: The Case of the English Higher Grade Schools', *Journal of Educational Administration and History*, 19 (1987).

Davis, J., *Reforming London. The London Government Problem, 1855–1900* (Oxford, 1988).

——, 'The Progressive Council', in Saint, A. (ed.), *Politics and the People of London* (1989).

Emy, H. V., *Liberals, Radicals and Social Politics, 1892–1914* (Cambridge, 1973).

Foster, R., *Lord Randolph Churchill. A Political Life* (Oxford, 1981).

France, J., 'Salisbury and the Unionist Alliance', in Blake, Lord and Cecil, H. (eds), *Salisbury:The Man and His Policies* (1987).

Fraser, W. H. and Maver, I., 'Tackling the Problems', in Fraser, W. H. and Maver, I. (eds), *Glasgow, Vol. 2: 1830 to 1912* (Manchester, 1996).

Gailey, A., *Ireland and the Death of Kindness. The Experience of Constructive Unionism, 1890–1905* (Cork, 1987).

Green, E. H. H., *The Crisis of Conservatism. The Politics, Economics and Ideology of the British Conservative Party, 1880–1914* (1995).

Griffiths, P. C., 'The Caucus and the Liberal Party in 1886', *History*, 61 (1976).

Hanham, H. J., 'The Sale of Political Honours in Late Victorian England', *Victorian Studies*, 3 (1960).

——, *The Nineteenth Century Constitution, 1815–1914. Documents and Commentary* (1969).

Harcourt Williams, R. (ed.), *The Salisbury–Balfour Correspondence, 1869–1892* (Hertford, 1988).

Harris, J., *Unemployment and Politics. A Study in English Social Policy, 1886–1914* (Oxford, 1972).

——, *Private Lives, Public Spirit: A Social History of Britain, 1870–1914* (Oxford, 1993).

Hennock, E. P., *British Social Reform and German Precedents* (Oxford, 1987).

——, 'Technological Education in England 1850–1926: The Uses of a German Model', *History of Education*, 19 (1990).

Hollis, P., *Ladies Elect. Women in English Local Government, 1865–1914* (Oxford, 1987).

Holton, S. S., *Suffrage Days. Stories from the Women's Suffrage Movement* (1996).

Howell, D., *British Workers and the Independent Labour Party, 1888–1906* (Manchester, 1983).

Hurst, M., *Joseph Chamberlain and Liberal Reunion. The Round Table Conference of 1887* (1967).

Hutchison, I.G.C., *A Political History of Scotland, 1832–1924* (Edinburgh, 1986).

Jackson, A., *The Ulster Party. Irish Unionists in the House of Commons, 1884–1911* (Oxford, 1989).

Jay, R., *Joseph Chamberlain. A Political Study* (Oxford, 1981).

Jenkins, T. A., *Gladstone, Whiggery and the Liberal Party* (Oxford, 1988).

Joyce, P., *Work Society and Politics* (Brighton, 1980).

Kellas, J. G., 'The Liberal Party in Scotland, 1876–1895', *Scottish Historical Review*, 44 (1965).

Kinnear, M., *The British Voter. An Atlas and a Survey since 1885* (2nd edition, 1981).

Lipman, V. D., *Local Government Areas, 1834–1945* (Oxford, 1949).

Loughlin, J., *Gladstone, Home Rule and the Ulster Question, 1882–1893* (Dublin, 1986).

Machin, G. I. T., *Politics and the Churches in Great Britain, 1869–1921* (Oxford, 1987).

MacKay, T., *A History of the English Poor Law, Vol. 3: From 1834 to the Present Time* (1899).

Marsh, P., *The Discipline of Popular Government. Lord Salisbury's Domestic Statecraft, 1881–1902* (Hassocks, 1978).

——, *Joseph Chamberlain. Entrepreneur in Politics* (New Haven, 1994).

Martel, G., *Imperial Diplomacy: Rosebery and the Failure of Foreign Policy* (Kingston, 1986).

Matthew, H. C. G., *The Liberal Imperialists. The Ideas and Politics of a Post-Gladstonian Elite* (Oxford, 1973).

—— (ed.), *The Gladstone Diaries*, Introduction to vol. XII (Oxford, 1994).

——, *Gladstone, 1875–1898* (Oxford, 1995).

Morgan, K. O., *Wales in British Politics, 1868–1922* (Cardiff, 1963).

Oakeshott, J. F., *The Humanising of the Poor Law* (1894).

O'Callaghan, M., *British High Politics and a Nationalist Ireland. Community, Land and Law under Forster and Balfour* (Cork, 1994).

Offer, A., *Property and Politics, 1870–1914* (Cambridge, 1981).

Pinto-Duchinsky, M., *British Political Finance, 1830–1980* (Washington, DC, 1981).

Price, R., *Labour in British Society* (1986).

Rover, C., *Women's Suffrage and Party Politics in Britain, 1866–1914* (1967).

Rubenstein, D., *Before the Suffragettes. Women's Emancipation in the 1890s* (Brighton, 1986).

Salisbury, Lord, 'Disintegration', *Quarterly Review*, 312 (October, 1883).

Savage, M., *The Dynamics of Working-Class Politics. The Labour Movement in Preston 1880–1940* (Cambridge, 1987).

Shannon, R., *The Age of Salisbury, 1881–1902* (1996).

Smith, P. (ed.), *Lord Salisbury on Politics* (Cambridge, 1972).

Stedman Jones, G., *Outcast London. A Study in the Relationship between Classes in Victorian Society* (Oxford, 1971).

Steele, E. D., 'Salisbury and the Church', in Blake, Lord and Cecil, H. (eds), *Salisbury: The Man and His Policies* (1987).

Sutherland, G., *Policy-Making in Elementary Education, 1870–1895* (Oxford, 1973).

Thane, P., 'Non-Contributory versus Insurance Pensions, 1878–1908', in Thane, P. (ed.), *The Origins of British Social Policy* (1978).

Waller, P. J., *Town, City and Nation. England 1850–1914* (Oxford, 1983).
Webb, S. and B., *English Local Government, Vol. 8: English Poor Law History, II. The Last Hundred Years, I* (1929).
Weston, C. C., 'Salisbury and the Lords, 1868–1895', *Historical Journal*, 25 (1982).

Chapter 3: Tariff Reform

Note: Sykes (1979) provides the standard modern analysis of the Tariff Reform controversy at the high political level, augmented now by the broader Green (1995). Marrison (1996) assesses the impact of tariff reform upon the business community and the work of the Tariff Commission. Bebbington (1982) and Pugh (1990) make the furore over the 1902 Education Act more comprehensible. Bealey and Pelling (1958) and the relevant sections of Marquand (1977) explain the evolution of the 1903 Lib–Lab arrangements.

Asquith, H. H., *Trade and the Empire. Mr Chamberlain's Proposals Examined* (1903).
Bahlman, D. W. R. (ed.), *The Diary of Sir Edward Walter Hamilton, 1885–1906* (Hull, 1993).
Bealey, F. and Pelling, H., *Labour and Politics, 1900–1906* (1958).
Bebbington, D., *The Nonconformist Conscience, 1870–1914* (1982).
Bew, P., *Conflict and Conciliation in Ireland, 1890–1910. Parnellites and Radical Agrarians* (Oxford, 1987).
Brown, B. H., *The Tariff Reform Movement in Great Britain, 1881–1895* (New York, 1943).
Brown, K. D., 'The Trade Union Tariff Reform Association', *Journal of British Studies*, 9 (1970).
Clarke, P. F., *Lancashire and the New Liberalism* (Cambridge, 1971).
Clegg, H. A., Fox, A. and Thompson, A.F., *A History of British Trade Unions since 1889, Vol. I: 1889–1910* (Oxford, 1964).
Cornford, J. P., 'The Political Foundations of the Hotel Cecil', in Robson. R. (ed.), *Ideas and Institutions of Victorian Britain. Essays in Honour of George Kitson Clark* (1967).
Crewe, Marquess of, *Lord Rosebery* (1931), vol. II.
Daglish, N., *Education Policy-Making in England and Wales. The Crucible Years, 1895–1911* (1997).
Emy, H. V., *Liberals, Radicals and Social Politics, 1892–1914* (Cambridge, 1973).
Fair, J. D., *British Inter-Party Conferences. A Study of the Procedure of Conciliation in British Politics, 1867–1921* (Oxford, 1980).
Freeden, M., *The New Liberalism* (Oxford, 1978).
Gailey, A., *Ireland and the Death of Kindness. The Experience of Constructive Unionism, 1890–1905* (Cork, 1987).

Green, E. H. H., *The Crisis of Conservatism. The Politics, Economics and Ideology of the British Conservative Party, 1880–1914* (1995).

Harris, J., *Unemployment and Politics. A Study in English Social Policy, 1886–1914* (Oxford, 1972).

——, *William Beveridge* (Oxford, 1977).

——, 'The Transition to High Politics in English Social Policy, 1880–1914', in Bentley, M. and Stevenson, J. (eds), *High and Low Politics in Modern Britain* (Oxford, 1983).

Headlam, C., *The Milner Papers*, vol. I (1931).

Hobson, J. A., *Imperialism. A Study* (1902).

Howell, D., *British Workers and the Independent Labour Party, 1888–1906* (Manchester, 1983).

Jackson, A., *The Ulster Party. Irish Unionists in the House of Commons, 1884–1911* (Oxford, 1989).

Kendle, J. E., *The Colonial and Imperial Conferences, 1887–1911* (1967).

Kennedy, P., *The Rise of the Anglo-German Antagonism, 1860–1914* (1980), 262.

Kesner, R. M., *Economic Control and Colonial Development* (Oxford, 1981).

Kinnear, M., *The British Voter. An Atlas and a Survey since 1885* (2nd edition, 1981).

Kubicek, R. V., *The Administration of Imperialism: Joseph Chamberlain at the Colonial Office* (Durham, N.C., 1969).

Lowndes, G. A., *The Silent Social Revolution. An Account of the Expansion of Public Education in England and Wales, 1895–1965* (second edition, Oxford, 1969).

Machin, G. I. T., *Politics and the Churches in Great Britain, 1869–1921* (Oxford, 1987).

Mackenzie, J. M. (ed.), *Imperialism and Popular Culture* (Manchester, 1986).

Marquand, D., *Ramsay MacDonald* (1977).

Marrison, A., *British Business and Protection, 1903–1932* (Oxford, 1996).

Marsh, P., *The Discipline of Popular Government. Lord Salisbury's Domestic Statecraft, 1881–1902* (Hassocks, 1978).

Marsh, P. T., *Joseph Chamberlain. Entrepreneur in Politics* (New Haven, 1994).

Matthew, H. C. G., *The Liberal Imperialists. The Ideas and Politics of a Post-Gladstonian Elite* (Oxford, 1973).

McKibbin, R., *The Evolution of the Labour Party, 1910–1924* (Oxford, 1974).

O'Halpin, E., *The Decline of the Union. British Government in Ireland, 1892–1920* (Dublin, 1987).

Pelling, H., *A Social Geography of British Elections, 1885–1910* (1967).

Porter, A. N., *The Origins of the South African War. Joseph Chamberlain and the Diplomacy of Imperialism, 1895–1899* (Manchester, 1980).

Pugh, D. R., 'English Nonconformity, Education and Passive Resistance, 1903–6', *History of Education*, 19 (1990).

Russell, A. K., *Liberal Landslide. The General Election of 1906* (Newton Abbot, 1973).
Savage, M., *The Dynamics of Working-Class Politics. The Labour Movement in Preston, 1880–1940* (Cambridge, 1987).
Shannon, R., *The Age of Salisbury, 1881–1902* (1996).
Sykes, A., *Tariff Reform in British Politics, 1903–1913* (Oxford, 1979).
Taylor, T., 'Lord Cranborne, the Church Party and Anglican Education, 1893–1902: From Politics to Pressure', *History of Education*, 22 (1993).
Webb, S. and B., *English Local Government, Vol. 8: English Poor Law History, Part. II. The Last Hundred Years, I* (1929).
Williams, K., *From Pauperism to Poverty* (1981).
Wilson, J., *C.B. A Life of Sir Henry Campbell-Bannerman* (1973).

Chapter 4: Liberalism and Welfare

Note: The historiography of this period is exceptionally rich. Peter Clarke's pioneering study of New Liberalism in Lancashire is a work of inexhaustible insight, as is Blewett's study of the 1910 elections: both range far beyond their nominal subjects. So, in a sense, does the excellent Tanner (1990), which has almost as much to say about Liberalism as about the Labour Party, and is particularly valuable as a guide to the local development of Lib–Lab relations. Freeden (1978) is a powerful piece of intellectual history. Murray (1980) and Adonis (1993) provide skilful accounts of the 1909–10 crisis. Offer (1981) describes both rural and urban land campaigns. McBriar (1987) analyses the intricacies of the Poor Law reform debate, while Harris's important (1983) article examines the translation of social politics from the local to the national arena. Holton's (1987) study of the NUWSS is probably the single most useful work on the politics of the suffrage movement.

Adonis, A., *Making Aristocracy Work. The Peerage and the Political System in Britain, 1884–1914* (Oxford, 1993).
Allett, J., *New Liberalism. The Political Economy of J.A. Hobson* (Toronto, 1981).
Blewett, N., *The Peers, the Parties and the People: The General Elections of 1910* (1972).
Campbell, R. H. and Devine, T. M., 'The Rural Experience', in Fraser, W. H. and Morris, R.J. (eds), *People and Society in Scotland, Vol. II: 1830–1914* (Edinburgh, 1990).
Cassis, Y., *City Bankers, 1890–1914* (Cambridge, 1994).
Clarke, P. F., *Lancashire and the New Liberalism* (Cambridge, 1971).
Clegg, H. A., Fox, A. and Thompson, A. F., *A History of British Trade Unions since 1889, Vol. I, 1889–1910* (Oxford, 1964).
Collini, S., *Liberalism and Sociology. L.T. Hobhouse and Political Argument in England, 1880–1914* (Cambridge, 1979).

Cronin, J. E., 'Strikes, 1870–1914', in Wrigley, C.J. (ed.), *A History of British Industrial Relations, 1875–1914* (Brighton, 1982).

Den Otter, S., *British Idealism and Social Explanation. A Study in Late-Victorian Thought* (Oxford, 1996).

Dutton, D., *'His Majesty's Loyal Opposition.' The Unionist Party in Opposition, 1905–1915* (Liverpool, 1992).

Emy, H. V., *Liberals, Radicals and Social Politics, 1892–1914* (Cambridge, 1973).

Eustance, C., 'Protests from Behind the Grille: Gender and the Transformation of Parliament, 1900–1918', in Green, E.H.H. (ed.), *An Age of Transition: British Politics 1880–1914* (Edinburgh, 1997).

Fair, J. D., *British Inter-Party Conferences. A Study of the Procedure of Conciliation in British Politics, 1867–1921* (Oxford, 1980), 84 and ch. IV.

Fenton, A., *The Turra Coo. A Legal Episode in the Popular Culture of North-East Scotland* (Aberdeen, 1989).

Freeden, M., *The New Liberalism* (Oxford 1978).

——, *Reappraising J.A. Hobson. Humanism and Welfare* (1990).

Gilbert, B. B., *The Evolution of National Insurance in Great Britain* (1966).

——, *David Lloyd George. A Political Life, Vol. I: The Architect of Change, 1863–1912* (1987); *Vol. II: Organiser of Victory, 1912–16* (1992).

Green, E. H. H. (ed.), *An Age of Transition: British Politics 1880–1914* (Edinburgh, 1997).

——, *The Crisis of Conservatism: The British Conservative Party, 1880–1914* (1995).

Harris, J., *Unemployment and Politics. A Study in English Social Policy, 1886–1914* (Oxford, 1972).

——, *William Beveridge* (Oxford, 1977).

——, 'The Transition to High Politics in English Social Policy, 1880–1914', in Bentley, M. and Stevenson, J. (eds), *High and Low Politics in Modern Britain* (Oxford, 1983).

Hennock, E. P., *British Social Reform and German Precedents. The Case of Social Insurance, 1880–1914* (Oxford, 1987).

Hirshfield, C., 'Fractured Faith: Liberal Party Women and the Suffrage Issue in Britain, 1892–1914', *Gender and History*, 2 (1990).

Hollis, P., *Ladies Elect. Women in English Local Government, 1865–1914* (Oxford, 1987).

Holton, B., *British Syndicalism, 1900–1914* (1976).

Holton, S. S., *Feminism and Democracy: Women's Suffrage and Reform Politics, 1900–1918* (Cambridge, 1987), 37.

——, *Suffrage Days. Stories from the Women's Suffrage Movement* (1996).

Howell, D., *British Workers and the Independent Labour Party, 1888–1906* (Manchester, 1983).

Hutcheson, J. A., *Leopold Maxse and the National Review, 1890–1914. Right-Wing Politics and Journalism in the Edwardian Era* (New York, 1989).

Jalland, P., *The Liberals and Ireland. The Ulster Question in British Politics to 1914* (1980).

King, D., *Actively Seeking Work? The Politics of Unemployment and Welfare Policy in the United States and Great Britain* (Chicago, 1995).

Laffan, M., *The Partition of Ireland, 1911–1925* (Dublin, 1987).

Lewis, J., *Women and Social Action in Victorian and Edwardian England* (Aldershot, 1991).

Liddington, J. and Norris, J., *One Hand Tied Behind Us. The Rise of the Women's Suffrage Movement* (1978).

McBriar, A. M., *An Edwardian Mixed Doubles. The Bosanquets versus the Webbs. A Study in British Social Policy, 1890–1929* (Oxford, 1987).

McKibbin, R., *The Evolution of the Labour Party, 1910–1924* (Oxford, 1974).

Mallet, B., *British Budgets, 1887–1913* (1913).

Marquand, D., *Ramsay MacDonald* (1977).

Marrison, A., *British Business and Protection, 1903–1932* (Oxford, 1996).

Morgan, D., *Suffragists and Liberals. The Politics of Women's Suffrage in Britain* (1975).

Morris, A. J. A., *Radicalism Against War, 1906–1914* (1972).

——, *The Scaremongers. The Advocacy of War and Rearmament, 1896–1914* (1984).

Murray, B. K., *The People's Budget, 1909–10: Lloyd George and Liberal Politics* (Oxford, 1980).

Offer, A., *Property and Politics, 1870–1914* (Cambridge, 1981).

Packer, I., 'The Liberal Cave and the 1914 Budget', *English Historical Review*, 111 (1996).

——, 'The Conservatives and the Ideology of Landownership', in Francis, M. and Zweiniger-Bargielowska, I. (eds), *The Conservatives and British Society, 1880–1990* (Cardiff, 1996).

Pugh, M., *Electoral Reform in War and Peace, 1906–1918* (1978).

——, 'Yorkshire and the New Liberalism', *Journal of Modern History*, 50 (1978).

——,' Labour and Women's Suffrage', in Brown, K.D. (ed.), *The First Labour Party, 1906–1914* (1985).

Ridley, J., 'The Unionist Social Reform Committee, 1911–1914: Wets Before the Deluge', *Historical Journal*, 30 (1987).

Rosen, A., *Rise Up, Women! The Militant Campaign of the Women's Social and Political Union, 1903–1914* (1974).

Rover, C., *Women's Suffrage and Party Politics in Britain, 1866–1914* (1967).

Royal Commission on the Poor Laws, *Parliamentary Papers* 1909, XXXVII, Majority and Minority Reports.

Russell, A.K., *Liberal Landslide. The General Election of 1906* (Newton Abbot, 1973).

Savage, M., *The Dynamics of Working-Class Politics. The Labour Movement in Preston, 1880–1940* (Cambridge, 1987).

Sykes, A., *Tariff Reform in British Politics, 1903–1913* (Oxford, 1979).

Tanner, D., *Political Change and the Labour Party, 1906–1922* (Cambridge, 1990).

Thane, P., 'The Labour Party and State Welfare', in Brown, K.D. (ed.), *The First Labour Party, 1906–1914* (1985).

Vincent, A. and Plant, R., *Philosophy, Politics and Citizenship. The Life and Thought of the British Idealists* (Oxford, 1984).

Webb, S. and B., *English Local Government, Vol. 8: English Poor Law History, Part. II. The Last Hundred Years, I* (1929).

Williams, K., *From Pauperism to Poverty* (1981).

Wrigley, C. J., 'The Government and Industrial Relations', in Wrigley, C.J. (ed.), *A History of British Industrial Relations, 1875–1914* (Brighton, 1982).

——, 'Labour and the Trade Unions', in Brown, K. D. (ed.), *The First Labour Party, 1906–14* (1985).

Chapter 5: Transformation by War

Note: So far as the drift to war is concerned, Kennedy's holistic diplomatic history (1981) remains a *tour de force*. Wilson's (1985) essays demonstrate the real constraints created by entente policy. Williamson (1969) remains valuable. John Turner's massive political history of wartime Britain (1992) makes evident how skimpy earlier work on war politics had been. David French's volumes on the evolution of strategy have also broadened our understanding of the political implications of total war. DeGroot (1996) is useful for the home front, and the essays in Burk (1982) remain valuable. Pugh (1978) is a good study of the evolution of the electoral reform issue and the emergence of the 1918 Reform Act. The relevant chapters of Bentley (1977) capture well the disintegration of the Liberal mind under the pressure of war.

Amery, L. S., *My Political Life, Vol. 2: War and Peace, 1914–1929* (1953).

Babbington, A., *For the Sake of Example* (1983).

Bentley, M., *The Liberal Mind, 1914–1929* (Cambridge, 1977).

Bonzon, T. and Davis, B., 'Feeding the Cities', in Winter, J. and Robert, J.-L. (eds), *Capital Cities at War: London, Paris, Berlin, 1914–1919* (Cambridge, 1997).

Burk, K., *Britain, America and the Sinews of War, 1914–1918* (1985).

—— (ed.), *War and the State* (1982).

Cline, P., 'Winding Down the War Economy: British Plans for Peacetime Recovery', in Burk, K. (ed.), *War and the State* (1982).

Crewe, Lord, 'Memorandum on the Break-Up of the Coalition Government, December, 1916', reprinted in Pope-Hennessy, J., *Lord Crewe, 1858–1945. The Likeness of a Liberal* (1955).

DeGroot, G. J., *Blighty. British Society in the Era of the Great War* (1996).

Englander, D., *Landlord and Tenant in Urban Britain, 1838–1918* (Oxford, 1983).

French, D., *British Economic and Strategic Planning, 1905–1915* (1982).

——, *British Strategy and War Aims, 1914–16* (1986).

French, D., 'The Rise and Fall of "Business as Usual" ', in Burk, K. (ed.), *War and the State* (1982).

——, *The Strategy of the Lloyd George Coalition, 1916–1918* (Oxford, 1995).

Gilbert, B. B., *David Lloyd George. A Political Life, Vol. II; Organiser of Victory, 1912–16* (1992).

Gill, D. and Dallas, G., 'Mutiny at Etaples Base in 1917', *Past and Present*, 69 (1975).

Grieves, K., *The Politics of Manpower, 1914–1918* (Manchester, 1988).

Guinn, P., *British Strategy and Politics, 1914 to 1918* (Oxford, 1965).

Harris, J., 'Bureaucrats and Businessmen in British Food Control, 1916–19', in Burk, K. (ed.), *War and the State* (1982).

Hartley, S., *The Irish Question as a Problem in British Foreign Policy, 1914–1918* (1987).

Hinton, J., *The First Shop Stewards' Movement* (1973).

Howard, M., *The Continental Commitment* (1972).

Jeffery, K., *The British Army and the Crisis of Empire* (Manchester, 1984).

Kennedy, P. M., *The Rise of the Anglo-German Antagonism, 1860–1914* (1980).

Kennedy, P., *The Realities Behind Diplomacy* (1981).

Laffan, M., *The Partition of Ireland, 1911–1925* (Dublin, 1987).

McDowell, R. B., *The Irish Convention, 1917–18* (1970).

Magri, S., 'Housing', in Winter, J. and Robert, J.-L. (eds), *Capital Cities at War: London, Paris, Berlin, 1914–1919* (Cambridge, 1997).

Marsh, P. T., *Joseph Chamberlain. Entrepreneur in Politics* (New Haven, 1994).

Martel, G., *Imperial Diplomacy. Rosebery and the Failure of Foreign Policy* (1986).

Matthew, H. C. G., *The Liberal Imperialists. The Ideas and Politics of a Post-Gladstonian Elite* (Oxford, 1973).

Middlemas, K., *Politics in Industrial Society. The Experience of the British System since 1911* (1979).

Monger, G. W., *The End of Isolation. British Foreign Policy, 1900–1907* (1963).

Monroe, E., *Britain's Moment in the Middle East, 1917–1956* (1965).

Morris, A. J. A., *Radicalism Against War, 1906–1914* (1972).

O'Halpin, E., *The Decline of the Union. British Government in Ireland, 1892–1920* (Dublin, 1987).

Pugh, M., *Electoral Reform in War and Peace* (1978).

Scally, R. J., *The Origins of the Lloyd George Coalition. The Politics of Social Imperialism 1900–1918* (Princeton, 1975).

Swartz, M., *The Union of Democratic Control in British Politics During the First World War* (Oxford, 1971).

Tanner, D., *Political Change and the Labour Party, 1906–1918* (Cambridge, 1990).

Triebel, A., 'Coal and the Metropolis', in Winter, J. and Robert, J.-L. (eds), *Capital Cities at War. London, Paris, Berlin, 1914–1919* (Cambridge, 1997).

Turner, J., *Lloyd George's Secretariat* (Cambridge, 1980).
——, 'Cabinets, Committees and Secretariats: The Higher Direction of War', in Burk, K. (ed.), *War and the State* (1982).
——, *British Politics and the Great War* (New Haven, 1992).
——, (ed.), *Britain and the First World War* (1988).
——, and Dockrill, M., 'Philip Kerr at 10 Downing Street, 1916–1921', in Turner, J. (ed.), *The Larger Idea. Lord Lothian and the Problem of National Sovereignty* (1988).
Waites, B., *A Class Society at War* (Leamington Spa, 1987).
Williamson, S. R., *The Politics of Grand Strategy* (Harvard, 1969).
Wilson, K. M., *The Policy of the Entente. Essays on the Determinants of British Foreign Policy, 1904–1914* (Cambridge, 1985).
Winter, J., *Socialism and the Challenge of War* (1974).
——, and Robert, J.-L. (eds), *Capital Cities at War. London, Paris, Berlin, 1914–1919* (Cambridge, 1997).

Chapter 6: Losing the Peace: Coalition Politics, 1918–22

Note: Morgan's (1978) monograph on the Lloyd George Coalition remains indispensable. The older Johnson (1969) is less digestible but contains much good material. The articles by Whiting (1990) and Daunton (1996) provide valuable coverage of the previously neglected fiscal aspect of wartime and post-war policy, essential to keep the failure of reconstruction in perspective. McDonald (1989) throws new light on the operations of the Geddes Committee.

Boyce, D. G., *Englishmen and Irish Troubles* (Cambridge, Ma., 1972).
Cain, P. J. and Hopkins, A. G., *British Imperialism: Crisis and Deconstruction, 1914–1990* (1993).
Clegg, H. A., *A History of British Trade Unions since 1889, Vol. II: 1911–1933* (Oxford, 1985).
Cleveland, W. L., *A History of the Modern Middle East* (Boulder, 1994).
Cowling, M., *The Impact of Labour* (Cambridge, 1971).
Daunton, M., 'How to Pay for the War: State, Society and Taxation in Britain, 1917–24', *English Historical Review*, 111 (1996).
Deacon, A., *In Search of the Scrounger. The Administration of Unemployment Insurance in Britain, 1920–1931* (1976).
Drummond, I. M., *British Economic Policy and the Empire, 1919–1939* (1972).
——, *Imperial Economic Policy, 1917–1939. Studies in Expansion and Protection* (1974).
Garside, W. R., *British Unemployment, 1919–1939. A Study in Public Policy* (Cambridge, 1990).
Hicks, U. K., *The Finance of British Government, 1920–1936* (Oxford, 1938).

Howson, S., *Domestic Monetary Management in Britain, 1919–1938* (Cambridge, 1975).

Hutchison, I. G. C., *A Political History of Scotland, 1832–1924* (Edinburgh, 1986).

Johnson, P. B., *Land Fit for Heroes. The Planning of British Reconstruction, 1916–1919* (Chicago, 1968).

Kinnear, M., *The Fall of Lloyd George. The Political Crisis of 1922* (1973).

——, *The British Voter. An Atlas and a Survey since 1885* (2nd edition, 1981).

Lawrence, J., 'Material Pressures on the Middle Classes', in Winter, J. and Robert, J.-L. (eds.), *Capital Cities at War. London, Paris, Berlin, 1914–19* (Cambridge, 1997).

Lowe, R., *Adjusting to Democracy. The Role of the Ministry of Labour in British Politics, 1916–1939* (Oxford, 1986).

McDonald, A., 'The Geddes Committee and the Formulation of Public Expenditure Policy, 1921–1922', *Historical Journal* (1989).

Moggridge, D. E., *British Monetary Policy, 1924–1931. The Norman Conquest of $4.86* (Cambridge, 1972).

Morgan, K. O., *Consensus and Disunity. The Lloyd George Coalition Government, 1918–1922* (Oxford, 1980).

——, and Morgan, J., *Portrait of a Progressive* (Oxford, 1980).

Phillips, G. and Whiteside, N., *Casual Labour. The Unemployment Question in the Port Transport Industry, 1880–1970* (Oxford, 1985).

Pugh, M., *Electoral Reform in War and Peace* (1978).

Rasmussen, J., 'The Political Integration of British Women: The Response of a Traditional System to a Newly Emergent Group', *Social Science History*, 7 (1983).

Searle, G. R., *Corruption in British Politics, 1895–1930* (Oxford, 1987).

Shannon, C. B., *Arthur J.Balfour and Ireland, 1874–1922* (Washington, D.C., 1988).

Sherington, G., *English Education, Social Change and War, 1911–20* (Manchester, 1981).

Stockwell, A. J., 'The War and the British Empire', in Turner, J. (ed.), *Britain and the First World War* (1988).

The Third Winter of Unemployment. The Report of an Enquiry undertaken in the Autumn of 1922 (1923).

Tomlinson, J., *Problems of British Economic Policy, 1870–1945* (1981).

Turner, J., *British Politics and the Great War* (New Haven, 1992).

Waites, B., *A Class Society at War* (Leamington Spa, 1987).

Whiting, R., 'Taxation and the Working Class, 1915–24', *Historical Journal*, 33 (1990).

Chapter 7: Three-Party Politics, 1922–31

Note: Boyce's (1987) study of the failure of economic liberalism and Williamson's (1992) work on the run-in to the (1931) crisis are both weighty and densely textured but magnificent. So is Self (1986), though it is lamentably hard to find. Ball's (1988) assessment of the Tories' difficulties during the Second Labour Government also enhances our understanding of the politics of the 1920s. Marquand (1977) offers what is probably still the best entrée to the politics of the Labour Party. Clarke (1988), Howson (1975) and Moggridge (1972) are essential for unravelling the development of economic policy, as are Deacon (1976) and Lowe (1986) for the even more tortuous history of welfare policy. Phillips (1976) was the best of a clutch of books commemorating the fiftieth anniversary of the General Strike, and remains invaluable.

Bakke, E. W., *The Unemployed Man. A Social Study* (1933).

Ball, S., *Baldwin and the Conservative Party. The Crisis of 1929–31* (New Haven, 1988).

Ball, S. (ed.), *Parliament and Politics in the Age of Baldwin and MacDonald: The Headlam Diaries, 1923–1935* (1992).

Bentley, M., *The Liberal Mind, 1914–1929* (Cambridge, 1977).

Blake, R., *The Unknown Prime Minister. The Life and Times of Andrew Bonar Law, 1858–1923* (1955).

Booth, A. and Pack, M., *Employment, Capital and Economic Policy. Great Britain, 1918–1939* (1985).

Bourke, J., *Working-Class Cultures in Britain, 1890–1960: Gender, Class and Ethnicity* (1994).

Bowley, M., *Housing and the State, 1919–1944* (1945).

Boyce, R. D., *British Capitalism at the Crossroads. A Study in Politics, Economics and International Relations* (Cambridge, 1987).

Burns, E. M., *British Unemployment Programs, 1920–1938* (Washington, DC, 1941).

Clarke, P. F., *Lancashire and the New Liberalism* (Cambridge, 1971).

——, *The Keynesian Revolution in the Making, 1924–1936* (Oxford, 1988).

Committee on National Expenditure, 1931 (Cmnd 3920), *Report*.

Cooper, A. F., *British Agricultural Policy, 1912–1936. A Study in Conservative Politics* (Manchester, 1989).

Cowling, M., *The Impact of Labour* (Cambridge, 1971).

Crowther, M. A., *The Workhouse System 1834–1929* (1981).

Deacon, A., *In Search of the Scrounger. The Administration of Unemployment Insurance in Britain, 1920–1931* (1976).

Deacon, A. and Briggs, E., 'Local Democracy and Central Policy. The Issue of Pauper Votes in the 1920s', *Policy and Politics*, 2 (1973–4).

Dilks, D., *Neville Chamberlain. I. Pioneering and Reform, 1869–1929* (Cambridge, 1984).

Dintenfass, M., 'The Politics of Producers' Co-operation: The FBI–TUC–NCEO Talks, 1929–1933', in Turner, J. (ed.), *Businessmen and Politics. Studies of Business Activity in British Politics, 1900–1945* (1984).

Drummond, I. M., *Imperial Economic Policy, 1917–1939. Studies in Expansion and Protection* (1974).

Dutton, D., *Simon. A Political Biography of Sir John Simon* (1992).

Francis, M. and Zweiniger-Bargielowska, I. (eds), *The Conservatives and British Society, 1880–1990* (Cardiff, 1996).

Freeden, M., *Liberalism Divided: A Study in British Political Thought, 1914–1939* (Oxford, 1986).

Garside, W. R., *British Unemployment, 1919–1939. A Study in Public Policy* (Cambridge, 1990).

Gilbert, B. B., *British Social Policy, 1914–1939* (1970).

Havinden, M. and Meredith, D., *Colonialism and Development. Britain and its Tropical Colonies, 1850–1960* (1993).

Hewins, W. A. S., *Apologia of an Imperialist* (1929), vol. II.

Hicks, U. K., *The Finance of British Government, 1920–1936* (Oxford, 1938).

Holland, R., *Britain and the Commonwealth Alliance, 1918–1939* (1981).

Howson, S., *Domestic Monetary Management in Britain, 1919–1938* (Cambridge, 1975).

Hutchison, I.G.C., *A Political History of Scotland, 1832–1924* (Edinburgh, 1986).

Jarvis, D., 'The Conservative Party and the Politics of Gender, 1900–1939', in Francis, M. and Zweiniger-Bargielowska, I. (eds), *The Conservatives and British Society, 1880–1990* (Cardiff, 1996).

Kinnear, M., *The British Voter. An Atlas and a Survey since 1885* (2nd edition, 1981).

Lowe, R., *Adjusting to Democracy. The Role of the Ministry of Labour in British Politics, 1916–1939* (Oxford, 1986).

Lyman, R. W., *The First Labour Government, 1924* (1957).

McKibbin, R., *The Evolution of the Labour Party, 1910–1924* (Oxford, 1974).

——, *The Ideologies of Class. Social Relations in Britain, 1880–1950* (Oxford, 1990).

MacNichol, J., *The Movement for Family Allowances, 1918–1945* (1980).

Mallet, Sir B., and George, C.O., *British Budgets. Third Series 1921–2 to 1932–3* (1933).

Marquand, D., *Ramsay MacDonald* (1977).

Middlemas, K. (ed.), *Thomas Jones: Whitehall Diary*, vol. II (1969).

——, *Politics in Industrial Society. The Experience of the British System since 1911* (1979).

——, and Barnes, J., *Baldwin. A Biography* (1969).

Mishkin, L., *The Contentious Alliance. Trade Unions and the Labour Party* (Edinburgh, 1991).

Moggridge, D. E., *British Monetary Policy, 1924–1931. The Norman Conquest of $4.86* (Cambridge, 1972).

Morris, M., *The General Strike* (1976).

Phillips, G. A., *The General Strike. The Politics of Industrial Conflict* (1976).

Pinto-Duchinsky, M., *British Political Finance, 1830–1980* (Washington, DC, 1981).

Powell, A. and Blight, E. C., 'Poor Law Relief', in Llewellyn Smith, H. (ed.), *The New Survey of London Life and Labour* (1930), Vol. I, Forty Years of Change.

Pugh, M., *Women and the Women's Movement in Britain, 1914–1959* (1992).
Ramsden, J., *The Age of Balfour and Baldwin, 1902–40* (1978).
Self, R.C., *Tories and Tariffs. The Conservative Party and the Politics of Tariff Reform, 1922–32* (1986).
Theakston, K., *The Labour Party and Whitehall* (1992).
Thorpe, A., *The British General Election of 1931* (Oxford, 1991).
Wasserstein, B., *Herbert Samuel. A Political Life* (Oxford, 1992).
Whiteside, N., 'Counting the Cost: Sickness and Disability among Working People in an Era of Industrial Recession, 1920–39', *Economic History Review*, second series, 40, 1987.
Williamson, P., *National Crisis and National Government. British Politics, the Economy and the Empire* (Cambridge, 1992).

Chapter 8: The Thirties

Note: Regrettably there is no single study of the National Government, though aspects of its work are well covered by Howson and Winch (1977), Lowe (1986) and Rooth (1992). Middleton (1985) is a strong study of the evolution of economic policy after the 1931 debacle. Garside (1990) is the definitive modern work on inter-war unemployment, detailed but accessible. Nicholas (1986) is an engrossing study of the effects of unemployment in one blackspot, and the contemporary Pilgrim Trust report (1938) remains valuable. On Ottawa and its aftermath the first two Drummonds (1972 and 1974) are important economic studies, while Holland (1981) captures well the political nuances of the Commonwealth relationship. On appeasement, Parker's (1993) superb revision of 1980s revisionism has to be the starting point. The Mommsen and Ketternacker (1981) collection contains much of value, and Howard's (1972) lectures were once considered important.

Anderson, G.D., *Fascists, Communists and the National Government. Civil Liberties in Great Britain, 1931–1937* (Columbia and London, 1983).
Ball, S., *Baldwin and the Conservative Party. The Crisis of 1929–31* (New Haven, 1988).
Beales, H.L. and Lambert, R.S., *Memoirs of the Unemployed* (1934)
Blaazer, D., *The Popular Front and the Progressive Tradition* (Cambridge, 1992).
Boyce, R.D., *British Capitalism at the Crossroads. A Study in Politics, Economics and International Relations* (Cambridge, 1987).
Briggs, E. and Deacon, A., 'The Creation of the Unemployment Assistance Board', *Policy and Politics*, (1973–4).
Burns, E.M., *British Unemployment Programs, 1920–1938* (Washington, DC, 1941).
Cain, P.J. and Hopkins, A.G., *British Imperialism. Crisis and Deconstruction, 1914–1990* (1993).

Crafts, N. F. R., 'Long-term Unemployment in Britain in the 1930s', *Economic History Review*, second series, 40 (1987).

Crowson, N., *Facing Fascism. The Conservative Party and the European Dictators, 1935–40* (1997).

Crozier, A., *Appeasement and Germany's Last Bid for Colonies* (1988).

Curran, J., Smith, A. and Wingate, P. (eds), *Impacts and Influences. Essays on Media Power in the Twentieth Century* (1987).

Davison, R. C., *British Unemployment Policy. The Modern Phase since 1930* (1938).

Deacon, A. and Bradshaw, J., *Reserved for the Poor. The Means Test in British Social Policy* (1983).

Dowse, R. F., *Left in the Centre. The Independent Labour Party, 1893–1940* (1966).

Drummond, I. M., *British Economic Policy and the Empire, 1919–1939* (1972).

——, *Imperial Economic Policy, 1917–1939. Studies in Expansion and Protection* (1974).

——, *The Floating Pound and the Sterling Area, 1931–1939* (Cambridge, 1981).

Eichengreen, B., 'Sterling and the Tariff, 1929–1932', in his *Elusive Stability. Essays in the History of International Finance, 1919–1939* (Cambridge, 1990).

Eleven Unemployed, *Time to Spare. What Unemployment Means* (1935).

Foreman-Peck, J., 'The British Tariff and Industrial Protection in the 1930s. An Alternative Model', *Economic History Review* (1981).

Garside, W. R., *British Unemployment, 1919–1939. A Study in Public Policy* (Cambridge, 1990).

Gilbert, B. B., *British Social Policy, 1914–1939* (1970).

Harmer, H., 'The Failure of the Communists, the National Unemployed Workers' Movement, 1921–1939: A Disappointing Success', in Thorpe, A. (ed.), *The Failure of Political Extremism in Inter-War Britain* (Exeter, 1989).

Holland, R. F., *Britain and the Commonwealth Alliance, 1918–1939* (1981).

Howard, M., *The Continental Commitment* (1972).

Howell, D., *British Social Democracy. A Study in Development and Decay* (1976).

Howson, S., *Domestic Monetary Management in Britain, 1919–1938* (Cambridge, 1975).

Howson, S. and Winch, D., *The Economic Advisory Council, 1930–1939. A Study in Economic Advice During Depression and Recovery* (Cambridge, 1977).

Lowe, R., *Adjusting to Democracy. The Role of the Ministry of Labour in British Politics, 1916–1939* (Oxford, 1986).

MacDonald, C. A., *The United States, Britain and Appeasement, 1936–1939* (1981).

McHenry, D. E., *The Labour Party in Transition, 1931–1938* (1938).

McKibbin, R., 'Class and Conventional Wisdom: The Conservative Party and the "Public" in Inter-War Britain', in his *The Ideologies of Class. Social Relations in Britain, 1880–1950* (Oxford, 1990).

Marquand, D., *Ramsay MacDonald* (1977).

Middlemas, K. and Barnes, J., *Baldwin. A Biography* (1969).

Middleton, R., *Towards the Managed Economy* (1985).

Miller, F., 'The British Unemployment Crisis of 1935', *Journal of Contemporary History*, 14, 1976.

Mommsen, W. J. and Ketternacker, L (eds), *The Fascist Challenge and the Policy of Appeasement* (1983).

Nicholas, K., *The Social Effects of Unemployment on Teesside, 1919–1939* (Manchester, 1986).

Ovendale, R., *Appeasement and the English-Speaking World* (Cardiff, 1975).

Parker, R. A. C., *Chamberlain and Appeasement. British Policy and the Coming of the Second World War* (1993).

Peden, G.C., *British Rearmament and the Treasury, 1932–1939* (Edinburgh, 1979).

PEP, *Report on the British Social Services* (1937).

Pilgrim Trust, *Men Without Work* (Cambridge, 1938).

Pimlott, B., *Labour and the Left in the 1930s* (Cambridge, 1977).

Pollard, S., *The Development of the British Economy, 1914–1990* (1992).

Porter, B., *The Lion's Share. A Short History of British Imperialism, 1850–1983* (2nd edn., 1984).

Pronay, N., 'Rearmament and the British Public. Policy and Propaganda', in Curran, J., Smith, A. and Wingate, P. (eds), *Impacts and Influences. Essays on Media Power in the Twentieth Century* (1987).

Ramsden, J., *The Age of Balfour and Baldwin, 1902–1940* (1978).

Reynolds, D., *The Creation of the Anglo-American Alliance, 1937–1941* (1981).

Rooth, T., *British Protectionism and the International Economy. Overseas Policy in the 1930s* (Cambridge, 1992).

Savage, M., *The Dynamics of Working-Class Politics. The Labour Movement in Preston, 1880–1940* (Cambridge, 1987).

Scannell, P. and Cardiff, D., *A Social History of Broadcasting* (1991), *Vol. I: 1922–1939, Serving the Nation*.

Schmidt, G., *The Politics and Economics of Appeasement* (English translation, Leamington Spa, 1986).

Self, R. C., *Tories and Tariffs. The Conservative Party and the Politics of Tariff Reform, 1922–32* (1986).

Smith, M., *British Air Strategy Between the Wars* (Oxford, 1984).

Thorpe, A., ' "The Only Effective Bulwark Against Reaction and Revolution". Labour and the Frustration of the Extreme Left', in Thorpe, A. (ed.), *The Failure of Political Extremism in Inter-War Britain* (Exeter, 1989).

Thorpe, A. (ed.), *The Failure of Political Extremism in Inter-War Britain* (Exeter, 1989).

Thurlow, R., 'The Failure of British Fascism, 1932–40', in Thorpe, A. (ed.), *The Failure of Political Extremism in Inter-War Britain* (Exeter, 1989).

Wark, W. K., *The Ultimate Enemy. British Intelligence and Nazi Germany* (2nd edn., Oxford, 1986).

Watt, D. C., 'The European Civil War' in Mommsen, W. J. and Ketternacker, L. (eds), *The Fascist Challenge and the Policy of Appeasement* (1983).

Webster, C., 'Healthy or Hungry Thirties?', *History Workshop Journal*, 13 (1982).

White, J., '"Penniless and Without Food". Unemployment in London between the Wars', in Alderman, G. and Holmes, C. (eds), *Outsiders and Outcasts. Essays in Honour of William J. Fishman* (1993).

Williamson, P., *National Crisis and National Government. British Politics, the Economy and the Empire* (Cambridge, 1992).

Wright, P., *Spycatcher. The Candid Autobiography of a Senior Intelligence Officer* (1987).

Yelling, J., *Slums and Redevelopment. Policy and Practice in England, 1918–1945* (1992).

Conclusion: A Conservative State?

Bentley, M. (ed.), *Public and Private Doctrine. Essays in British History Presented to Maurice Cowling* (Cambridge, 1993).

Boyce, R. D., *British Capitalism at the Crossroads. A Study in Politics, Economics and International Relations* (Cambridge, 1987).

Fair, J. D. and Hutcheson, J. A., 'British Conservatism in the Twentieth Century: An Emerging Ideological Tradition', *Albion*, 19 (1987).

Jarvis, D., 'British Conservatism and Class Politics in the 1920s', *English Historical Review*, 111 (1996).

Morley, J., *The Life of William Ewart Gladstone*, vol. III (1903).

Steele, E. D., 'Salisbury and the Church', in Blake, Lord and Cecil, H. (eds), *Salisbury: The Man and His Policies* (1987).

Williamson, P., 'The Doctrinal Politics of Stanley Baldwin', in Bentley, M. (ed.), *Public and Private Doctrine. Essays in British History Presented to Maurice Cowling* (Cambridge, 1993).

Index